On the Breeze of Canadian Literature

On the Breeze of Canadian Literature

International Reviews and Essays

Editor

MSc Miguel Ángel Olivé Iglesias

First Edition

QuodSermo Publishing
www.QuodSermoPublishing.com
QuodSermo@gmail.com

On the Breeze of Canadian Literature:
International Reviews and Essays

Editor – M.Sc. Miguel Ángel Olivé Iglesias
Associate Professor, Holguin University, Cuba

Proofreading – Miguel Ángel Olivé Iglesias,
– Jorge Alberto Pérez Hernández
Translations from Spanish – Miguel Ángel Olivé Iglesias, Jorge Alberto Pérez Hernández
Cover Design – Richard M. Grove
Cover Photograph – Richard M. Grove
Layout and Design – Richard M. Grove

Typeset in Garamond
Printed and bound in Canada
Library and Archives Canada Cataloguing in Publication

Library and Archives Canada Cataloguing in Publication

Title: On the breeze of Canadian literature : international reviews and essays / editor, MSc Miguel Ángel Olivé Iglesias.
Names: Olivé Iglesias, Miguel Ángel, 1965– editor.
Description: First edition.
Identifiers: Canadiana (print) 20210370769 |
Canadiana (ebook) 20210370874 |
ISBN 9781989786451 (softcover) |
ISBN 9781989786468 (ebook)
Subjects: LCSH: Canadian literature—History and criticism. |
LCGFT: Literary criticism. |
LCGFT: Reviews.
Classification: LCC PS8601 .O5 2021 |
DDC C810.9—dc23

Acknowledgements

I am deeply indebted to many key players in the original conception and making of this book. I thank the publisher for his generosity and long-sighted understanding of the book´s intentions. I thank every contributor whose work I received and honored these pages.

Heartfelt acknowledgement to the reviewed writers, who give us a world of wonders through their words, thus opening a vast territory for our humble appreciation of their work.

A special thank you to first publishers, who kindly allowed authors to republish essays and reviews. Finally, I thank Jorge for joint revision and collaborative translation, and the layout and design artist for his fine job.

Thank you all for your full support to the project.

I thank Amanda, my daughter, who lights up my life in so many ways. I still marvel how I could even breathe before she was born.

I wish to acknowledge my wife's contribution to my writings. Without her support, understanding and realization of the concentration I need to bring my books to fruition, it would be impossible to finish them.

Dedicated to:

My mother, an avid reader who planted in me
the seed of reading for edification

My English and Lit teachers in high school and university, and
my college students all these past 33 years. They have made
me feel proud and led me to study and learn more and more

My many poet friends in Canada and Cuba.
Their advice and suggestions are in these pages

The perfect triangle writer-critic-reader
in Cuba, Canada and everywhere

The wide, inexhaustible, loyal readerships worldwide
that keep the flags of literature high up in the wind

The Editor
MSc Miguel Ángel Olivé Iglesias

Table of Contents

Editor's Foreword

On the Breeze of Canadian Literature: International Reviews and Essays is a necessary tribute to writers, readers and those who read, enjoy, feel and serve as mediators between the writer and the reader, critics, who are inspired by the literary piece they have absorbed, understood and been moved by. I remember gratefully John B. Lee´s generous comments about the title of my Hidden Brook Press review book, *In a Fragile Moment: A Landscape of Canadian Poetry* (2020), and the role reviewers play:

"For those creative individuals who are gifted by time and opportunity to vanish into the fragile moments when we commune with the inner voice, the voice through which the poem flows from within the deep wells of the self, and from there onto the page, we know that we are blessed with the occasion to vanish into the work, to partake in that state of creative grace which all too often collapses into consciousness, self-awareness, and worldliness... And if this mind is vivid, reliable, and capable of a luminous comprehension of the experience contained within the primary work, then the world is enriched. This dreamspeaker, this shaman, is as important as the one gifted by the original impulse to create. Let us call this individual someone from the priestly class. How we struggle with our own weak light to understand and appreciate and communicate the fragile experience of the written word. The luminous writer and the illuminating reader join hands with the third reader, the one who returns to the original work carrying **the** light candling the mind. And in the fragile moments, we shine, however briefly, with understanding and communion in service of deep need. We are all the more human for the rarity of those complimentary voices. The original voice, and its radiant echoing when the critic and the poet sing in harmony, we hear perhaps the voice of angels as we join the choir."

This is what the book we present is about: poetry or prose, poet or prose writer, pulsing in the critic´s pen, urging him/her to further decode for readers the magic of words thus becoming a middleman favoring enlightenment. I have always been emphatic on the meaningfulness of art and literature to foster education and values. The book concentrates, precisely, on essays and reviews about contemporary Canadian poets and prose writers whose work is a landmark to pursue virtuous, aesthetical and spiritual enrichment.

Literature gives us enjoyment, an insight into what surrounds us that maybe we did not have before; also a sense of associations with this universe we inhabit, natural, social and mental. In my profession as a university professor I know that contents to be taught must relate and be passed on one way or another to our students´ life experiences and sentiments. If this is not achieved, there is no education, no imprint left to transcend and influence them so they, in return, help in the continuity of a life of personal cultivation

But it is John B. Lee who makes it so clear for us: "Great literature broadens our knowledge, deepens our understanding, clarifies our emotions, and connects us to the inner wells of the self where deep need is served. In great literature we also find a meaningful connection with our fellow humans." (Taken from his essay *Einstein's Hammer and the Painting Pachyderm: Reading Alice Munro in the Digital Age (every day is trying to teach us something)*, first published in Alice Munro Country, ed. J.R. (Tim) Struthers (Guernica Editions, 2020). Reprinted here in this book with the kind permission of the publisher). The works herein are proof of that.

The essays and reviews contributed by the critics follow their expert interpretations and respected assessment on the writers reviewed, their lives and oeuvre. The critics take us through a sharp academic study of author and work; very personal, affective interpretations and valuable insights, offered with skilled penmanship, emotion and communicativeness. The value of works under analysis transcends sometimes the literary frontier to enter didactic explorations, which show how relevant they are and their specialized ramifications. Critics and academics dissect and provoke, reveal and throw light upon – and definitely motivate – thus handing out to readers the gift of realizing "What a wonderful writer!" they are about to read or have been reading (the quote is Shane Joseph´s, from his essay *Margaret Atwood and the Labour of Literary Celebrity (by Lorraine M. York)* included in this book).

Many essays (*) follow these same notions based on criteria concerned with and conducive to the trends of literary analysis traditionally taught in class in the Teacher Education English Major of Holguín University. The analyses aim at disclosing motivations, evocations and effects of the language chosen by the writers (a reflection of their interpretations and how these affect them) that led them to trek up and down the labyrinths of language and transfer thought and impressions onto their pieces.

The perspective then is that of the writers´ nexus with the outside world and with themselves. One side of the poems and novels or stories is surveyed from a literary-stylistic reflection and how they relate to the writers´ feelings and intimate lives, how they express their emotions, death, life, loss, events, their contemplation and identification/taxonomy of those abstract/concrete realities, and how they seek out to understand and present what lies within and without. In doing so, they have to resort to what I call "languageware." I tell my students: language is there in the cupboard, you open its doors and choose depending on your needs, background, urges, capacity, motivations, contexts and goals; consciously or not.

All essays and reviews in this book (50) written by 24 essayists and reviewers are, as a whole, a personalized, historic, literary, didactic, linguistic-stylistic, textual and social-cultural examination, surgically disclosing the backdrop and undercurrents driving the writers, as is discussed in some of the papers, plus a knowledgeable understanding of human urges and how these are poured out. As I said, there is also a welcome, innovatively didactic spin in some cases, as an example of how relevant the literary piece is and how it transcends the publication moment. I am positive both academics and general readers will feel at home with them and, allow me to say, at ease too with an all-inclusive perspective of many authors (35 poets or prose writers reviewed), poetry and prose analysis. Anthologies and magazines inclusive of a large number of poets and prose writers are also reviewed.

This book is intended to be, in addition, a kind of heartfelt homage to *the word* (*quodsermo*) at the service of values and culture, at the service of friendship and love, at the service of human edification to preserve our most sacred possession, ourselves, and our aesthetic-literary legacy. While within the boundaries of academic studies, the papers honor the writers´ indefatigable efforts and concrete achievements in "wordland."

Notes:

Authors are fully responsible for their language, views, opinions, statements, copyright regulations and legal actions of any kind in their papers. Neither the publisher nor the editor has accountability for any transgressions detected in the future. There are no royalties implied in or ensuing from the publication of their papers in this book. Authors were properly notified since the issuing of the book´s call.

Academic and scientific degrees are generally translated into English as *BEd* (or B.Ed.); *Prof.* (in Cuba it is a first-level college degree similar to a BEd or BA); *BA* (or B.A.); *MSc* (or M.Sc., M.S.); *Spec.* (in Cuba it is a second-level college degree similar to an MSc); and *PhD* (or Ph.D.).

To be in line with international titles, we include a practical reference guide for worldwide readers. The first three denominations (*BEd; Prof.*; *BA)* are similar to the terms we use here (As was noted, *Prof.* is not a teaching rank in Cuba). The fourth one (*MSc*) may be found as MSc, Master of Education (M.Ed.), MA (Master of Arts) or Master of Arts in Teaching (M.A.T.). The fifth one (*Spec.*), Educational Specialist (Ed.S.); and the sixth one (*PhD*), similar to the terms we use here, or Doctor of Education (Ed.D.), or Dr.

MSc Miguel Ángel Olivé Iglesias
Associate Professor. Holguin University, Cuba
Canada Cuba Literary Alliance Cuban President
Editor, Author, Poet, Writer, Essayist

(*) Some of these essays and reviews are part of two books,

***A Shower of Warm Light** and*

***In a Fragile Moment: A Landscape of Canadian Poetry**,*
Hidden Brook Press, 2020, about Canadian
authors, included in Holguin University´s Teacher Education English
Department´s undergraduate curriculum, and the grad courses´
map of the Canadian Studies Department

"The luminous writer and the illuminating reader

join hands with the third reader, the one who returns to the original work

carrying the light candling the mind"

John B. Lee, Canadian Poet

"Great literature broadens our knowledge, deepens our understanding, clarifies our emotions,

and connects us to the inner wells of the self where deep need is served.

In great literature we also find a meaningful connection with our fellow humans"

John B. Lee, Canadian Poet

Bruce Meyer and the Tradition

James Deahl. Professor, Poet, Critic, Editor

The International Students' Centre of the University of Toronto had long been a focal point of many literary events for both students and the general public. One day in June of 1977, I met the then-twenty-year-old Bruce Meyer at the Centre, and through him other young undergraduate poets. Four decades ago I was confident at least one of them would become a major writer, perhaps a leader of his generation. I was not mistaken.

While these young poets were reading the collections of the Great Generation of Canadian poets — Irving Layton, Al Purdy, Gwendolyn MacEwen, Milton Acorn, Margaret Avison, Louis Dudek, Jay Macpherson — what set Bruce Meyer apart from the others was his interest in living British poets. It was through Meyer that I encountered initially the poetry of Howard Sergeant (editor of *Outposts Poetry Quarterly*), Hilary Davies (editor of *Argo*) along with her husband of that time, Bill MacDougall, and Eddie S. Linden (editor of *Aquarius*) and, later, the poets themselves when they came to Toronto. At that time, it was uncommon for young Canadian poets to study the work of British writers or to read journals like *Outposts*, *Argo*, and *Aquarius*.[1]

In general, British poets during the 1970s and 1980s were keenly interested in formal poetry and the long poetic tradition they inherited. By contrast, Canadian and American poets were deeply involved in free verse and in rejecting "old-fashioned" traditions. They considered rejecting traditions to constitute a signal virtue. This is not to say that all North American poets were writing free verse. There were Richard Wilbur and Robert Lowell. And there was the young James Wright. But the focus was more on Beat Generation, Black Mountain, and Deep Image poetics. To many North American readers, the British poetry of the 1970s and 1980s seemed somewhat out of date. Meyer thought otherwise.

One problem with much of what passes for poetry today is that it does not "feel" like poetry. Poetry has a certain way of employing language that is different from prose, and poetry should never sound like prose. This is not to suggest that all poetry should be written as strictly formal verse. But our poetry should be rooted in the English-language traditions of poetic usage, if not starting with Geoffrey Chaucer and other English writers of the late Middle Ages, then surely with George Herbert or Thomas Gray. Modern British poets tend to be aware of this vital legacy. Not so Canadian poets.

From his initial chapbooks, *The Tongues Between Us* (1981) and *The Aging of America* (1982), it was clear that Meyer had a true feel for the texture of the English tradition. His poems struck a different tone. Some of Meyer's poetry is indeed formal poetry, and some is written as free verse, but it is all clearly *poetry* and never prose posing as poetry. One would expect this from a man whose doctoral thesis was on Howard Sergeant and his *Outposts Poetry Quarterly*.

As an example of what I am getting at, please consider the "Glanmore Sonnets"[2] of Seamus Heaney and the *American Sonnets*[3] of Gerald Stern. Heaney's sonnets would never please purists because of their irregularities, but they definitely *feel* like sonnets. The Stern sonnets are not sonnets at all, although they are free verse poetry, and in many cases quite good. Other examples are Milton Acorn's *Jackpine Sonnets*[4] and Robert Lowell's poems in *Notebook*.[5] While both Lowell's "roomier" sonnet and Acorn's jackpine sonnet feel more like the sonnet tradition than the Stern variant, neither feels as sonnet-like as a Heaney sonnet. Much like the Irish master, Meyer's poems catch the flavour of the poetic tradition even when he writes free verse or semi-free verse.

From the above discussion of British, Irish, and American poets, I certainly do not suggest that Meyer only looks elsewhere and is not grounded in our Canadian tradition. He knows our Confederation Poets, and knows them well. Canada is a new nation; our English-language poetry starts in 1880 when Sir Charles G.D. Roberts published *Orion and Other Poems*. (*The Canterbury Tales*, circa 1390, was published some five hundred years earlier.) But our emerging poet was also drawn to his British contemporaries.

During the 1980s as Meyer was publishing his early collections, he was also doing the groundwork for his Ph.D. thesis on the British poet, editor, and critic Howard Sergeant (1914 – 1987)[6] and Sergeant's journal, *Outposts Poetry Quarterly*, which he edited for over forty years. While Sergeant accepted many types of poetry for *Outposts*, he became known for promoting members of two important British schools: The Movement and The Group.[7] These poets became central to Meyer's work on his doctorate.

The Movement began in the mid-1950s and featured such major poets as Philip Larkin, D.J. Enright, Elizabeth Jennings, and Donald Davie. Aside from Larkin, whose last poetry collection, *High Windows* (a Bruce Meyer favourite), appeared in 1974, they were publishing major collections[8] during the 1980s while Meyer was busy investigating their relationship with *Outposts*. The Movement was, at least in part, a reaction against and a rejection of Modernist poetics as practiced by T.S. Eliot, Ezra Pound, and Wallace Stevens. It was very English and tended to avoid non-English influences, which Movement poets considered Modernism to be. In some respects, The Movement embraced many of the features of the earlier Georgian Poetry, but was much more intellectual, more rigorous, and less sentimental. It also tried to accept, or at least come to terms with, the existence of Modernism, and in this regard was more realistic than Georgianism. And, like all literary schools should, The Movement produced its anthology, *New Lines: An Anthology*.[9]

The Group — in some quarters viewed as a result of, or as a reaction to, The Movement and its concerns — also dates from the mid-1950s. The Group's leading members, not to be upstaged by the literary stars of The Movement, included Peter Porter, Peter Redgrove, Fleur Adcock, and Alan Brownjohn. In general, the poets associated with The Group were less conservative than the members of The Movement. While The Movement was suspicious of non-English movements, several members of The Group took up the New Criticism.[10] In so doing they made common cause, so to speak, with John Crowe Ransom, Allen Tate, and Robert Lowell. Although meetings had started in the mid-1950s, The Group earned a more heightened public profile with the publication of *A Group Anthology*.[11] As was the case with The Movement poets, members of The Group were also busy publishing important collections[12] while Meyer was doing his research.

In general, The Movement promoted formal poetry and they favoured classical themes over autobiography-in-verse, which had become more prominent in magazines following World War II, and by the 1950s was to be found everywhere. The term "conventional" would apply to much of their poetry, not that that is such a bad thing. By contrast, The Group was more open to non-English influences, welcomed poetry of direct experience, and, while in no way experimental, was less rigid in terms of adherence to traditional poetic forms or received concepts. "Autobiographical" was never a term they shunned. (As an interesting footnote, future Poet Laureate Ted Hughes was loosely associated with both groups.) Meyer, while perhaps more strongly attracted to The Movement poets, has been in his own practice more like the poets in The Group.

During the period when Meyer was forming his own ideas of what a poem should be — roughly until he published his first full-sized collection, *The Open Room*, in 1989 — he was deeply engrossed by British poetry, especially the books by members of The Movement and The Group. I know of no other poet in the Toronto area who was reading the British as much as Meyer. This had a lasting impact on the poetry he would write.[13] Having his poetic roots planted so firmly in the English literary tradition has set him apart from other Canadian poets of his generation.

This Canadian aversion to, or ignorance of, literary tradition is odd and difficult to explain. The British Victorian poets knew the traditions of the 17th and 18th centuries. And the poets of post-World War II Britain also knew their Victorian forebears. In Canada it was different. While our Confederation Poets knew the traditions of the 17th and 18th centuries, the Canadian poets of Meyer's generation commonly knew next to nothing of their poetic tradition. For too many, poetry started with T.S. Eliot in the 20th century. Meyer's deeper understanding (so like his British cohort) has always set his poetry apart.

The signal qualities of Meyer's poetry are (1) a true feeling of poetry, even when he writes free verse, (2) a fulsome appreciation for the traditions of English-language poetry, formal or otherwise, both British and Canadian, (3) a seriousness of intent, and (4) an unusual degree of intellectual rigour for a poet writing today. Meyer's books shun the use of "filler poems" to flesh them out. And while his seriousness of intent has been present since he broke onto the CanLit scene during the 1980s, it was enhanced a decade and a half ago when Meyer converted to Catholicism. This happened in 2004 under the guidance of Fr. Robert Madden, a Milton scholar and English professor at the University of Toronto. As Meyer has stated, "I loved the intellectual tradition of the Basilian Brothers at St. Michael's (where I took up teaching for several years in their Continuing Education Program)."[14] One early result of his conversion was the publication of *Bread*.[15]

Prior to his conversion, Meyer had been, like many people in the late 20th century, vaguely Christian/vaguely Jungian. That is, he tended to experience Christianity more as a cultural presence, or even as a psychological expression in inner realities, than as a living religion to have faith in and to follow in daily life. The results of such a mid-life conversion — the poet was in his mid-forties — are often profound. In a true conversion the structure of consciousness is altered. And this new structure is illustrated by the order of service during worship and by Catholic ritual. This helped the poet come down on the side of Christianity rather than on the side of Carl Jung and his theories.[16]

In his pre-conversion poetry, Meyer tended to ground his poems in human history, current events, and/or human psychological experiences. Much of our contemporary literature is rooted in these things. But a writer connected by faith to Judeo-Christian theology will understand that the entire universe is based on Divine order. This order then becomes the foundation of one's life and work, infusing one's poetry. Today Meyer has more in common with Thomas Merton than with Northrop Frye. The foregoing is not to suggest that Meyer's poetry is traditionally devotional. Rather, it is based on a belief in Divine order instead of on human perception.

One quality that distinguishes Meyer from other academics who write poetry is that Meyer, although a scholar all his life, is a poet first. It was as a fellow poet, not as a professor, that Bruce Meyer introduced me to the poetry of Philip Larkin, especially *The Whitsun Weddings* and *High Windows*, his last two collections.[17] Several of Meyer's finest poems display common qualities with the poems found in Larkin's final books. These features include the structure, or the organization, of the content of individual poems and a rather conventional approach to revealing that content to the reader. These poems also evidence a dignified tone that at times verges on the stately. (Not bad qualities in my opinion.) What a Meyer poem does not share with the poetry of Larkin is most important. Larkin too often comes across as bitter and cynical. Bitterness and cynicism hold no place in Meyer's poetry.

Whatever individual readers think of Philip Larkin and his poetry, I believe all will agree that Larkin's poems are extremely well crafted. His poems are never simply thrown together. And Larkin leads his reader through the poem's content in a clear, if conservative, process to its conclusion — a conclusion that, when reached, seems inevitable. This is something Meyer learned.[18] Meyer's longer poems hang together very well, and seldom contain extraneous material.

In addition to the effect of British poets like Philip Larkin, Meyer was also deeply influenced as a young man by Northrop Frye,[19] who was lecturing at Victoria College,

University of Toronto. Frye's masterwork, *The Great Code*, appeared in 1981, while Meyer was a student. In *The Great Code*, Frye considers the impact of the Bible on shaping Western imagination and, by extension, our entire civilization. Frye views the Bible not so much as theology, but as a *story* that helped inform Western culture, including our literary culture. In Frye's opinion, one cannot fully understand our traditional literature unless one studies the Bible. Most importantly, many different national cultures are interconnected through the story of the Bible. Thus, the general Judeo-Christian culture and ethical system that English-language literature has always been part of remains central to us.

One aspect of the Bible Professor Frye investigated was its structure. Thus, Meyer learned the importance of considering the *structure* of all literary works from fourteen-line sonnets to massive novels. This attention to structure is apparent in Meyer's poetry and fiction. Unlike some poets who start to write and wait to see where the poem takes them, Meyer "builds" poems so that their form reveals their meaning. And this practice also lends a more traditional tone to his writing.

When Frye's focus on structure, which Meyer learned during the 1980s as a university student, is combined with the Catholic insistence on an orderly life, which he embraced much later, the result can only be beneficial. This can be seen in Meyer's most recent writing. Yet another aspect to Meyer's traditionalism is his bestselling study, *The Golden Thread*.[20] Within its 456 pages, Meyer seeks the unity within the entire tradition of Western literature, a most invidious task when one considers that the theology of the Bible is generally at odds with the ideas upon which Modernism is based.

The Golden Thread was published in 2001 and, as noted above, Meyer became a Catholic three years later in 2004. This forced him to move away from Frye's thought. Northrop Frye, although once an ordained United Church minister,[21] had become a Jungian at heart, and his ideas were therefore inconsistent with Christianity. This break from Frye has been another step in the correct direction for Meyer as well as for his poetry because it has forced him to re-think some of his long-standing assumptions, ideas he had developed during his student years, and has added greater clarity to his thought.

Meyer should properly be considered a traditionalist in both structure and in practice. Although Meyer has written on the New Formalism as a literary movement, he is not really a Formalist in the mould of Dana Gioia, Molly Peacock, or Mark Jarman. Rather, Meyer is a literary traditionalist. His finest poetry has always exceeded the limits of narrow classifications — traditionalist, formalist, modernist, or whatever. And it continues to escape easy assignment to this or that supposed movement or school or faction. It would be too facile to suggest that Meyer is some sort of 21st century rebirth of The Movement for in many respects, and although he certainly values tradition, he is a Modernist in a way they would not endorse. On the other hand, Meyer does admire the poetry of that school, as well as the poetry written by some members of The Group. But he is not simply "going back" to 20th century London.

Bruce Meyer is completely Canadian. Within the context of late 20th and early 21st century writing, his voice is unique because of its mixture of British formalism and Roman Catholicism, this mixture being fully grounded on his detailed understanding of Canada's literary history. His use of form and language is at once serious, dignified, and at its best, elegant. And, although he has turned sixty, good reasons exist to expect his best work lies ahead.

Notes:

1. One result of having met Meyer on the University of Toronto campus was my first publication in a British literary journal. Shortly after meeting Hilary Davies and Bill MacDougall at Meyer's Toronto home, Argo (Oxford, England) published my poem "The 690 Level" and this was followed by other British periodicals like Envoi, iota, Lines Review, and Acumen. I quickly discovered poets like William Oxley, John Heath-Stubbs, Sebastian Barker, and Nicholas Bielby, and eventually went on a poetry tour of England, Scotland, and Wales.

2. Heaney, Seamus. Field Work. London: Faber and Faber, 1979. Print. See pages 33 – 42.

3. Stern, Gerald. American Sonnets. New York: W.W. Norton & Company, 2002. Print.

4. Acorn, Milton. Jackpine Sonnets. Toronto: Steel Rail Educational Publishing, 1977. Print.

5. Lowell, Robert. Notebook. New York: Farrar, Straus and Giroux, 1970. Print.

6. Bruce Meyer was awarded his Ph.D. by McMaster University in 1988 and completed his post-doctoral fellowship at McMaster in 1990.

7. Of interest to Canadian readers, Howard Sergeant developed an interest in Canadian poetry, notably the work of Margaret Atwood, Earle Birney, and Fred Cogswell.

8. D.J. Enright's Collected Poems was issued in 1981; Donald Davie's Selected Poems appeared in 1985; the Collected Poems, 1953-1985 of Elizabeth Jennings was published in 1986.

9. Conquest, Robert, ed. New Lines: An Anthology. London: Macmillan & Company, 1956. Print. It featured the poetry of Kingsley Amis, Robert Conquest, Donald Davie, D.J. Enright, Thom Gunn, John Holloway, Elizabeth Jennings, Philip Larkin, and John Wain.

10. In 1941 the American writer and academic John Crowe Ransom published The New Criticism. (New York: New Directions, 1941. Print.) Professor Ransom's literary theory soon attracted followers in the form of American poets Robert Lowell, Allan Tate, Randall Jarrell, Robert Penn Warren, and many others. A movement was born. The New Criticiam was, for the most part, highly formalist, although some poets, most notably Robert Lowell and James Wright, would break with strict formalism.

11. Lucie-Smith, Edward and Philip Hobsbaum, eds. A Group Anthology. London: Oxford University Press, 1963. Print. The poets represented include Alan Brownjohn, Zulfikar Ghose, Philip Hobsbaum, Adrian Mitchell, Peter Porter, Peter Redgrove, Anthony Smith, David Wevill, and others.

12. Peter Redgrove's The Apple Broadcast and Other New Poems was issued in 1981; both Fleur Adcock's Selected Poems and Alan Brownjohn's Collected Poems, 1952-1983 appeared in 1983; Peter Porter's Fast Forward was published in 1984.

13. Meyer's reading affected me, too. I had never read Philip Larkin, David Wevill, Howard Sergeant, Peter Porter, and Donald Davie until Meyer encouraged me to do so. Sadly, magnificent poets like John Heath-Stubbs, Jenny Joseph, William Oxley, and Sebastian Barker are almost never read this side of the Atlantic.

14. Letter from Bruce Meyer to the present author dated May 30, 2018.

15. Meyer, Bruce. Bread. Toronto: Lyricalmyrical, 2009. Print. This small collection is a meditation on the Sacraments and the Catholic service.

16. Both Meyer's wife, Kerry, and his friend and literary colleague, Brian O'Riordan, are Catholic. They probably helped Meyer over the hump.

17. Larkin, Philip. The Whitsun Weddings. London: Faber and Faber, 1964. Print. Larkin, Philip. High Windows. London: Faber and Faber, 1974. Print. These two collections have always been among Meyer's personal favourites.

18. The main American poet to achieve such highly structured and excellent poems might be Richard Wilbur. While their content is quite different, in terms of a serious attention to form, Larkin and Wilbur are similar.

19. Of especial interest to the young poet were Frye's books The Bush Garden: Essays on the Canadian Imagination (Toronto: House of Anansi, 1971, Print.) and The Great Code: The Bible and Literature. (Harvest Books, an imprint of Harcourt Brace Jovanovich, 1981. Print.). Frye's theories influenced two generations of Canadian poets including Margaret Atwood and Dennis Lee.

20. Meyer, Bruce. The Golden Thread: A Reader's Journey Through the Great Books. Toronto: HarperCollins Canada, 2001. Print. In this study, Meyer covers literature from the Bible and Homer to the 20th century Modernists. By starting with the Bible, Meyer shows his debt to the ideas of Northrop Frye.

21. The Rev. Frye served briefly in Saskatchewan in this capacity.

Simply Ray: an Introduction

James Deahl. Professor, Poet, Critic, Editor

When I moved to Canada during the spring of 1970, an obscure, scarcely published American poet of twenty-four, I knew of virtually no Canadian poets, and those few by reputation only. It has been my great good fortune to have had many Canadian poets befriend me over the past four decades. Several of these poets became long-term friends, our friendships ending only with their deaths: Milton Acorn, Dorothy Livesay, Ted Plantos, Al Purdy, and Raymond Souster. No poet learns the craft without help and sage advice from those who have already achieved a higher level of writing. As my poetry slowly developed, I learned a great deal from the poets who took me under their wings: Irving Layton, Milton Acorn, and Ray Souster chief among them.

I was honoured to be invited to contribute both prose and poetry to the Al Purdy tribute anthology, *And Left a Place To Stand On*, and it was my privilege to edit Milton Acorn's tribute anthology, *The Northern Red Oak*. Now Ray Souster has died. No anthology can come close to celebrating the life and work of such an important, indeed *essential*, figure in the history of Canadian literature; several large books would be required. But my publisher and I will do our best.

Raymond Holmes Souster, OC, was born in Toronto on January 15, 1921 to Norma and Austin Souster. He died in the city of his birth on October 19, 2012 at the age of ninety-one. Ray spent his entire life in Toronto except for the years during which he saw active duty with the Royal Canadian Air Force during World War II. He served from November 11, 1941 until the end of hostilities, being based first in eastern Canada and later in England. His military experiences would result in his two novels: *The Winter of Time* (published in 1949) and *On Target* (1972). When not serving his country in uniform, he spent his entire working life at the Canadian Imperial Bank of Commerce, from 1939 until his forced retirement. (I say forced because Ray would have kept working had not retirement been mandatory in those days.)

I will briefly cover the principal aspects of the literary life of this seminal poet. These will fall into eight areas: Poetry, Fiction, Editing (both books and magazines), Book Publishing, Organizing Readings, the League of Canadian Poets, Mentorship, and the Souster Legacy. I will start with his own poetry and fiction because Ray was, first and foremost, a *writer*. Strictly in terms of his own books, and excluding all of his other major accomplishments, Ray can be placed among the most important dozen poets of 20th

Century Canada. A final section will deal with his character. I will also refer to him simply as Ray because that is how my friend would wish to be known.

1. **Poetry**

From his initial magazine appearances to his final poem written on October 5, 2012, Ray was a working poet for seventy-two years. Between 1946 and 2012, Ray published some fifty-eight books and chapbooks of original poetry (not counting the ten-volume *Collected Poems of Raymond Souster* from Oberon Press, which is essential reading for anyone interested in fine poetry).

Ray launched his professional publishing career in 1946 when John Sutherland's First Statement Press issued his chapbook *When We Are Young*. With First Statement, Ray joined other young poets such as Irving Layton, Miriam Waddington, and Patrick Anderson, all active within the Montreal literary community at the time. It was via this connection to Montreal that Ray formed his extremely important friendships with Louis Dudek and Layton. Ray was among the first Canadian poets to be inspired by the Populist Poetry of the Chicago School. His major early influences were Kenneth Fearing, Kenneth Patchen, and Carl Sandburg. To a much lesser degree, the influence of Kenneth Rexroth, who was not really part of the Populist movement, can be discerned. Indeed, it was Ray who introduced Milton Acorn, Al Purdy, and several other Canadian People's Poets to American Populism. What appealed to Ray was the mixture of image-based poetry with realism. Such poems would utilize plain speech, and avoid Classical or academic references. This poetry could easily embrace both urban and rural themes, both social-political issues and nature.

Terry Barker has argued in his unpublished paper "Raymond Souster: Compact Canadian Chesterton?" that Ray could be seen as the "father" of People's Poetry in Canada because it was Ray who introduced his fellow poets to Midwest Populist Poetry, especially the work of Fearing and Patchen. Ray was avidly reading books by the American Populists, which he bought mail-order from New York while serving in the RCAF, a few years before he met Irving Layton during the summer of 1943, as well as other young Montreal poets such as Louis Dudek. Indeed, not only can one see many echoes of Fearing in Ray's own poetry, as conclusively demonstrated in Hugh Cook's unpublished M.A. thesis, "The Poetry of Raymond Souster", one can see the same echoes in the early poetry of Irving Layton, Milton Acorn, and Al Purdy, along with other members of Ray's literary circle.

It was in the United States, not Canada, where Ray found his initial success and, more importantly, *encouragement*, publishing poetry in the *Sunday Journal* (Providence, Rhode Island) and the *New York Herald Tribune* (which reprinted a Souster poem from the *Sunday Journal*). Interestingly enough, the editor of the *Sunday Journal* who was so welcoming to the unknown Canadian poet was poet and literary critic Winfield Townley Scott (who would himself later write for the *Herald Tribune* in praise of Carl Sandburg). It was Ray's early interest in the American poets that attracted him to the *First Statement* group rather than to the more British-influenced *Preview* group, the dueling literary movements in Montreal during the first half of the 1940s.

While Fearing, whose poetry Ray discovered in 1939-40 (according to Ray's own account), was the first powerful influence on Ray's mature work, it would be Patchen who would provide the lasting influence. (Ray read Fearing during his RCAF service. Fearing's *Dead Reckoning* had been published in 1938 and his *Collected Poems* two years later. Both were important books for Ray.) Ray developed his poetics throughout the 1940s and 1950s. That is to say, he became better and better at his craft while deepening his vision of Canada. The next big change came in the 1960s after he came across Robert Lowell's *Life Studies* (published in 1959). Throughout the 1960s Ray read Lowell, and by the publication of *Change-Up* (1974) Ray had fully absorbed Lowell's discursive, off-hand, chatty style, which he used for his own purposes. (Always shy and reserved, Ray would write no Confessional poetry.)

Another Chicago-born (but New York-raised) poet who influenced Ray a bit later on during the middle of his career was Harvey Shapiro, whose *This World* (1971) and especially his *National Cold Storage Company* (1988) impressed Ray greatly. Unlike Lowell's *Life Studies*, Shapiro's poetry was tighter and more controlled. This was much like Ray's own pre-*Life Studies* work, and the Shapiro influence was, in my opinion, most beneficial. Indeed, I believe it was Shapiro's poetry that helped reintroduce Ray to the shorter, sharper poetry he had perfected during the 1940s and '50s. Among the many gifts Ray gave to me was a copy of *National Cold Storage Company*.

The final evolution in Ray's poetics demonstrates the continued influence of Patchen. Starting with three collections published during 2006 — *Uptown Downtown*, *Wondrous Wobbly World*, and *Down to Earth* — Ray began to adopt the brief, imagistic and/or epigramatical poetry that he first discovered in collections like Patchen's *Cloth of the Tempest* (1943). While it is true that he had experimented with this style many years before, in the 21st Century it became a major feature of his poetry. By doing this, Ray was able to focus on wry, witty, and ironic statements, often on aging (his), cultural decay (Toronto's), and corruption (political). In these short pieces, Ray could be at once pithy and humorous, wise and silly. Indeed, he titled many of them "Silly Little Poem No. __". These tiny poems, some of only a single line, could deal with death, religion, beauty, crime, and, quite often, love. Ray never allowed the short form to imprison his vision or in any way to limit his content.

The poetics adopted by Ray were largely, but *not* exclusively, those of the different strands of American Modernism. He was, for example, influenced by a few of the Georgian Poets, Edward Thomas for one, W.W. Gibson for another. And Ray closely read Rainer Maria Rilke. (One must look long and hard to find any Rilke in Ray's later poetry, but it was Rilke's Romanticism that caught Ray's attention. And Ray always had a notable streak of Romanticism in his work.) The Edward Thomas influence is readily found in Ray's nature poetry, both his celebrated "backyard" poems and his Humber River valley poems. The Gibson influence is more in the way of content and poetic stance.

When Oscar Peterson died, both Ray and I were upset when some foolish commentator (supposedly an expert on jazz) claimed that Peterson had been "a great imitator, but *not* a great innovator." It is not my purpose here to dismiss my friend as merely an imitator of American Populist Poetry or any such thing. What Ray took from Kenneth Fearing, Kenneth Patchen, Carl Sandburg, Robert Lowell, Harvey Shapiro, William Carlos Williams, the Georgian Poets, Rilke, etc. he made his own. He used his own creative brilliance to extend their literary ideas. Moreover, Ray was Canadian through and through, his poetry being rooted in our history and literary traditions, especially our Confederation Poets.

Lest my comments be put down as the special pleadings of a personal friend, please consider the following. Just as it is highly unlikely that Oscar Peterson won a Grammy Award for Best Improvised Jazz Solo because he was merely imitating Art Tatum, it is also unlikely Ray won the Governor General's Award for Poetry (in 1964), the Centennial Medal (1967), the City of Toronto Book Award (1979), or was presented with the Order of Canada (1995) because he was imitating Fearing or Patchen. In an era when Canadian poetry was largely unknown in the U.S., Ray's books were read and admired by such poets as Louis Zukofsky, Denise Levertov, Cid Corman, and Larry Eigner. I suspect that back then, Ray and Irving Layton might have been the only Canadian poets widely read by American poets.

While Ray's chosen topics — love, nature, war, social injustice, jazz, religion, and beauty — are universal, he sticks close to Canada and his beloved Toronto. He fully shares a belief in "good common sense" with his Populist Poet cousins. And like them, Ray also believed in the basic goodness of his fellow humans. His life and work were sustained by three pillars: his love for his wife Rosalia, his Christian faith, and his confidence in the power of sharp and decisive poetry. Ray was no Pollyanna, however; as a Christian he fully recognized the action of evil in this world.

Love poetry — Like all real poets, Ray wrote love poems throughout his career. The better pieces, including an entire book of them (*The Eyes of Love*, 1987), date from his marriage to Rosalia, to whom he was devoted. In fact, the romance of Ray and Rosalia is a love story for the ages.

Nature poetry — Striking nature images appear in Ray's poetry from the very beginning. Examples: the rain in "Night of Rain" and the crickets in "The Invaders", both included in *Unit of Five* (1944). The natural world is used in two main ways, as accents to remind the reader of beauty in poems that deal with other, often less pleasant, concerns and in poems directly about the joy, or heartless cruelty, of fallen nature. Ray's pure nature poems are usually set not far from home: in the Humber River valley or in his own backyard on Baby Point Road. In my reading of Canadian poetry, only Milton Acorn wrote nature poems, and poems highlighting natural images, that were equal to Ray's poetry at its best. When it comes to the backyard poetry from his years on Baby Point, Ray became a Canadian Emily Dickinson.

War poetry — Ray wrote on the horror of war all his life. Most of the poems in *Unit of Five* and much of the poetry in *When We Are Young* (1946) relate to his years in the Air Force during the war. In addition to numerous short poems, Ray wrote a 154-page poem about the ill-conceived raid on Dieppe (August 19, 1942), *Jubilee of Death*, and a 398-page poem, *What Men Will Die For,* about the French war in Vietnam (November 1946-May 1954). The latter was written between February 2001 and March 2007, and is a true epic poem. It was published in 2007.

Jubilee of Death was published in 1984, just a couple of years after I first met Ray. At the time we became friends, Ray was still with the Canadian Imperial Bank of Commerce and I was a financial analyst on Bay Street. To put it another way, we were both paid to look after other people's money. Upon occasion we would meet for lunch. It was at one of these luncheons that Ray gave me a copy of his just-published *Jubilee of Death*. Then, as now, I enjoyed getting into bed with a book to read for half an hour before the arrival of sleep. That night it was *Jubilee of Death*. I admit I was daunted by a 154-page poem, but I thought I would read fifteen pages or so. Ray's poem was so compelling that I read the entire thing, staying up all night, and going to the office the next morning without having slept.

Social poetry — Ray commented on social/political issues from his first publications until the end of his life. Poverty, oppression, violence, racism, anti-Semitism, avarice, and human degeneration were all targets of his poetry. Politically, Ray was well within the spectrum of large "L" liberalism – social democracy. I suspect he always voted N.D.P. once the N.D.P. was created, and he was a passionate supporter of Jack Layton. This was in keeping with his United Church faith. Ray believed that Christians have a social duty. He was a People's Poet from day one, and never wavered in his defense of human dignity.

Jazz poetry — From boyhood Ray was a jazz fan, becoming an expert on the topic. One of his early, and successful, jazz poems is "Salute to Bobby Hackett" (collected in *Cerberus*, 1952). Among his last is "Vic Dickinson" (collected in *Easy Does It*, 2012). He wrote poems referring to jazz in general or about specific jazz players regularly for decades, with what was perhaps his finest hour coming in the eleven-section "No Sad Songs Wanted Here: The Life & Death of the Colonial Bar & Grill", the title sequence of a book Oberon published in 1995.

Religious poetry — While Ray published very little religious poetry, he did write more in his final few years. In his 2011 collection *Big Smoke Blues*, published a year and a half before his death, Ray offered five poems concerning his Christian faith. In "This Man of April" he affirms the presence of Jesus within our lives in this Easter meditation:

> This Man of April
> lives here
> with us still

The poet states in "At Peace" that he has found solace in the arms of Jesus:

he's found peace
nestled in
to his saviour's
all compassionate grace.

(Throughout *Big Smoke Blues* as a whole, Ray habitually referred to himself in the third person.) Ray was a longtime member of Runnymede United Church.

His final collection of short poems, *Easy Does It* (2012), contains more meditations on mortality and even one on Divine forgiveness. One fine example is "Judgement Day". And there is another Easter meditation, "Good Friday, 2011", in my opinion Ray's finest religious poem.

Beauty — Ray believed (as I do) that the existence of beauty, and the ability of humans to see and appreciate it, is a proof of the basic goodness of creation in general, and of mankind in particular. Beauty has redemptive qualities that are needed in this defiled world. Ray often opposed the city with all its faults and blemishes to the pure beauty of trees, flowers, rivers, sunsets, and birds. Until he became old and unstable on his feet, Ray would often walk by the Humber River, which flows quite near his home on Baby Point. He especially enjoyed Étienne Brûlé Park, the Old Mill area, and Lambton Woods.

An excellent example of how Ray contrasted natural beauty with the corrupt, dispiriting city is "Nocturnal" from 1940. Another, written sixty years later, is "Black Trillium" (from *Of Time & Toronto*, 2000). In the latter piece, a single flower can "spread a welcome veil of peace / across the battered face / of a despairing world".

In terms of literary quality alone, I place Ray among the finest dozen or so Canadian poets of the 20th Century, and certainly well into the Top Ten Canadian poets of the post-World War II period. And I write here only about his poetry. Between *When We Are Young* (First Statement Press, 1946) and *Never Counting the Cost* (The Battered Silicon Dispatch Box, 2012), Ray published fifty-six other books and chapbooks of poetry.

While it is not my intention to write a critical essay on Ray's poetry, allow me to close this section with my personal observation. Some critics are of the opinion that Ray began to write his really good poetry only during the very late 1950s-early 1960s, perhaps around the time he wrote the poems included in *A Local Pride* (published in 1962). This opinion, in my view, is in error. Ray's section of *Unit of Five* offers the reader several poems of remarkable quality, "Night of Rain", "Ten PM", "Hunger", "Search", and "Reality" being five examples. Because *Unit of Five* was published in 1944, all of Ray's poems were written during his stint with the RCAF. And *When We Are Young* (1946) has numerous fine pieces. "The Hunter", "The Lagoon", "Waiting", and "The Barracks" are, in my opinion, as worthy of praise as any poetry being written at the time by anyone else in Canada. And this just takes us to the close of World War II. By the time *For What Time Slays* appeared in 1955, Ray had published so many excellent poems that they are too numerous to list here.

But you need not take my word for this. Prof. Francis Mansbridge locates the start of the good, mature poetry as early as "The Penny Flute", first published in 1941 (and collected in *When We Are Young*, 1946). Hugh Cook considers "Night Watch", "Air Raid", and "Apple Blow" to be among the first of Ray's poems to display lasting quality (published in 1943). Ray's choice would be the aforementioned "Nocturnal", first published in 1940.

I fully agree with Ray. "Nocturnal" surely must count among the outstanding poems to be published that year in Canada. Although published in the *Canadian Forum* in 1940, it was not to appear in book form until Ray's *Go to Sleep, World* (1947). To understand just how strong Ray's poetry was when he was still quite a young man, I highly recommend the *Collected Poems of Raymond Souster, Volume One, 1940-55*. Not many poets write major poems prior to the age of twenty. But Ray did.

I have read the forty-seven books and chapbooks of Ray's poetry I own. I have also read his two novels. It is my personal taste in poetry — and only my personal taste — that prompts these next statements. I prefer the poems Ray wrote before the influence of Robert Lowell's *Life Studies*; these early poems are often great, as fine as any poems written in Canada. I also like reading the longer, more discursive poems Ray wrote after he had read and digested *Life Studies*, but not as much. I feel that Ray was at his best when he wrote shorter, more imagistic poems. (I feel I must note here that many critics believe exactly the opposite.) Finally, I am much less interested in Ray's post-Oberon poems (2004-2012), but would like to make it clear that there are a great many good poems in Ray's final books, all published by The Battered Silicon Dispatch Box. Among these final sixteen titles the reader will find *What Men Will Die For*, which is compelling reading. The longer, looser line served Ray well when he wrote of war.

As I have stated above, Ray wrote first-rate poetry from 1940 until his death in 2012. Not one of his sixty books is a bad book, some are just better than others. All are worth reading. I eagerly await the publication of a truly definitive *Selected Poems of Raymond Souster, 1940-2012*. It will be an exceedingly fine book by any standards.

2. **Fiction**

Ray wrote two novels: *The Winter of Time* (published under the *nom de plume* Raymond Holmes in 1949, re-published in 2006) and *On Target* (published under the *nom de plume* John Holmes in 1972, re-published in 2006). The first is a short novel, the latter ninety pages longer. Both deserve to be read.

The Winter of Time is a coming of age tale set against the backdrop of World War II. *On Target*, also set during the war, is largely based on the flight log and wartime experiences of one of Ray's comrades-at-arms in the Air Force. In the opinion of the present writer, *The Winter of Time* is quite a good, well-written book; *On Target* is a major achievement. Clearly Ray was a gifted novelist as well as a gifted poet, although Ray's fiction does fall short of the true excellence his finest poetry achieved.

Both of these novels use the realistic, straight-forward storytelling perfected by Morley Callaghan and James T. Farrell. If you like a well-told story of the human drama of young men caught up in a war they did not start and may not live to finish, a tale of blind courage and heartbreak, of clinging to life with raw determination, buy and read *On Target.*

3. **Editing** (both books and magazines)

Through his textbooks as well as volumes like *100 Poems of Nineteenth-Century Canada, Comfort of the Fields, Vapour and Blue, Powassan's Drum*, and *Windflower*, Ray established himself as a leading expert on Canadian poetry from the Confederation period to the emerging poets of 1980.

Five volumes of 19th Century poetry (three co-edited by Douglas Lochhead):

100 Poems of Nineteenth Century Canada, with Lochhead (Macmillan of Canada, 1974), *Vapour and Blue: the poetry of William Wilfred Campbell* (Paget Press, 1978), *Comfort of the Fields: Archibald Lampman, best-known Poems* (Paget Press, 1979), *Powassan's Drum: Selected Poems of Duncan Campbell Scott*, with Lochhead (Tecumseh, 1985), and *Windflower: Poems of Bliss Carman*, with Lochhead (Tecumseh, 1985).

Unfortunately, I have only two of these, the selections from Archibald Lampman (*Comfort of the Fields*) and the selections from W.W. Campbell (*Vapour and Blue*). Both are quite fine representations of these two major poets. I certainly wish I had the three that were co-edited by Douglas Lochhead, but I have never found them in any used bookshop. I do not understand how I missed out on the final two volumes because Ray and I were good friends by 1985.

Four textbooks (all co-edited by Richard Woolatt):

Generation Now (Longman Canada, 1970), *Sights and Sounds* (Macmillan of Canada, 1973), *These loved, these hated lands* (Doubleday Canada, 1975), and *Poems of A Snow-Eyed Country* (Academic Press, 1980). Between 1970 and the early 1980s it is quite likely that a student in Ontario would meet one of the textbooks edited by Ray and Richard Woolatt. The first one, *Generation Now*, like the other three, is entirely poetry. It includes work from Canadian, American, and British writers. It is no surprise that Souster favourites Kenneth

Patchen, William Carlos Williams, Carl Sandburg, W.W. Gibson, Edward Thomas, Kenneth Fearing, and Kenneth Rexroth are well represented.

Sights and Sounds is also international, but with a much tighter focus on American and Canadian poets, including Milton Acorn, Carl Sandburg, Gwendolyn MacEwen, and Robert Frost. This textbook also includes one of the rare poems by Ray's mentor Winfield Townley Scott.

Spanish-language and French-Canadian poets play a prominent role in *These loved, these hated lands*. Examples are Salvador Diaz Miron, Octavio Paz, Jose Juan Tablada, Jacques Brault, Roland Giguère, Anne Hébert, Gilles Hénault, Gatien Lapointe, Hector de Saint-Denys-Garneau, and Pierre Trottier.

The final textbook Richard Woolatt and Ray edited is entirely Canadian, with a strong French-Canadian presence. *Poems of A Snow-Eyed Country* introduces several poets of the (then) younger generation: Tom Howe, Hans Jewinski, Sid Marty, Joseph Sherman, Andrew Suknaski, Peter Van Toorn, Tom Wayman, and Dale Zieroth.

I own copies of all four books. As a former teacher of Canadian literature at the high school and college levels, I can attest to their excellence. Had I been teaching during the 1970-1985 period I would have wanted to use them with my students. I can also report that my three daughters were not given such finely-edited books when they attended high school in Ontario during the post-1985 years. Although these were edited and published for school children, they would be enjoyed and valued by adult readers. These books certainly refuse to talk down to their intended audience simply because they are teenagers. If only today's textbooks would treat students like intelligent people. I know I liked reading them and can recommend them to readers of all ages.

Four literary magazines:

Direction, 1943-1946, *Enterprise*, 1948, *Contact*, 1952-1954, and *Combustion*, 1957-1960.

Of these magazines, the latter two were truly important, and not simply for Canadian poets. Both *Contact* and *Combustion* attracted readers and contributors from outside Canada. Among the regular readers of *Contact* were Americans Larry Eigner, Louis Zukofsky, Theodore Holmes, Robert Creeley, and Donald M. Allen. Readers of *Combustion* included Denise Levertov and Eigner. As noted by Cook in his M.A. thesis, *Contact* would publish the work of Canadians Dudek, Layton, and Alfred G. Bailey, Americans Charles Olson, Robert Creeley, Paul Blackburn, Lawrence Ferlinghetti, and Cid Corman, as well as leading non-English-language poets in translation: Octavio Paz, Jacques Prévert, Guillaume Apollinaire, Gottfried Benn, Jean Cocteau, Anna Akhmatova, and George Seferis.

Combustion, like *Contact*, was also international in scope. Contributors included Gary Snyder, Robert Duncan, Fielding Dawson, Zukofsky, and Creeley. Denise Levertov's *With Eyes in the Back of Our Heads*, for one example, includes poems initially published in both *Contact* and *Combustion*. And poems in Gary Snyder's *The Back Country* first appeared in

Combustion. Indeed, Frank Davey has written that "*Combustion* made a significant contribution to U.S. literature". Prof. Davey also wrote that "*Contact* was thus the first Canadian magazine to publish U.S. poets of the Black Mountain school."

What Ray was able to do was place Canadian poetry before the world and introduce foreign poets to Canadians. In my view, *Contact* and *Combustion* were the most important Canadian poetry magazines of the 1960s, an opinion shared by Donald M. Allen and several U.S. poets.

Three anthologies of contemporary poetry:

Poets 56: Ten Younger English-Canadians (Contact Press, 1956), *New Wave Canada: The New Explosion in Canadian Poetry* (Contact Press, 1966), and *Made in Canada: New Poems of the Seventies*, with Douglas Lochhead (Oberon Press, 1970). I own only one of these anthologies, *Made in Canada: New Poems of the Seventies*, which I bought as soon as it was published. This was my first, serious introduction to Canadian poetry, and it was through this volume that I, as a brand new immigrant in 1970, got to know the poetry of Milton Acorn, Margaret Atwood, Earle Birney, bill bissett, David Donnell, Paul Dutton, Doug (now George) Fetherling, Patrick Lane, Dennis Lee, Dorothy Livesay, Gwendolyn MacEwen, Ray himself, Francis Sparshott, Colleen Thibaudeau, and Robert Zend prior to becoming acquainted with, and in many cases close friends with, the poets themselves. This was an eye-opening anthology, and one of the best-edited in Canada, then or now.

As he would do a decade later with his textbook *Poems of A Snow-Eyed Country*, Ray included no fewer than twenty young, emerging poets in with Governor General's Award-winning poets Margaret Atwood, Earle Birney, Dorothy Livesay, Eli Mandel, Alden Nowlan, P.K. Page, and Ray himself. Three of these young poets — David Donnell, George Fetherling, and Dennis Lee — have contributed to the present anthology.

No editor could discover talented poets like Ray. At least fifteen of the poets introduced to the public in *Made in Canada* had yet to publish their first full collections, and a good many others had only a single publication to their credit. Of the previously "unknown" poets, some half a dozen have seen their poetry installed in the CanLit canon, eight would have their poetry appear in *The New Oxford Book of Canadian Verse in English* (as early as the 1983 edition), and at least two have gone on to win the Governor General's Award for Poetry. A good many of today's leading poets owe a great deal to Ray's editing and/or publishing genius. If the two Contact Press anthologies are as valuable as Oberon's *Made in Canada*, I wish I had them.

4. **Book Publishing**

Contact Press, established by Ray, Louis Dudek, and Irving Layton, ran for fifteen years (1952-1967). Authors published include Milton Acorn, Margaret Atwood, George Bowering, Leonard Cohen, Frank Davey, Louis Dudek, George Ellenbogen, Eldon Grier, Daryl Hine, D.G. Jones, Irving Layton, Gwendolyn MacEwen, Eli Mandel, Kenneth

McRobbie, John Newlove, Alden Nowlan, Al Purdy, Gael Turnbull, and Phyllis Webb. Sometimes their Contact Press book was the first professional publication these poets had. Almost all are now firmly ensconced in the canon of major Canadian poets, yet most were unknown when Contact Press published them.

5. **Organizing Public Readings**

As a direct outgrowth of *Contact* magazine, for many years Ray organized and hosted dozens of poetry readings in Toronto, initially at the Isaacs Gallery, and finally, decades later, at the University of Toronto in the mid-1980s. As with *Contact*, Ray featured Canadian poets from all regions across our vast country, Leonard Cohen, Al Purdy, Alden Nowlan, and James Reaney among them, as well as such major American poets as Charles Olson, Denise Levertov, Robert Creeley, LeRoi Jones (as he was known then), Louis Zukofsky, Frank O'Hara, and Cid Corman. In many cases, this would be the first Canadian reading for the Americans and the first Toronto reading for the Canadians. These readings Ray organized were the most important in the Toronto-area until Greg Gatenby built the Harbourfront Reading Series into one of the finest and most comprehensive in the world.

Ray even worked poems by Levertov, Creeley, and O'Hara into his textbooks for Ontario schools. Through poetry readings, magazines, and textbook anthologies, Ray introduced the general public and students to a wide and eclectic variety of Canadian, American, British, and non-English-language writers. As I recall, one of the readings Ray hosted at the University of Toronto (University College) was my first appearance at that university.

6. **The League of Canadian Poets**

The founding of The League of Canadian Poets dates from August 20, 1966 when Ray along with Louis Dudek, Ronald G. Everson, and Michael Gnarowski met with Ralph Gustafson at the latter's home in North Hatley, Quebec. The LCP grew out of that meeting, and Ray served as its first President (then called Chairman), 1967-1971. It's doubtful if the LCP would exist without Ray's dedicated work during its early, formative years. (The reader may wish to consult *Making the Damn Thing Work* by Raymond Souster, published for the 35th birthday of the League of Canadian Poets.)

7. **Mentorship**

Ray had unlimited time and energy when it came to encouraging other writers. During the thirty years I knew Ray he spent as much energy, if not more, helping and promoting other poets than he spent on his own writing. Contributors Sam Simchovitch and Carleton Wilson are but two examples of poets Ray assisted, either by mail (Sam) or in person (Carleton). Others included Gwendolyn MacEwen and Alden Nowlan. Poets who have praised Ray's support are countless; Michael Ondaatje has written, "He brought many of us to the surface and we owe him everything."

8. **The Souster Legacy**

Two of the poets who have generously contributed to this tribute anthology — Simcha (Sam) Simchovitch and Norma West Linder — are among the leading Sousterian poets writing today. Sam was born in Poland the same day as Ray, January 15, 1921, and Ray always referred to Sam is his "poet-twin". Norma was born later that same decade, and was inspired to write poetry by reading Ray's work. Both of these poets have, of course, made their own significant contributions to Canadian letters, both in poetry and prose. And both carry on the literary tradition Ray started some 65 years ago. The Souster legacy extends far beyond these two writers, however. One can clearly see Ray's influence on the poetry of Milton Acorn, for example. And I have also learned a great deal from Ray and his poetry, as have contributors such as Kent Bowman and Michael Fraser.

In addition, such public appreciation as exists for the work of Confederation Poets Archibald Lampman (Ray's favourite Canadian poet), William Wilfred Campbell, Duncan Campbell Scott, and Bliss Carman can be largely traced to the volumes of their work Ray so painstakingly edited, some on his own and some with Douglas Lochhead.

9. **The Man Himself**

Ray was a true gentleman of the old school as well as a man of honour in the full sense of the word. The terms "gentleman" and "honour" might sound odd these days, but they have real meaning. When I think of Ray, as I often do, certain words like courage, compassion, honesty, generosity, and strength leap into my mind. The poetry world is, sad to say, populated by sharp operators. Ray was never among them. Ray believed in cooperation, not competition, among writers. As a poet, editor, and publisher he was strikingly honest. A hallmark feature of his writing was his social commitment to, and deep compassion for, his fellow humans.

Ray faced many hardships throughout his long life that I need not go into here. A tribute anthology is no place to rehearse this modest man's personal trials. I will mention only the three that many of his readers already know about. Ray went blind, and despite becoming blind, which he expected to happen, he kept on with his usual daily life as long as possible. He wrote hundreds of poems after he lost his sight. Every time I visited him, Ray was in a good mood. He accepted his condition, and did not allow it to depress or define him.

Prior to going blind, Ray lost all his teeth. For several years he was reduced to eating puréed baby food. Around this time he had to stop drinking beer and wine. All readers of Ray's poetry or fiction will know how attached he was to the pleasures of the table. With the loss of his sight and the loss of his teeth, his world became very narrow. Again,

I never heard him complain. I assure my readers that his blindness and the loss of his teeth were not the greatest of his burdens.

The third thing was death. It was Ray's fate to suffer what the Irish call a hard death. During his last three years he was often in pain, and sometimes his pain was quite severe. On the rare occasions when he mentioned his physical sufferings he did so as if merely recounting a fact. I never heard him complain. The details of his ninety-one years in this world were the actions of Providence. The pains and the pleasures were to be equally accepted.

One of the results of living for nine decades is that most of your friends die before you. Almost all of Ray's friends and colleagues who were born during the 1920s and 1930s are gone. Were they still with us, I am certain this anthology would contain work by Milton Acorn, Earle Birney, Fred Cogswell, Cid Corman, Louis Dudek, Ronald G. Everson, Ralph Gustafson, Irving Layton, Denise Levertov, Douglas Lochhead, Charles Olson, Al Purdy, James Reaney, and John Sutherland to mention a few of Ray's buddies.

Even ignoring all of his literary achievements, Ray was a great man. He was a rare and true example of how to fully *live* a life. I consider it to have been a privilege and a blessing to have been his friend. Given Ray's humility, he would no doubt think I have gone on far too long. He would much rather praise other poets than have us praise him. So I had better turn this over to the other contributors.

To be or not to be: problems of modern human existence in Richard M. Grove's *The Importance of Good Roots*

PhD Shireen Huq. Full Professor

In a casual conversation with Richard Grove one day, I had asked the author if there was any significance in how he had interspersed poems with the fictional pieces in his book *The Importance of Good Roots* and whether he had consciously done so. He answered that there had been nothing conscious from his side. However, an attentive reading of the book suggests a close connection between the poems and the fictional pieces in the development of the main theme. This essay will first explore the theme that runs through the book. In the preface, the author suggests that the stories are about the ties of family and friends and the roots that bond people in spite of a hostile environment. This essay will look particularly into how these roots grow and thrive in a subversive soil. Who are the people whose voices we hear here? The essay will mainly discuss "Cemetery Walk", "The Slivers of Life", "5:20 p.m. Toronto", and "Never Coming Back", "What Could have Been", "What Might have Been", and the title story "The Importance of Good Roots".

Let's take a look at some of the poems first. We begin with "Cemetery Walk".

"Cemetery Walk" begins with the poet/persona taking a walk through a cemetery with his camera, musing on the transience of time. We notice that the camera is 'poised' (*p.1*) to take pictures. Things are etched in our memories but pictures often trigger the memory and much attention has been given here on how memories are captured, retained, and erased. The camera suggests a wish to capture and build memories. Throughout the poem, he mourns the passage of time and the individual's futile attempt to hold it back. Eventually, time is the great destroyer. When Shakespeare wrote his memorable Sonnet 55 "Not marble nor the gilded monuments "he had upheld the power of the 'word' (his poetry) that would outlast time but Grove does not express such beliefs. References to the headstones as "listing slabs" (*p.1*) made of "pitted white granite" (*p.1*) conjure before us images of such memorials (as headstones) eroded and destroyed by time. The slabs are already tilting with time and the granite has been beaten by time and hollowed by weather and erosion. In his words from the first stanza; "through a century of listing slabs / pitted white granite, / time-stained grey." (*p.1*) Death claims the human life and time claims man-made memorabilia! Through a skilful use of sound and visual imagery, Grove makes his poetic statement here. Everything will fall victim to time at some point or other. We'll all be forgotten. Grove end's his poem with these poignant lines; "no matter how deeply carved / no matter how deeply felt / will eventually fade / like graying goldenrod forever / past its prime / forgotten." (*p.1*) So the poet hears the whistle of a train, a commonplace sound, often irritating but now in the poet's musing about time, this common sound becomes uncommon and reminds him of the movement of time. Like the clinging red lichen, humans desperately humans battle time. People put fresh flowers on the graves, but fresh flowers wilt and die, so then they place plastic ones ; they chisel inscriptions on the granite headstones hoping granite will beat the destructive process of weather/time but they, too, are eventually eroded and words etched with so much love are lost forever. The poetic voice is despondent, filled with a sense of hopelessness. The rhythm, meter, and imagery of the poem work together to create this feeling of despondency.

If the reader is disappointed with the despondent note on which the poem seemingly ends, then I would suggest that the poem should be read through again for the ring of warning in the last line cannot be ignored! This could be taken as a reminder to *wake up* and *Seize the Day**!

In "The Slivers of Life", we have a poem whose theme is boredom, frustration with life and above all, with human mortality. So we see the (poet?) wake up late, tired after *another* "late night" (*p.4*) and sit down with obviously nothing better to do than to watch the *Dini Petti Show* in midmorning which then rolls into night, midnight, and finally dawn (The show, as we know, reflected popular culture in Canada in the 1990s, featuring interviews with celebrities, actors, authors, singers and performers, as well as politicians, and local celebrity). Day rolls into night with no meaningful activity and at 4:00 a.m. he finds himself still awake sitting, with cold hands and feet, on the toilet, fully clothed, with the just loaded dishwasher whirring behind him. The author is blunt in his presentation of banality. "I sit on the toilet, now late at night, / 4:05 am to be exact. / The dishwasher that I had just loaded whirs / in the background, / my face pressed into hands, feet cold, naked." (*p.4*)

The image is so real, so every day that it hits us with the question: Is our existence as hollow as this! The whirring dishwasher and the television connect modern life with technology, as does the camera and the train in the poem" Cemetery Walk", discussed previously in this essay. In this poem "Slivers of Life", the connection becomes stronger, the poetic voice emerges clearer, the slivers of wax beside the burning candle reminding him of his own mortality. The wax and candle image is not new but the image of the toilet, the man sitting on the toilet, flushing the toilet, hauling up his pants and simultaneously thinking a profound thought hits us strongly. "The idea of a fragment of wax comes to mind, / you know the tiny pieces / that you peal up from a candle / or scrape with thumbnail from the tablecloth / beside a burning candle / those fragments that one can neither wash / nor even scrub away but / they beg to be picked or poked." (*p.4*)

This profundity of a thought about human mortality and the so very commonplace act of hauling up one's pants after flushing the toilet, clash so hard that it startles the reader. And yet, the image is also so very realistic the reader cannot fail to understand the plight of modern life where there is a constant battle between the 'littleness' of man and the 'greatness' of man, the 'meaninglessness' of life and the 'profundity' of life. The next day, as he looks at the slivers of wax and how they rekindle the candle, he is filled with the realization that it may be possible to still pick up the pieces and give meaning to life. To give meaning or not to give meaning to life is a human choice left to the individual will.

"5:20 p.m. Toronto" gives a grim picture of the reality of existence in Toronto, a city Richard Grove obviously knows much about. It reminds us of Eliot's London in *The Wasteland.* Suffocating, claustrophobic are the two best words to describe this city. Using direct references, Grove situates his poem, not only by naming the city in the title but also through mention of places like University Ave or King Street car. Ironically, we know that Toronto is bordered by the sparkling blue Lake Ontario, but the poet chooses to ignore it and instead highlight on small, still dirty collections of water like "gutters" (*p.7*), toilets and tin cans of food to build up the image of a terrible lack of space for the individual's emotional growth. Darkness prevails in every image, be it when the Torontians are "flushed (*p.7*) down the subway stairs or as they are packed like "captured" (*p.7*) trouts in "cans" (*p.7*). In every stanza, Grove builds up the image of a lack of space, spatial, emotional, and intellectual. Their world is stunted, and sadly, they have mutely accepted their individual anonymities. The 'comfort zone' of their world is a 'pond' which, as is commonly known, is a small body of 'still' water! It is an apt metaphor for the confined and shallow lives of the urban people of Toronto. Grove ends his poem with these sad but enlightened words. "…buried as deep as humanly possible / in their private knowledge that they / will sooner or later spill / from the urban river / into the comfort of their own pond." (*p.7*)

Every piece in this book, both poetry and prose, is filled with thoughts of life and 'death-in-life', and the individual's choice to either continue with this situation or surmount it and beat it. The short stories explore how the individual can do it. And so we move to the prose pieces. Let's look at, "And never Coming back" gives a telephone conversation between two friends. It is in the form of a dramatic monologue with one friend, Bob, continuing the conversation but Frank's presence is both seen and heard by the reader. The two friends have obviously not been in touch for some time. It is a story of one friend (Frank) dying and in the course of the conversation we notice how the human connections between the two friends disintegrate gradually.

It's interesting to note the breakdown step by step.

First, human connection by vision and touch. "Can I come and see you sometime?" (*p.9*). The answer is "No" from the other end.

Next, connection across space. 'Email? How about email can I still email you " (*p.9*)?

Again a 'No' from the other end.

Then it comes down to the outdated modes of communication: snail mail, phone. Finally, the Force that is the Creator and Destroyer of all relationships in the modern world: Money.

"What's the problem? Money, I'll send you some money, how much do you need? Money_makes all problems disappear" (*p.10*).

In this case, money, too, is of no use, so this final comment comes from Bob.

"If you don't need money and you can't have email you might as well be dead man." (*p.10*)

We understand that Frank is dying and will soon join the people in the cemetery in the poem "Cemetery walk". But did he, before dying, reach out to relight his own candle, as in "The Slivers of Life"?

When we move to "What Could have Been What Might Have Been", we are faced with the question, Does the individual have a choice to decide his own life or is he simply the victim of his circumstances? If we think back about the faceless people in the poem "Toronto 5.30 p.m.", we wonder how much inner force (or Life Force, as D.H. Lawrence would have said) they have, if at all, to surmount their circumstances and make human choices in life.

We see two friends meeting in an upscale Toronto café. Important to note, they 'slump' (*p.20*) and have 'joyless, somber looks on their faces (*p.19*). Mark obviously has done well in life for he wears a high- end pinstripe three-piece suit and gold cuff links. Mark also likes to throw his weight around. He takes business calls even during his conversation with Bob, a friend of 25 yrs. he has obviously not been in touch with for some time. There are numerous references in the text to his self- importance. Bob, on the other hand, is dressed casually and does 'little bit of this and that' "Whatever brings in some cash…like that" (*p.20*). So these two friends meet to reminisce over their friend Billy who had passed away and whose funeral perhaps they have come to attend.

Now what do they reminisce about Billy? And what do these reminiscences tell us about Billy? Each friend remembers what he wants to remember. Mark remembers Billy sprouted 100 weed plants in their living room so much so that the friends were afraid of getting caught. However, Bob remembers Billy to have sprouted only 10 weed plants, so Billy is different in the memories of the two friends. To Mark, Billy is a 'stoner', to Billy, he is another friend who smokes some weed. Why this happens, we can understand, when we understand the characters of the two friends. Mark lives, has lived within boundaries always as is evidenced by his clothes and, even in his youth, he was always careful, watching his step, not taking risks. When, in youth, this group of friends, including Billy, visited the waterfalls, Mark restrained himself from jumping off the cliff like the others; later, as young men, the friends planned to invest in land together but Mark did not agree to the proposition for he did not believe in the viability of the business. Nothing wrong in that, for materially he has done better than the others. Mark lives by his head. Bob, on the other hand, is less rigid than Mark but he has his boundaries. He lives in the past and is unable to move on. Billy was spontaneous and lived by his heart. He's the one who jumped off the cliff first to save a kid who was lying face down in the water; he was the one who dove head first off the waterfalls where the friends went for fun and frolic; he was the one "who wanted to push it just a bit further than the rest of us" (29). He was the one who went out into a storm in a canoe, without a life jacket and died. Why did he do it? Was he simply daring nature like Hemingway's old man in *The Old Man and the Sea*? Or did he choose to commit suicide because he didn't want to live like a captured trout in a can (5:20 p.m. Toronto)? The answer is open-ended. But the reader comes away with the feeling that of the friends Billy is the one who was not bogged down by codified restrictions but by his own choices. This moving story ends with these last lines; "*Maybe we just gotta accept him for who he was. We'll have to do a proper toast to Billy Boy later with a beer at the Rex but for now coffee will have to do. Here's to the silly bastard and all the times we had together. I guess it's not a matter of what could have been or might have been." They both raised their coffees, clinked them together over the centre of the low table and slumped heavy back into their chairs. They sat ponderously quiet for the longest time.*

Finally, we come to the novella "The Importance of Good Roots". Spread over eight brief chapters, this novella explores, once again, the complicacies of human existence in modern life. The story is mainly narrated by Mike but there is a third person narrator who steps in at times to fill in the gaps. The time span moves from the time Mike is a schoolboy to when he is a grown man showing how he evolves to maturity through the various stages. The title, at first glance, is flat. Good roots as is commonly understood, refers to good family origins. However good is a relative term and for our analysis of this novella we will not go by the traditionally understood meaning. The novella gives us Mike's relationships with his mother, grandmother and Mr. Barker. Both he and his mother have abusive relationships; him at the hands of his grandmother and her client Mr. Barker and his mother at the hands of Mr. Barker. Yet he brings himself to forgive both his grandma and Mr. Barker, both for his sufferings and his mother's. Where does he acquire this great quality of forgiveness toward those who made him suffer the most? Does it come from the people around him: his much-abused mother who showed her private parts to local boys for 25 cents, or his grandmother who ran a 'whorehouse' or Mr. Barker who seemed to derive special pleasure from beating him? Is it possible? More likely, from the bonding he sees between his mother and grandmother when they ate Kentucky Fried chicken together or when he sees his grandmother's pain at his mother's death.

Grove does a fine job painting a full picture for the reader as exampled here at the beginning of chapter 6. "*Don't you just love corn season? I love strawberries; I love the sweet tiny peas when they first come out and I love fresh tomatoes sun hot off the vine but oh my gosh I love corn season the most. Some like their corn with butter, salt and pepper but I like my corn naked." Ma Reilly laughed out loud and slapped her thigh. "Katharine, I can just picture you eatin' your corn naked. Since you was just a little girl you always liked bein' naked. I would put you out on the clothes line in your harness so you could play and have the run of the backyard and I didn't have to watch you every minute. I would come out a few minutes later and find you naked as a jay bird. The only thing that you would have on is your harness. You always had to be naked no matter who was around. I would put you in your swim suit and put you in your little pool and you would get naked. I would put you to bed in your*

PJs and I would find you naked in the morning. I bet you still sleep in your nudity. I couldn't keep your clothes on you. There was nothin' bashful about you girl. You was as sweet and innocent as a little bug back then. I don't know what happened. One day you was a sweet child and the next you was pregnant."

But let us not overrule the impact of nature on a growing boy, nature with all its lushness, and splendor .The most important and confessional conversations Mike had with his friend were in open space, amid nature, beside a waterfall or lake, on the grass. We find him running from his abusive home and school and take refuge in a quiet corner on the grass with his friend. Nature has a tremendous healing and restorative power which may have impacted positively upon the young boy. Billy, too, before him, had run played amid nature with his friends. This ultimately leads us to conclude that urbanization does not allow for growth of the individual whereas nature allows for space to the individual which leads to growth and fulfilment. Strong roots are bred in conducive environment and not through prestigious family origin unlike in popular belief.

The story ends with a compassionate conversation with his deceased mother. "*Well there's not much else to say. I guess I had better go now. I got to drive north in the morning and I got a few things to do before I go. Oh I forgot to tell you that I ran into old man Barker. I told you that Grams had kicked him out sometime ago. Well I stopped to help an old guy who had a flat tire on the highway and it turned out to be him. He's just a harmless old guy now. I know you didn't like him much but somehow he turned ok. He just looked like any nice old man you would see. He didn't recognize me none and I didn't want to get into anything with him so I just let him drive off. I figure it would have cost me too much to drag up the past. I was trying to forgive him for the longest time. Now that I have seen him as an old man, fragile and even kind of innocent I just can't hold a grudge anymore. Ma, it turns out he has good roots after all. I just want to move on and not think about him and how nasty he was. It's kind of like tossing a slug into the bushes to see if he will live or not. It doesn't take any energy to toss him and it doesn't take any energy to just let him go on his way and forgive him. Anyway Ma, I gotta go now. I'll come back and visit again sometime soon. I love you, Ma.*"

From cover to cover this book is an excellent example of the author's preoccupations with human life, its transience, and the need, therefore, to live life on one's own terms; more specifically, to have the courage to make the right choice. Richard Grove is an author who has not lost his faith in humankind though he is aware of the dangers all around.

References

Grove, Richard M. 2013. *The Importance of Good Roots.* SandCrab Books: USA (All references from Richard Grove's poetry and prose have been taken from this book).

* *Seize the Day: title of Saul Bellow's acclaimed novel.*

It means to make the most of the present moment

Margaret Atwood and the Labour of Literary Celebrity (by Lorraine M. York)

Shane Joseph. Author, Critic

An interesting study of literary celebrity and what it takes to build, grow, and maintain a whole cast behind the icon: publisher, editor, publicist, secretarial staff, agents, marketing assistants *et al.* The celebrity becomes both the labour and the product, but the benefits are not distributed equally—they flow more to the celebrity side, and the pressure to sever labour from product is constantly prevalent for the writer in order to return to him to the isolation of creating (and attaining even more celebrity from these new creations). "Rock concerts and T-shirts are not an option for the writer," says Atwood. Yet, with her Year of the Flood circus, she does just that: traverse across the disinterestedness of art (i.e. once being the classic poet and literary writer) into commodity capitalism. Many other authors stoked indirect publicity by their withdrawal from public life, albeit they did it by becoming recluses, not celebrities: Thomas Pynchon and J.D. Salinger among others.

Atwood got her first agent in 1965 for her book Red Shoes, and it was, ironically, a British agent. Publishers were hostile to agents at the time who created another gate in the chain. But agents have managed to carve important territory that publishers have retreated from: editing, business promotion, translation rights, slush pile manager for publishers; they even do jacket design and marketing copy production today. A good agent also needs to tell her client when to stop writing, when literary powers are declining. York defends agents against the charge that they are the venial handmaids of capital.

The best compliment for an editor would be, "What a wonderful writer!" The editor is invisible in the work. In that sense, the editor epitomizes the disinterestedness of art. The editor is supposed to work on the structural, copy, style and proofing components of the editing process. Publishers' editors also work on Product Development which requires interfacing with sales and marketing groups, but it sometimes also includes commissioning titles and recruiting authors. They are encouraged to look for promotional points when editing books— the inevitable seepage of the commercial into the artistic. The loyalty of the author to the editor is well known; authors often leave publishers to follow their editors. Atwood is well "edited," for teams from various publishing companies convene in Toronto for ten days to review her new work.

But I thought this was a book about Margaret Atwood, not a book about the current roles within publishing? We conclude at the end that she has transcended the disinterestedness of art to achieve the full scale celebration of it. If you consider that she has full time staff interact with interest groups such as academic readers, film industry executives, translators, agents, etc., she is not your stereotypical writer starving in a garret. She also stages plays that adapt her novels (The Handmaid's Tale, The Year of the Flood *et al*) that only feed into the hype of her celebrity. Her website and social media platforms can take on other heavyweight social media types in terms of response rates from followers to a single (in her case, thought provoking) tweet. I was left with the impression that every book about an author is a subtle marketing plug for that author, whether we couch it in critical, academic or satirical terms. And this book was no different.

And yet, there is one nugget of wisdom that she leaves us who trail in her long shadow: in this celebrity culture, she sees authors forming small presses as the way forward, just as she and a bunch of start-up authors began in the 1960's. This cycle seems to repeat as writers mature and move up the chain and new ones have to create their own opportunities. I am glad that I started my small press eight years ago and have gone on to publish not only some of my work, but that of other deserving writers. Now, thanks to Margaret, I can dream (note: it's only a dream) of the wings of celebrity encircling me one day. But then do so many other writers dream the same way. The authors' dream world must be saturated with these swirling desires. This is like the Lord's Feast: many are called, few are chosen. Perhaps, Margaret, sitting at her prominent seat at the guest table, will throw me a bone!

https://www.goodreads.com/review/show/2539970583

The Erotics of Restraint: Essays on Literary Form (by Douglas Glover)

Shane Joseph. Author, Critic

This collection of essays comes from a lifelong absorption in the literary form. Some are broken out into the minutia of formulae that could be delivered to a class on short story writing, while others cover books and writers that appear to be the author's favourites, among them Alice Munro, Jane Austen and Albert Camus.

Glover opens with Munro and two stories in her book *The Lives of Girls and Women.* Munro's style is focussed on chronological threads, repetitions, parallels, constraints and reflectors more than on story and closure. Austen on the other hand, given the tumultuous time she lived in (American Revolution, Industrial Revolution, French Revolution etc.) contrasted with the pastoral and secluded life she led as the unmarried daughter of a not-so-well-to-do clergyman, advocated restraint in her characters. Fanny the heroine in *Mansfield Park*, the book that Glover dissects, is a heroine by default due to her self-restraint and non-action. Camus (the novel in question being *L'Etranger*) strays into Hemingway territory with his ellipsis style of showing character actions but not thoughts, often mistaken for Existentialism but vehemently denied by the French-Algerian author.

The extensive essay on the short story resembled a college lecture to me, where three short stories of varying length and voice are broken out into their minutia. The old anchor of "plot" around which stories were traditionally built seems to be giving way to other emphases like image patterning, word repetition, thematic passages, backfill and conflict formulae. I wondered whether this drift was due to the increasing influence of poetry on fiction, or whether readers were getting tired of "story" within "short story." Other essays also get into the craft of fiction, like the ones on time control in narrative prose and on building sentences, and they too resemble classroom lectures. In the very short essay titled "The Literature of Extinction," experimental literature is discussed; again the old must-haves of plot, setting and theme are discarded in favour of repeated events and images, patterns, sound, dream, and the accidental.

The final essay titled "Consciousness and Masturbation" in which Glover examines the short novel *Cosmos* by Witold Gombrowicz was the most interesting to me. It reminded me of Kafka's work. Here, there is a chaos of events, with no apparent meaning, taking place, with the protagonist trying to create order. Gombrowicz's novel brings into focus all the points hitherto raised by Glover in this collection of essays: imagery, repetition, and cross references that usurp a nonsensical and parodic plot. Masturbation is presented as a way to create a private world from the chaotic one outside one's control. Some of the other imagery borders on the obscene. Although dubbed a quasi-detective novel, Cosmos ends up a horror story.

Reading this book of essays I realized that if I were to be conscious of all the elements of fiction as outlined here while creating a short story or novel, I might be so self-conscious and paralyzed that I might not write a single word. It is therefore better for the writer to create and the academic to analyze. The creator is free to take the analysis, or reject it. However, keeping these learnings in mind during revision and sculpting of a first draft can help to deepen and enrich it. It is a tribute to an author like Glover who is able to balance both roles of creator and academic in his presentation of this work.

With the rapid evolution of fiction, one wonders whether it is easy to become dated quickly. However, Glover provides one nugget of hope: "What is old and discarded becomes fashionable again." Testament to Austen's renaissance 200 years after her passing!

https://www.goodreads.com/review/show/3430428963

Warlight (by Michael Ondaatje)

Shane Joseph. Author, Critic

A testament to memory, an extension of The Cat's Table, where mysterious adults surround impressionable kids, to protect or to harm, leaving those kids permanently altered in adulthood. 15 year-old Nathaniel and his older sister Rachel are abandoned by their parents in 1945 England at the end of the war, the father to go off to South East Asia on assignment for a multi-national corporation and the mother to follow. But does she? The teenagers are raised by shadowy but caring characters nicknamed Moth and Darter and others who flit in and out of their home in London. They pick up some interesting jobs: washing dishes in restaurants, recovering art treasures from tunnels, and ferrying illicit greyhounds on barges to populate the 150 unregulated dog racing tracks around England. As an adult, the cloistered and secretive Nathaniel, enters the British Secret Service and is given the job of poring over old war files to extract information that may still be of interest to authorities. In the process, he decides to track down what happened to his mother.

Rose, the mother, emerges as the most enigmatic character in the book. A secretive sort herself, who was recruited into the secret service by a man who fell off a roof and whom she fell in love with but never married, Fallon. She went onto become a legend in that world of secrets, codenamed Viola. Her marriage to Nathaniel's father gets short mention, in fact the father disappears after the first chapter and is dismissed as "smart but damaged." Along with Fallon, who was also a ladies man with not only Rose among his conquests, she ranges across the world on secret missions, acquiring enemies along the way. For the safety of her children she has them entrusted to buddies in her cohort, such as Moth and Darter. When her children are threatened with harm, Rose quits the service and takes to a life of solitude and exile in her family home in Sussex. But her reputation tragically catches up with her. All this emerges from a combination of the service files and from Nathaniel's memory and imagination, and the picture of Rose's life is completed in a series of chapters that jump forward and back in time and place.

This was not one of Ondaatje's stronger books for me. While uncovering a mystery in fragmented memory recall is an effective device, the danger and menace implicit in this story is dulled and leaves more questions. For instance, how did Rose escape her torturers? Rose comes across as a cold-hearted person, hated by her daughter, and unknown by her son. Her duty to country overrides her care for family. The British stiff-upper lip and reticence is quite evident in this family of secrets. That she and Fallon had sex while on mission is clear, but did they love each other? Why was he living in exile not too far away from her and not getting in touch? A lover's rift, perhaps?— not explained, and subject to the failure of memory, which also becomes an easy out for the author from having to tie loose ends.

Just like with previous Ondaatje novels, I learned new things that do not fall under the popular radar: WWII-spawned vendettas that went on long after the war ended, the canal system of England, the area called the Saints in Sussex, and the peculiar and unsanitary habits of British boarding schools.

On the credit side, this is an unusual angle at which to approach the old WWII story, from the eyes of a 15-year old looking upon his world which the adults are doing their darndest to destroy, leaving him a solitary in his adulthood, content to live in a house with a large wall around it. I wonder whether millennials today view their climate-destroying boomer parents in the same way?

https://www.goodreads.com/review/show/3212109298

Confessions of a Small Press Racketeer (by Stuart Ross)

Shane Joseph. Author, Critic

I attended one of Stuart Ross' solo performances recently where he carried us through for nearly two hours (impressive) replete with anecdotes from his life, jokes (lots of them) and writing exercises, accompanied by wine, cheese and plenty of book selling (including this one). He is the quintessential starving writer who made it to the safe shore (i.e. teaching and editing gigs to supplement his writing and publishing income) through perspiration and perseverance, and he has now won a prestigious literary award that threatens to make him respectable, politically correct and boring. We pray that he does not go over to the dark side.

His book Confessions of a Small Press Racketeer is a distillation of his life over 25 years (the book was published in 2005, so there are still many more years in his life to chronicle, that I suspect come out in the sequel) as a writer, poet, magazine publisher, book editor, and general encyclopedia on the small press literary scene in Canada. His dedication to his craft is total, spending years selling thousands of chapbooks on the streets of Toronto, attending every literary festival he got invited to, slumming around with every known and unknown poet and writer, irritating some and endearing himself to others. The picture of the small press world he paints is starkly funny: everyone knows everybody, everyone owns his own micro-press and publishes everyone else's writing under the aegis of a benevolent government funding program, everyone compliments and bitches about everyone else, everyone can't resist the temptation to perform their work in front of an audience, and everyone dreams of winning a big prize in the literary establishment that they are kept at bay from. His advice to budding writers:

1) Forget about making money.

2) Read like crazy, then steal.

3) Buy books, if you expect others to buy yours.

4) Start your own magazine or press.

5) Don't take creative writing courses, unless your instructor is Stuart Ross.

6) Start performing your work (although he doesn't really like open mics for their accent on performance" over "quality").

Being the owner of a micro-press myself, which Ross graciously elevates to "small press," because he too has one, I have to agree with him on all these points, although I would modify the second half of point # 5 to read "no matter who your instructor is." I believe that creativity is inherent and cannot be taught. The writing mills were just an industry that sprang up to supplement writers' incomes. Sorry Stuart, upon reading your book, I am starting to become an upstart, just as you are!

Small press poets and writers try to gain attention by writing about a crazy reality, and they use monikers that are spelled in combinations of upper case and lower case letters applied out of established grammatical norms – attention grabbers, or branding, as one would say today. Their readings can be bizarre, such as reading a failed grant application on open mic, or reading the table of contents of their book only, or just thumbing the pages of their manuscript in front of an audience while making rude noises before walking away. They are glad when someone, unknown to them, looks up their website or recognizes them in the street.

As to the evolution of the industry, more nuggets fall out:

a) American suck at most things such as world peace, but they produce great writers. b) Readers prefer funny and light instead of dark and heavy.

c) Poetry is more about personality and performance than about the writing (hence his disfavour of open mics).

This book was strangely re-assuring to me, a fellow small presser, for Ross candidly expresses what many of us suspect but are sometimes reluctant to voice. As for small press writers and publishers, I wonder what their purpose in the world is, given that so little of their work is read due to narrowed or suppressed distribution? Would they have created a better world with their work, or would they merely leave the world a duller place when their technicoloured personalities die out? Strangely, Ross didn't answer this question in his book. I think I'll read the sequel to find out.

https://www.goodreads.com/review/show/3153388348

The Boat People (by Sharon Bala)*

Shane Joseph. Author, Critic

A chilling tale that pits a black & white refugee determining process against the nuances of war, where civilians are trapped in the middle, not knowing that the decisions they make for self-preservation in their war ravaged homeland can make them inadmissible in the land they have fled to.

Based on a true incident, 500 Sri Lankan refugees arrive off the coast of Vancouver in a leaky ship and seek asylum. There is a rumour that many on board are part of the terrorist group, the Tamil Tigers, that recently lost its 26-year civil war to Sri Lankan Government forces. What follows is a lengthy and painstaking eligibility-determination process where the new arrivals are subjected to a battery of hearings while being housed in a prison in Canada. The mood of the Canadian political establishment is that they don't want refugees jumping to the head of the line, especially ones with terrorist ties, and the more of this batch that can be deported the better.

The narrative is covered from three viewpoints: Mahindan, a widowed mechanic in Sri Lanka who has escaped on the boat with his five-year old son Sellian; Priya, a Canadian-born law articling student whose Sri Lankan father and uncle share disparate views on the civil war back home; Grace, the third generation Japanese adjudicator who is battling her own family's demons caused by their incarceration during WWII.

Mahindan comes across as the most credible and interesting character, for through him we are able to visit the horrors of the final years of the Sri Lankan civil war. We witness the stranglehold the Tigers had on the freedom of their citizens, where forcible conscription took place for children as young as ten. We witness the fall of Kilinochchi, the Tiger stronghold, in 2009, and the retreat by surviving civilians to a strip of land between the ocean and a lagoon where the Tigers made their last tragic stand. Mahindan is a survivor, doing anything that will save his life and that of his son, whether that involves fixing Tiger vehicles, or stealing ID papers of dead people for resale to those looking for escape to foreign lands. Mahindan's "never give up attitude" and his unflagging love for his son are bright lights in this dark narrative. Priya is conflicted with her role as a budding lawyer and is more concerned with what field of law she should follow after she is called to the bar; her family history in Sri Lanka, which is dredged out slowly—especially her uncle's dark secret—is more colourful than her own life. Grace, politically appointed to "send them back," comes across as a cold-hearted, disinterested and distracted woman who has no sympathy for her refugee claimants. She suspects everyone; it is Grace's mother, Kumi, suffering from dementia, and Grace's twin teenage daughters, who keep alive the spectre of injustice that was committed by Canadian authorities on disenfranchised Japanese during WWII, and maintain a semblance of grounding for the adjudicator. What is clear is that whatever conflict it was that made a generation of refugees flee their homeland, living in Canada tends to dull those emotions over generations of that family's residence in this country.

Scenes alternate between prosaic ones in Canada (children organizing birthday parties, teenagers arguing with parents, families playing card games etc.) and diabolical ones in Sri Lanka (civilians being bombed to smithereens while forced to act as shields between the Tigers and the Sri Lankan military). The Canadians are unable to understand what these refugees have gone through as they view the foreigners' experiences through domestic lenses. Mahindan is exasperated, "These Canadians, with all their creature comforts, have such meagre imaginations." Gigovaz, the refugee lawyer, replies to Mahindan, "You have come to a place where people are spoiled. It is easier for them to call you a liar than to believe what you say is true." Mahindan sees that in his own son, who in a matter of months of arrival, is becoming "Canadian" by the day and distancing himself from the traumas that had once united them.

As the months go by, some refugees, especially the women and children, are gradually released into Canadian society while others go through many failed detention hearings, and others are summarily deported. Not everyone takes kindly to a deportation; some verdicts lead to tragic outcomes, and the adjudicators wonder whether they have indirectly become judge, jury and executioner through this process.

I was a bit disappointed in the inconclusive climax and wondered whether by ending where she did, the author was indicating to us where Mahindan's own case was headed, and therefore why not leave us with him enjoying his best day in Canada with his son? Or whether she wanted each reader to figure out Mahindan's fate given the flawed refugee determination system we had been exposed to in this novel? The one chilling certainty is that the process hasn't been refined yet, and the next boatload of refugees arriving from a war zone where allegiances are hard to determine will be faced with the same set of dilemmas.

https://www.goodreads.com/review/show/2841306610

** This review was originally published in the Sri Lankan Anchorman newspaper - May 2019 edition*

Einstein's Hammer and the Painting Pachyderm: Reading Alice Munro in the Digital Age (every day is trying to teach us something)

John B. Lee. Poet Laureate, Critic, Editor, Visiting Professor

"It was a great party until someone found a hammer."

— Neil Innes, Bonzo Dog Band

April 8, 2009, the day eight-year-old schoolgirl Victoria Elizabeth Marie "Tori" Stafford vanished, seemed an otherwise inauspicious day. For me it began in my home on Strathcona Avenue in Brantford on the Grand, performing my ablutions, shaving a stranger, noshing a modest breakfast of porridge laved in milk purpled by brambleberries. I was slated to read poetry to the students at College Avenue Secondary School at the corner of College Avenue and Fyfe Avenue in Woodstock, Ontario. Due at my destination at 8:30 a.m., I departed at 6:45 a.m. expecting to walk into the main office ready to begin my first session in the library with thirty minutes to spare.

I have always prided myself on being punctual. So, there I was driving west along Highway 403 with time on my hands. I'm often nervous before a performance, so I practised my craft as I drove, reciting from memory a poem I meant to present as the first poem of the day. As I spoke the words aloud behind the wheel, I imagined the promise of student amazement. Driving and declaiming, time ticking past, road signs blurring by, when suddenly I began to wonder as to my whereabouts. I hadn't been paying attention to the road. Had I blown past the Woodstock exit? Was I well on my way to London, the school of the day in my rearview mirror? Panic set in. My face flushed and my body began its anxious perspiration. I could feel the lather trickling down my rib cage drenching my shirt so it stuck to my spine like the clammy dampening of flop sweat.

I glanced at the green sign on the road. "Princeton." I didn't recognize the name of the town. Is Princeton before or after Woodstock? The terrain around me flashed foreign. Foreign! I didn't recognize a single landmark. Nothing to do but exit, turn around, and retrace my route. I pulled off the highway, re-entered by way of the ramp heading east, hoping to glimpse just one familiar feature. When I arrived at my starting point, I realized how foolish I had been. I exited at Brantford, re-entered the highway going west, having lost an hour. I hadn't been a daydreamer rhapsodizing in a warm window seat. No, I'd lost my way like a stranger on a lonesome highway and now I was guaranteed to be late.

When I arrived, Mr. Bryan Smith and his class were already waiting in the library. Had been there since 8:15. I'd been wrong about the starting time as well. I ran in, apologized, and told the students my sad tale. Trapped in the lustrum of secondary-school adolescence, they were amused to have the myth of the absent-minded writer confirmed by this sweaty, slightly dishevelled, wild-haired fellow standing before them with his pathetic explanation of tardiness for stock and trade.

Without missing a beat, I began the day reading poems, reciting, answering questions, selling a few books, before finishing, packing up, and saying farewell. Meanwhile, only a block away from where I was visiting, eight-year-old Victoria Elizabeth Marie "Tori" Stafford was spending her last day alive on the earth. She and her classmates were doing what schoolchildren do. She was studying, playing, talking, and dreaming of a future that would be denied her by a chance encounter with the monsters who would abduct her as she departed from the schoolyard of Oliver Stephens Public School on Fyfe Avenue making her way home through familiar streets. Of course, I did not know anything about her existence, nor did I observe her being enticed into an automobile by the girlfriend of the man on the hunt for a child to molest. Neither did those predators figure in my consciousness as I walked from the front door of College Avenue Secondary School to my car, parked in the turn-around on Fyfe Avenue.

I do have a vague recollection of young students thronging the street as they gathered in bunches, jostling and running and laughing along on their way going home from school. I remember noticing the elementary school students spilling over the sidewalk as I waited for an opportunity to depart. This youthful energy was peripheral to my primary attention – as, without my noticing, the woman in the white coat, the one on the hunt for a child to snatch as a gift for her 28-year-old boyfriend, was there close at hand, teasing little Tori with the promise of seeing newborn puppies – for Tori knew her abductor. She was there while I was there: she tantalizing the doomed youngster, I waiting patiently for a clear path to make the turn off Fyfe onto the main road home.

The Brantford Expositor would record that Tori was seen for the last time at about 3:32 p.m. on Wednesday, April 8, 2009 on Fyfe Avenue, walking past the high school up the street. She was wearing a black Hannah Montana jacket with white fur-lined hood, a green shirt, a denim skirt, black and white shoes and carrying a purple and pink Bratz bag.

She was walking with "a person of interest." On May 20, only forty days after Tori vanished, police charged Michael Thomas Rafferty, age 28, with first-degree murder and charged Terri-Lynne McClintic, age 18, as an accessory to murder. Tori's mutilated remains were discovered in July. And I was haunted by the fact that I was present on the day of the abduction. I realized as I read about it in the paper that I had been only a few feet away when this horrifying abduction had occurred.

***

Fifty-nine years ago to the very day, in the early hours of an uncommonly cold and rainy spring morning, April 8, 1950, my older sister Georgina Emily Lee was born. The farm lane was flooded, and Dad's car would not start. Rather inconveniently for all concerned, my mother went into labour in the middle of the night. Dad phoned local mechanic Spike McPhale. Spike owned a reliable car. He would meet them at the end of the lane and drive the thirty miles to the hospital in Chatham. I imagine George and Irene Lee wading knee deep in the chilly runoff flowing over the lane coming down from the house through deep country darkness of those early hours, down from the farm on the hill with the waters of the east and west muck joined in the middle. My grandfather Herb had joked about those fields: "Now I know how Moses felt fleeing Egypt." All worked out well in the end. And slightly less than a year later, I was conceived.

My mother, now in her ninetieth year, remembers nothing. A widow, suffering from dementia, she has forgotten us all. In a recent conversation I said to her:

"Mom, do you know who I am?"

"No."

"I'm your son, John."

"I don't know you."

"Do you remember your husband, George Lee?

"I was married?"

"Yes, you were married for nearly sixty years to George Lee."

"What happened to him?"

"He died."

"Well, why would he do that?"

"Do you know who George Lee was?

"My father?"

"No. He was your husband. That's why your name is Lee. You used to be a Busteed from Mull."

"Busteed? Busted. Mull's dull."

"Do you remember your children, Georgina and Johnny?"

"No."

"Do you remember Herb Lee? He lived in the other house on the farm."

"No."

"Do you remember Stella, his wife? You loved her and always called her the sweetest woman who ever lived."

"No."

"Do you remember Uncle John? He lived in the bedroom upstairs across the hall from your daughter Georgina. Sometimes we called him Redhocks because his hair was red. You and he did not get along, at least not until Dad died."

"No."

"Do you remember your sisters, Ruth and Dorothy?"

"No."

"So you don't remember your husband. You don't remember your children. You don't remember Grandpa or Grandma Lee. You don't remember Uncle John. You don't remember your sisters. Do you remember Tom Malott, the hired man?"

"Well, who could ever possibly forget Tom Malott?"

"Do you remember his dog, Wacky?"

"Of course I remember Wacky."

So, my mother has forgotten her husband of sixty years, both of her children, all of her closest relatives, yet she remembers the hired man. And she remembers his dog. Tom and Wacky remain vivid in her mind. Her face lights up in recalling these two. In the end, she stares at me for the longest while, saying: "I don't know you, do I?" When I say: "I'm your son, I'm John," she dismisses me with a wave of her hand. "No you're not. You can't be." We talk briefly of Tom and Wacky and she smiles to recall.

When first I read the Alice Munro story "The Bear Came Over the Mountain" from her book Hateship, Friendship, Courtship, Loveship, Marriage, about a woman losing her mind to Alzheimer's, and then when I saw the movie based on that story, *Away from Her*, I had no idea as to how I would find comfort and consolation in literature inspired by dementia. Great literature broadens our knowledge, deepens our understanding, clarifies our emotions, and connects us to the inner wells of the self where deep need is served. In great literature we also find a meaningful connection with our fellow humans. That essential empathy abides in well-written stories and poems.

***

I suppose as a writer I would have to say that I cherish memory over all other powers of the imagination. I once wrote: "We must imagine the past and remember the future." I say this because reliable memory is an act of the imagination. I also said in an interview: "It's memory that keeps us sane." I think I'm correct in this. And so I grieve the loss of my mother's memory, not for my own sake but for hers. Her personal past is vanishing one image at a time. Irene Lee is no longer a widow, no longer a mother, a grandmother, or a great-grandmother. She is simply an old woman sitting in a chair experiencing vague flickers of recognition concerning what it means to be Irene Lee.

For quite a while her short-term memory has been completely lost. I compare her recollection of immediate experience to the early morning tabula rasa of an empty schoolroom. Imagine someone writing on a blackboard being followed by someone with a chalk brush who is being followed by someone with a wet cloth. As the writing appears, it is being dusted to a white blur, and then washed away to leave only a black slate. As soon as someone is out of her field of vision, they vanish as though they had never been there. She might see my grandson and say: "Oh, look. A baby. Isn't he cute?" She looks away, then turning her head catches sight of him again repeating her remark: "Oh, look. A baby. Isn't he cute?" She says this as though he had only just arrived, though he'd been there for the whole visit.

When I teach writing I remind aspiring writers of the importance of memory, most especially old memory. Memory aged in the mind and deepened by time. The most evocative of all our five senses is the sense of smell. An uncapped fragrance can excite the most profound recollection of the past. And in writing of the present, as it is informed by the past, authors who attend to the olfactory in writing and who are masters of memory can write the smell of varnish, the perfume of apples, the pong of fresh-mown hay, the high sweet rose garden stink of manure, and the diesel burn of the city at the height of the day.

When I think of the great passages in literature that capture experience, I often reconsider a passage from Alice Munro's short story "Floating Bridge" from her book *Hateship, Friendship, Courtship, Loveship, Marriage.* A woman suffering from breast cancer finds herself on a farm at the edge of a field. She leaves her car and walks into the corn. Munro writes:

"The cornfield was the place she wanted to get to. The corn was higher than her head now, maybe higher than Neal's head – she wanted to get into the shade of it. She made her way across the yard with this one thought in mind. The dogs thank God must have been taken inside.

There was no fence. The cornfield just petered out into the yard. She walked straight ahead into it, onto the narrow path between two rows. The leaves flapped into her face and against her arms like streamers of oilcloth. She had to remove her hat so they would not knock it off. Each stalk had its cob, like a baby in a shroud. There was a strong, almost sickening smell of vegetable growth, of green starch and hot sap.

What she'd thought she'd do, once she got in here, was lie down. Lie down in the shade of these large coarse leaves and not come out till she heard Neal calling her. Perhaps not even then. But the rows were too close together to permit that, and she was too busy thinking about something to take the trouble. She was too angry." ("Floating Bridge" 71)

The line "There was a strong, almost sickening smell of vegetable growth, of green starch and hot sap" sings of memory reified and celebrated and true. I grew up on a farm and I know how profoundly moving it is to experience something in writing that has both the quality of personal familiarity and the ability to connect the inner world with the outer world. The cornfield is internalized, thereby evoking a connection to the character's past, all the while being a melancholy reminder of what is lost to us when we confront our own mortality. The smell is "almost sickening." Nostalgia, false memory, and every sentimental recollection of a world that never existed are unavailable to the reader.

We remember. We lament. We experience the nausea of being cloyed by the sweet sap of nature. For your consideration I offer a few examples of olfactory writing having simply combed through the stories appearing in Munro's book *Friend of My Youth*:

"When they walk side by side, she can smell his shaving soap, the barber's oil, his pipe tobacco, the wool and linen and leather smell of his manly clothes. The correct, orderly, heavy clothes are like those she used to brush and starch and iron for her father. She misses that job – her father's appreciation, his dark, kind authority. Jarvis Poulter's garments, his smell, his movements all cause the skin on the side of her body next to him to tingle hopefully, and a meek shiver raises the hairs on her arms." ("Meneseteung" 60)

"Her jeans had the smell jeans get when they've been worn a while without being washed – a smell not just of the body but of its labors. He could smell cleaning powder in them, and old cooking. And there was flour that she'd brushed off on them tonight, making the pastry for the pie. The smell of the shirt was of soap and sweat and perhaps of smoke. Was it smoke – was it cigarette smoke? … His mother's clothes would never smell this way, of her body and her life." ("Oranges and Apples" 131-32)

"In wet weather Karin could smell pig, and always she smelled another smell that she thought was blood." ("Pictures of the Ice" 143)

"Because she's got that coat, and is willing to wear it every day of the year, Mrs. Carbuncle never has to change her dress. A smell issues from her – camphorated, stuffy." ("Oh, What Avails" 189)

"Her smell was like something sweet cooking – spicy jam." ("Wigtime" 249)

***

After having been lost on the road on the way to Woodstock, I think of the importance of paying attention to the landscape going on without me. One of my mentors, poet/professor James Reaney, would sometimes interrupt a student in full flight as he or she was rhapsodizing in an academic exegesis of a poem. Reaney would compliment the aspiring scholar and then redirect his or her attention with this caution: "That's all very good, but what does this have to do with what is going on outside of the window?" The poem wasn't born in a library, and you won't unlock its deep mysteries with purely scholarly concentration. Reaney also encouraged his students to learn the name of everything between their front step and the city sidewalk. He also championed maps, geological surveys, anthropology, archaeology, and generally everything that contributes to a deep appreciation of place.

There is a wonderful passage in Alice Munro's short story "Wild Swans" from her book Who Do You Think You Are?, wherein the central character Rose is taking a journey by train to Toronto. It is very clear that Munro has paid studied attention to the landscape. She sees the environment through the filter of her character's point of view – that of an adolescent girl on her way from a small town to the big city. I take up Munro's description beginning in Brantford, the city where I began my own journey west to Woodstock as described at the outset of this essay. Munro writes: "The train was filling up. At Brantford a man asked if she would mind if he sat down" (59). Rose allows him to sit next to her as "She went on looking out the window at the spring morning. There was no snow left, down here. The trees and bushes seemed to have a paler bark than they did at home. Even the sunlight looked different. It was as different from home, here, as the coast of the Mediterranean would be, or the valleys of California" (59).

The man observes that the windows are filthy. He tells Rose that he is a United Church minister. The scene evolves. Rose pretends to fall asleep. The man pretends to read the paper. His hand creeps up her inner thighs crossing the line of the top of her stockings. Seemingly against her will her legs open. And Munro's description of the passing landscape continues:

"As the train crossed the Niagara Escarpment above Dundas, as they looked down at the preglacial valley, the silver-wooded rubble of little hills, as they came sliding down to the shores of Lake Ontario, she would make this slow, and silent, and definite, declaration, perhaps disappointing as much as satisfying the hand's owner. He would not lift his eyelids, his face would not alter, his fingers would not hesitate, but would go powerfully and discreetly to work. Invasion, and welcome, and sunlight flashing far and wide on the lake water; miles of bare orchards stirring round Burlington.

... she was borne past Glassco's Jams and Marmalades, past the big pulsating pipes of oil refineries. They glided into suburbs where bedsheets, and towels used to wipe up intimate stains, flapped leeringly on the clotheslines, where even the children seemed to be frolicking lewdly in the schoolyards, and the very truckdrivers stopped at the railway crossings must be thrusting their thumbs gleefully into curled hands. Such cunning antics now, such popular visions. The gates and towers of the Exhibition Grounds came to view, the painted domes and pillars floated marvelously against her eyelids' rosy sky. Then flew apart in celebration. You could have had such a flock of birds, wild swans, even, wakened under one big dome together, exploding from it, taking to the sky." (63)

In the next instant Rose "bit the edge of her tongue" (63). Difficult not to infer the strong connection between Rose's physical response to the man's hand and Munro's selective attention to what is occurring outside the window of the train as it comes shuddering to a halt at Union Station in Toronto.

Munro's use of precisely the right word at the right moment, her sense of the mot juste, sets a standard to which all writers might aspire. Her description of children "frolicking lewdly," or of the truckdrivers "thrusting their thumbs gleefully into curled hands," or the impossible to miss double meaning of the phrase "cunning antics," and that final image of wild swans "wakened … exploding … taking to the sky" amount to an accumulation of detail connecting what is occurring as Rose climaxes with exactly what is going on in the external world outside of that filthy train window. Memory and imagination allow for selective recollection of appropriate detail in service of the story and of the character's perspective within the story. And what a brilliant story "Wild Swans" is. Almost everyone who lives in Southwestern Ontario has taken the train that runs between Windsor and Toronto. This passage quoted here is something of an object lesson in the value of knowing everything there is to know about the world you inhabit so that you might call upon the essential details of the world in order to erase the barrier between the inner and the outer world.

***

I read a story in my local newspaper today. The article concerned the publication of a book by a woman who began writing in order to cope with a difficult life. She referred to poetry writing as therapeutic. She claimed to have written her way out of sorrow and to have struggled through adversity by putting pen to paper. As a result of her private crisis, she produced a small volume of poems called *Down Memory Lane*.

Although I contend that as a writer, and as a teacher of writing, one should never steal anyone's joy, and although I have argued in the past that it is better to write a bad poem than it is to make a good bomb, what sometimes shakes my confidence in the future of serious literature arises from the fact that there are so few contemporary readers who recognize the difference between a 'real' book and a purely self-serving project.

When I was in second year as a student of English literature at The University of Western Ontario, I had the good fortune to meet poet Margaret Avison. She had been appointed Writer in Residence and, as an aspiring young author, I visited her office during the second half of her residency. It had taken me most of a school year to work up the courage to show her my work. To my great delight, she saw a quality in my writing worth encouraging. I have written often about her excellence as a mentor. I have written how much I learned simply by noting the very first question Margaret Avison asked me before allowing me to show her a single piece of my own writing. She set my small folder of poems aside and inquired of me: "Whom do you read?"

After listening to me gushing for nearly an hour, she promised to read my poems. The next time I visited her, she left me with two pieces of advice that have stood me in good stead as a writer. "Mind your prepositions," she said. "Everything can turn on the smallest of words." And she added: "Figure out what your taboos are, and then – break them all." To cap off my day, she produced a poem she had written, inspired by the reading of my work. That poem, "To John Lee: Groundhog Day 1973," written in her hand, hangs framed on my office wall to this day.

Over the years, we stayed in touch. My wife and I visited her often in Toronto. I had the pleasure of reading with her on many occasions. And several of those times she spoke to me about certain poems of mine she cherished, ones she claimed to have shared with people she referred to as "real readers." And it is these "real readers" who concern me now.

In my book on writing, *Building Bicycles in the Dark: A Practical Guide to Writing*, I use the phrase "ideal readers" to describe the people for whom I write. These ideal readers, these "real readers" (to use Avison's phrase), know when they are in the presence of real writing. If I dare to suggest that Fifty Shades of Grey is not a real book, all I need do to confirm this caveat concerning the exploitative and awful erotica of this risible novel is draw the reader's attention to the aforementioned passage from Munro's story "Wild Swans." Or to this description of sex from the title story of *Friend of My Youth*:

"What made Flora evil in my story was just what made her admirable in my mother's – her turning away from sex. I fought against everything my mother wanted to tell me on this subject; I despised even the drop in her voice, the gloomy caution, with which she approached it. My mother had grown up in a time and in a place where sex was a dark undertaking for women. She knew that you could die of it. So she honored the decency, the prudery, the frigidity, that might protect you. And I grew up in horror of that very protection, the dainty tyranny that seemed to me to extend to all areas of life, to enforce tea parties and white gloves and all other sorts of tinkling inanities." (22)

Phrases like "gloomy caution," "dainty tyranny," and "tinkling inanities" abound in Munro's writing. A reader might not only luxuriate in the beauty of such phrases, but also consider how they plumb the depth and stir the murky complexity of human existence. A character might think of her life as having changed and yet not understand the nature of the change. A question may seem rhetorical on the surface, but it may also be an admission of confusion as in this question asked in "Goodness and Mercy" from Friend of My Youth: "How did you learn to be so stubborn and insistent and to claim your turn?" (161).

The reader of Munro's stories lingers in a moment, reads and re-reads a single phrase or observation or self-reflection or contemplation without resolution, remaining speculative and uncertain as in her comment on dreaming as it occurs in the title story of Friend of My Youth: "I used to dream about my mother, and though the details in the dream varied, the surprise in it was always the same. The dream stopped, I suppose because it was too transparent in its hopefulness, too easy in its forgiveness" (3). That pivotal verb, that word "suppose," withholds certainty of conviction, yet the character – and, through the character, the reader – is allowed insight.

***

When I mentioned to my friend Bryan Smith that I was writing this essay beginning with the reminder that I had been there the day that Victoria Elizabeth Marie "Tori" Stafford vanished from Fyfe Avenue in front of the high school where he taught, his face clouded over, his eyes saddened, his mouth turned down at the corners, and he said: "The community has never recovered from that, you know. I'm not sure it ever will. Everyone is still suffering."

I wondered for a moment if he thought my decision to use this horrifying event in my essay was a violation of basic human morality. Perhaps he is right. I don't know. I sometimes feel Atwood's words from her poem "Their attitudes differ" in Power Politics goading me on: "Please die, I said / so I can write about it." At least I am not in the camp of those life-shallowing pop culture shills who champion the painting pachyderm as though he were the next slapdash Picasso splashing paint on a piece of paper with a brilliant brush tucked into the curl of his trunk. And the monster intent on murder and mayhem who stopped at a hardware store to buy garbage bags and a hammer reminds us all that we may never understand the depravity of certain human beings and by comparison the abiding quality of others.

Consider the axiom: "To a man with a hammer everything looks like a nail," and then imagine that hammer in the hand of a genius. Imagine then Einstein's hammer, and what the hammer, what the nail – as you also might consider Alice Munro, pen in hand as she wrote: "They are driving between walls of corn. The stalks are eight or nine feet high. Any day now the farmers will start to cut them. The sun is low enough even by midafternoon to shine through the cornstalks and turn them to coppery gold. They drive through an orderly radiance, mile after mile" ("Oranges and Apples" 113).

Let me conclude this essay with a poem written the day I first read of the fate of young Tori Stafford. I confess I do not understand. But this is what we writers do. We write towards the light.

She Stops

she stops
the woman in the white coat
she stops
at the hardware
to purchase
a small bag of green bags
and one claw hammer
for her boyfriend, the ghoul
the ogre, the fiend, the monster
who bruised
the little girl's body
who broke
the bone of her skull

what is it that the thin radio waves sing from space
from the starry drumbeat
of dying pulsars
or what the weird
melancholia of lost whales
deep notes

peeping under water
where the sharp clack, clack sound
of struck-together rocks
might startle a silver school
of minnow shoaling away
in murky swirls of milting and gill-breathed water
a quickening galaxy of ugly gulps

I have also heard the static buzz
from mayfly swarms
smouldering above the alders of summer
and over
the lithe-waist poplars and thick-trunk beech
like the low hum of nightfall burning into darkness
all of these ephemeral blue and woeful songs of grace
gather into one profoundly sorrowful ululation
a singular lamentation for

the last Neanderthal
the last Beothuk
the last Taíno Arawak
toiling in the silver mines
of Hispaniola
listening for a greater grief than this

in the soft-hearted suffering
of each new dawn
I hear the voice of God
and whisper back
who stops the woman in the white coat
the one with the red hammer
in her hand
who stops her …

Essay first published in Alice Munro Country, ed. J.R. (Tim) Struthers (Guernica Editions, 2020). Reprinted with the kind permission of the publisher.

An Expectation of Enlightenment: walking the Camino (*The Way History Dries*. Keith Inman. Black Moss Press, 2020)

John B. Lee. Poet Laureate, Critic, Editor, Visiting Professor

"Than longen folk to goon on pilgrimages,

And palmers for to seken straunge stronds,

To ferne halwes koweth in sondre londes …"

(Lines from 'The General Prologue" to Canterbury Tales Geoffrey Chaucer)

I first met poet Keith Inman in Cuba. My impression of him was that of a soft-spoken man of high intelligence. By that time he was a retired factory worker dedicating himself to the craft of poetry. In his biography he speaks of a mentor encouraging him to "get that flowery shit" out of his writing and to dedicate himself to writing in a "blue-collar style." And he has had some considerable success since the occasion of that meeting, *The Way History Dries* being his sixth book of poems. And he has become one of the premier practitioners of what Canadian literary circles call Peoples' Poetry.

In this book of poems he tells the story of several Canadians walking the famous trail Camino-Frances, from their setting out to their arrival at their intended destination. In his epigram he unveils his commitment to the role of the poet as that of dispassionate observer. He quotes Andrew McMillan "The poet's job is to 'observe, to contemplate, to bear witness.'" And most interestingly he is absent from the story. He chooses four characters through whose eyes he relates the experiences of walking the Camino. They are Father Fred, a priest whose express purpose is to find a place to spread his daughter's ashes, and for travelling companions, self-confessed atheist Harv, Harv's wife Anne and their friend Barb. It is through the eyes of these pilgrims that we experience everything along the way.

In considering such a journey in the reading of this literary tour de force, I ask myself how much of where you are, where you're going, and where you're about to be depends upon the 'you' in the doing and the being, and how much of your experience depends upon your whereabouts and your whenabouts. And how much of who you are depends upon who you are with. The journey of the body on a spiritual quest involves the self, the soul, questions of the nature of faith, and the sensibility presented in studied attentiveness going for a walk, a trek, a hike, a pilgrimage, companionable and solitary. The journey along the Camino made into a previously unfamiliar landscape that promises inner transformation along with the consequence of accidental encounters.

Where Keith Inman's filter comes into play involves the presence of irony giving the reader a reliable glimpse into the truth of disappointed expectations that in his case avoid the honey trap of cynicism. These relatively well-healed travelers set out in hiker's gear. They enter a landscape in search of a bed to sleep on to soothe their fatigue and a restaurant meal to satisfy their hunger at the end of every day. There is beer and wine and good food, and the good cheer of meeting up with Ausies, Brits, Americans, and mendicants and merchants. One typical observation occurs in a poem close to the middle of the book, "They found the restaurant/ behind a laurel hedge." (from "the Book of Nature Mentions Humans Twice). In "Laundry" one trekker opines "What I really need is an American bank." After all, this pilgrimage of necessity is something of a credit-card journey, and these pilgrims are sometimes 'spiritual tourists.' But to Inman's credit, although he acknowledges this irony of the 'forced enlightenment', he never judges his characters. At one point, and this is not an expression of disappointment but rather a celebration of the beauty of small truths, he writes "The coffee was good and morning/ bright/ with a cool breeze of birds/ talking/ about the day." In heartbreaking simplicity Inman writes of these pilgrims "their pilgrimage carrying them/ inside the mountain/ of their hearts/ a journey among saints/ looking for a place/ of craftsmen.

In the end, Inman's genius involves putting irony to a deeper purpose. So often irony loops back on the subject of cosmic ridicule and thereby puts us all in our place. We are ridiculous as Lear who sees us "as flies to wanton boys are we to the gods." No. To Inman we may fall short, but in the end this is a book of affirmation. "… sure his people once danced/ before fire, threw spirits in the air,/ drew water, chopped wood, ate, drank,/ slept, wore animal skins, made hours for work,' tools for gardens, instructed, constructed,/ made music, rainbows and children/ like anyone full of rain." (Tending the Flowers of Tyrants). Pilgrim Anne raises a glass in celebration "We did it. We/ did it!" And the exclamation mark is not ironic. The 'it' of the doing is genuine and deeply felt. And the last act of the final poem involves a pseudo-sacramental gesture "slicing a tender medallion of braised/ boar with apricot jus de jour." In the closing lines of another book telling the story of pilgrims, Chaucer concludes "And as we diden, lat us laughe and pleye/ Anon they kiste and ryden forth hir weye."

Two Thousand Seventeen. Collection of Sesquicentennial Poems by Richard M Grove and John B. Lee. Publisher, Sunbun Publishers, New Delhi India (with Hindi Translation)

Syed Peeran. Professor

I am an Indian writing in English and I write poetry which in this Sub Continent is known as Indian English Poetry, with its own distinction, flavor, color, taste, emotions and an expression which is unique in itself. India is known as a poor country with extremes of poverty and people surrounded by squalor, and living in slums and sub human conditions. All of this has a profound influence on our poetry.

India was ruled first by conquering Muslims from Afghanistan and Persio-turks known as Mughals for almost 750 years; then we were ruled by the British for over 250 years. English was introduced as a medium of instruction and with teaching of English literature. The Indian Poets were influenced by Victorian and Elizabethan poets and their enormous writing. Even today in schools and colleges the poetry of Milton, Keats, Yeats, Shelly and a large majority of Poets of those eras is taught to students. Despite this influence, now Indian English has come to grow and flourish with Indians writing keeping in the back ground their age old culture and influence of their oldest civilization.

I have to admit that I have not read much of Canadian or American poetry or from other British influenced English countries like Australia and New Zealand. So now when Richard M. Grove sent me his work by email, I realized his mind boggling experience. His poetry is more about an expression of the poet facing the sub-zero temperature of his northern winter climate. Here is an example of his life in the freezing world: *A few days ago we experienced a winter storm. / Everything was covered with an inch of ice. / Shining branches bowed in submission, / my car a glistening sculpture. / Against my better judgment / I went out for a walk on that day and slipped / and fell hard. Picture this Blue Bear, / as Adonay calls me, flying in the air / winter boots three feet off the ground …*

His poems reveal that he is not living in a big town or in a populated city but in a place near a lake which freezes and the poems, in a large number, express his feelings with the environment he is facing, as is the case, with the poem "The Silence Between Notes". *I just returned from a long walk / out my back door into the park / west along the deserted road / two cold boulders that mark the path / heading south to the open lake. / It would be pitch black / if not for the bright snow / reflecting moonlight up / into a cloud-stippled sky. / Whipping snow / fills the -13oc air. / Trudging is almost perilous / as I push blindly through icy rutted path / under dark branches hanging low / making the snow vanish / into a timeless abyss.*

As I said we are totally immersed in our Indian culture, in our poverty and its attendant vicissitudes. We express our agony, chagrin, our despondency, frustration, our pain, anger, angst, our joys and sorrows, our privations under our religious and cultural influences. We Asians are much deeply influenced by our religious and superstitious upbringing and our ideology is fully marked in our writings, be it prose or poetry. In this book, Richard expresses himself, not in religious and cultural terms but in reference to weather. All the way through this sensitive book he talks about climatic conditions as is found in the poem "Kayaking on the Ripples of Indian Summer": *leaves chatter against gentle shoreline-lapping / sun warms bare legs after cold paddle-dipping sparks zing / east / home / resting / after restorative invigorating strokes into fall's black bay / yin and yang balance restored / soul sings*

The reading of Richard's poems brings us into his personal isolated experience. I am not an academician and my poetry is totally steeped in mysticism and of a practicing Sufi arising from a subject of Sufism which is Islamic Spiritualism. We believe in existence of a mighty Powerful, Magnificent and Beneficent Lord who has given us Divine decree to follow and surrender. My voice, as a poet, is the voice of my soul and my consciousness while I find the voice of Poet Richard is an experiential voice of facing the environment and living without a neighborhood. His poetry is bereft of interaction with humanity or of pain, anguish, anger, disgust, love, sexual feelings and emotions which we experience in this Indian temperate region with temperature shooting up to 45 degree centigrade with acute water and electricity shortage compared to the comforts of living in a super rich advanced country like Canada. Richard talks about leaving the comfort of his office to find yet another freezing experience that turns into the first stanza of his poem titled "Woodstock Invasion": *After a long arduous desk-hunched day / my darling wife beckoned me / for a -17oc wind whistling walk / to clear my frazzled monitor-flickered brain. / South towards the lake, wind-pelted, / head hunched, frosted glasses. / A half mile down the road / we see a distant black undulating V / stitching grey quiet sky, / fifty Canada Geese slowly swelling / towards us. The discord of dissonant honking / gradually filling the air.*

I will ultimately failing in my review of Richard's poetry for I have not experienced the life in a rich country and living in subzero temperature and harsh conditions. His experience and consequently his poetry is absent of color, smell and the excitement I find in my country. Our poems are marked with rhyme and nuances of British poets of earlier eras as taught to us though Richard does touch on the British influence which is in his poem "In the Deep Heart's Core" influenced by the Irish poet Yeats. He has respectfully dedicated the poem as such: *Owed to Yeats and his poem "The Lake Isle of Innisfree".* I will quote here only Richard's first stanza: *I will rise tomorrow and return / to our home on-the-frigid-shores / of Lake Ontario / snow-laden deck. Pines / in the back, looming, / will greet me and I will have / some peace there / where calm whispers / through the silent red / of dogwood, branches /*

perched upon by darting chickadees / foraging in winter solitude. / Midnight there will glow in quiet / silver moon's still beam, / a calm that will hush / into my long silence.

In any case the poems of Richard bring me the enjoyable experience of knowing a Canadian poetical voice. This style of poetry is new to me and I enjoyed it thoroughly, I shall try to emulate it. I congratulate the poet for getting his poetry translated into Hindi and getting it published in India for Hindi readers.

Of Ecological Connections and Rhapsodies: A Review of *Two Thousand Seventeen: Sesquicentennial Poems* by Richard M. Grove and John B. Lee

PhD Basudhara Roy. Professor, Poet, Editor, Critic

> *Here is magic. In the realm of a spell*
> *the common word seems lifted up above …*
> *and yet is really like the call of the male*
> *who calls for the invisible female dove.*
> *(from 'Magic' by Rainer Maria Rilke)*

Bonding in and through poetry, as most fellow-poets will concur, needs nothing less or more than a commitment to the word, a consecration of it on the soul's altar, and a subordination of everything else to its truth. *Two Thousand Seventeen: Sesquicentennial Poems* by Richard M. Grove and John B. Lee bespeaks just such a fertile, enigmatic and worthwhile bonding in words that spur the reader on to enter a landscape that is as bewitching as it is soothing, as real as it is metaphorical, as rooted as it is expansive, and as profound with truth as it is with wisdom.

What strikes one urgently in these poems is their grand spatiality - the immensity of space that they embody and through which existentiality is negotiated on a day-to-day basis. For readers unacquainted with the Canadian landscape, Grove's poems are bound to offer an almost photophilic access to it. In poem after poem in his twenty-nine pieces in the collection, Grove's poetic vision acquires a photographic lens as he zooms in upon the minutiae of a workaday life with astonishing clarity to reveal in glorious plenitude its irreplaceable splendours. In 'As If Just For Me', a "calm, placid day" is interrupted by a sudden spotting of Canada Geese in hundreds:

> *honking, mirrored*
> *by wing-tipped water arriving to splashdown*
> *squawking, talking*
> *as if they were there just for me.*

In 'A desk glance of a full moon', a glance over the computer reveals the unprepared-for glory of a full moon "past the spent orchid potted on my sill, past the compact florescent glare on windowpane, past the black silver traced cedar across the street, past the lamp post, past shifting clouds" and one startlingly realizes that here is a zooming out from the work-monitor which, while being literal, is richly metaphoric of an attempt to connect with the wonders of the wider world that envelops our circadian rhythms. The natural world, being at the centre of Grove's poetic vision, is ubiquitous in his poems. Not a single thought, action or observation in his lines is unmarked by the presence of trees, topography, birds, flowers, wind, weather or temperature. There is an intense awareness here of the vastness of the world and the fallible finitude of Man, a constant attempt to actively participate in nature's moods and processes, and to weave one's tiny being into this staggering beat of nature's loud and all-absorbing pulse. The poem, 'The Silence Between Notes', is an immensely powerful piece that describes the poet's attempts to

listen to "the song/ of ice and snow" and read the silence between " the notes of nature's cacophony" in a negative thirteen degree Celsius, snow-storming landscape "where earth ends/ and time never was". With a movement that is almost cinematic, the poem charts its speaker's journey through snow-covered woods to a frozen lake's edge where he sits motionless in the numbing cold while the "wind and snow hurled/ in every direction", in an attempt to acquire a oneness with this timeless world:

I listened until I could not hear
the waves or the wind.
I listened until I could only hear
the music in the silence between notes.
I sat without moving
until I was not even there.

Making the journey from Grove's poems to Lee's poetic world is travelling inwards from the world to the self, from meanings to symbols and from the clarity of language to the poignancy of expression. If Grove's poems offer a silhouette of the self in a world where the power of the natural landscape awes and overwhelms the soul, Lee's poems paint with lush, opulent strokes that invincible human soul that stands tall, empathetic, and aglow despite the pain, darkness and loss that inevitably comes one's way. In 'Walking the Trail Near Crawly Falls, New Hampshire', a dead tree becomes for the poet, a hallowed entity that he bids his grandsons not to disturb and to

let it sleep where it stands, for
time will soon enough find
a moment to fall into the shadow pull
when the light comes pushing through

Both Grove's and Lee's poems have their arms wide open with this only difference that while the former seeks to give himself over to the world, the latter yearns to merge the world within the infinitude of his own being , to lick "the earth like a wound". Across Lee's twenty pieces in this collection, the reader's gaze is gently directed to the underside of the most common human experiences in order to liberate to the vision an understanding that startles with its metaphoric accuracy and poetic logic.

In the poem 'The Human Skull for Sale on the Shelf of the Oddity Shop in Toronto', for instance, the skull on display triggers in the poet's mind, a train of thoughts that attempts to trace death to life, life to time, time to the world and the world that stands divided between the powerful and the powerless, to the need for divine grace:

consider how the nucleolus bloomed
ten fingered
in the milky hunger of an ancient moon
now found
upon a sheet of glass
the zygomatic curio
become the object of the rich man's purse

who shapes a meaning from the dead
what bites the earth away to grass
to seek the blue grave of the sky
or feel again the common kiss of God
a startlement sublime

Carved with inordinate beauty, Lee's poetry is suffused with a tenderness and calm that invite the reader to replenish her impoverished spirit at hope's springs and to bathe in its unalloyed light. His best poems, one realizes, are both odes and elegies that assert the invincibility of hope even as they lament the passing away of great goodness, certainty and faith. Poems like 'Now I am Become Death the Destroyer of Worlds', 'Dangerous to Say' and 'A Sandy Field in Syria' are deep laments for the passing away of a world that valued life, love and humanity leaving "a greedy overcoming/ a thickening/ invasion of toxic slog/…/ marching over the doomed landscape/ like the ghostly armies/ of some ancient death-bringing/ empire of dust." With images that have their roots in the earth and a cadence that is almost biblical in its faithful surrender to experience, Lee's poems bring the reader home to the eternal conscience of man - erroneous, fallible, even dead, perhaps, but not without immense possibilities of resurrection.

Undeniably universal, essentially Canadian, and thoroughly breathtaking in their images, these forty-nine poems in *Two Thousand Seventeen* are pieces that call for close, deep and reflective reading. Begotten by the spirit of a landscape that is as untameable as it is undecipherable, these poems can be termed, in Timothy Morton's words, as *ecological rhapsodies* with nature, in each of these poems, manifesting itself a narrator whose meaning is interpreted for us by the poem itself. Rejecting conventional temporality, these poems respond to earth-time where the whims and moods of nature are more significant than human need or convenience. One finds here a deeply ecological ethics of being where to be with the world, to cohere and to co-exist in love, peace, and wonder, is both joy and duty. In Lee's poem 'Mike Wilson's Chestnut', the thought of a neighbouring chestnut tree being cut, fills the poem with gloom, leading it to visualize the tree moving and attempting to seek shelter:

> *Mike swears the tree is moving*
> *his way its shadowline sidling closer*
> *like a widow slow dancing for grief*

Similarly, in Grove's poem, 'Raining', an invading raccoon becomes a "four-legged son" being driven "to a forest where he can live/ in peace with nature".

Each poem in this collection offers an unforgettable dialogue between man and the ecological world, affirming in art what Morton terms as 'ambient poetics'. In his essay 'Why Ambient Poetics?' Morton offers the following definition of ambience:

> Ambience is a poetic enactment of a state of nondual awareness that collapses the subject-object division, upon which depends the aggressive territorialization that precipitates ecological destruction. Furthermore, this collapse of subject-object dualism, however temporary in experience, spontaneously gives rise to howsoever weak a sense of warmth towards one's world, in which one is included. This world, to say more, is a world without centre or edge that includes everything.

Ambient poetics, according to Morton, involves the deconstruction of human identity to replace it with an extended environmental awareness of the self in space and this is exactly what Grove and Lee set out to do between them – to extricate the soul from its slips, sins and ignorance and to place it in its native ecosophy so that it may learn to grow into its immortal and immense infinitude.

This collection, published in India and being a bilingual edition that carries accompanying translations of these rich poems in Hindi, a word must be said for the astonishing cultural diversity and the grand semantic and epistemological wealth that these poems bring into the Hindi language. Many of the expressions contained here would have presented a daunting task to the Hindi translator for the sole reason that linguistic and cultural equivalences would have been hard to find. However, close approximations have been creatively discovered and many bridges have been built that will bring the reader of these poems in Hindi closer to the spirit of the Canadian landscape and the spiritual wisdom of Grove and Lee. The book, long after it has been read, will continue to watermark the reader's consciousness with its powerful images, its poetic profundity, and its ecomimetic beat and therein lies its undiminished accomplishment.

Traveler, What Do You Seek? A Review on P.K. Page's Life and Work

Anna Yin. Poet, Reviewer

I walk in rain, I wake in dark, I ask myself: "What do you seek?" Sometimes I seem to know, most times I am not sure. Many people have similar experiences, especially during difficult times. My own question turns me toward poetry. Reading a biography of iconic Canadian poet and painter P.K. Page, *Journey with No Map -A life of P.K. Page* by Sandra Djwa, as well as poetry by the intrepid traveler Page herself, I find multi-threads to map a maze that I, too, have lived in. I see some light shed-on answers both as Page lived her life, and as she wrote.

Patricia Kathleen "P. K." Page (1916-2010) published more than thirty books including poetry, fiction, travel diaries, essays and works for children. She won the Governor General's Award in 1954 for *The Metal and the Flower*, and the Canadian Authors association Award in 1985 for *The Glass Air*. Her last collection, *Coal and Roses*, was posthumously shortlisted for the Griffin Poetry Prize. Her art is in the permanent collections of the National Gallery of Canada, the Art Gallery of Ontario and the Burnaby Art Gallery.

I read Page's poetry in my late thirties. Unlike her, and other poets who wanted to be writers, from a very young age, I had no ambition in this regard. My background was neither dramatic nor dynamic, and in fact, I was from a practical family and a Confusion culture. For a long time I assumed it was accidental that I became a poet. But more and more, I saw it was destiny just as Page experienced. As Rumi says: "Not only the thirsty seek the water, the water as well seeks the thirsty." When Page was three, her family moved from England to the Prairies of Canada, then following her father's posts, they moved again and again, to Mountain areas and to the East Coast. These constant changes and moves stimulated Page's sense of restlessness and uncertainty. She started reading her father's books on time, life and death (*An Experiment with Time* by J.W. Dunne and *The Fountain* by Charles Morgan), then more books on psychology, such as Jung's *Modern Man in Search of a Soul.*

From her teenage years, Page wondered about concepts of reincarnation, the life journey, the spiritual life, the possibility of parallel worlds, and the final affirmation of love. Most of all she started to view man as a traveler who could be in the infinitive of flexible time. In her adolescent mind, Page also thought of the idea of invulnerability and hoped one could be invulnerable if one was like water for no knife could harm water… I find personal resonance with the water in her metaphor and agree that the most powerful force can be as soft as water. This kind of fountain blessed me decades later when I started writing poetry in a dark time. Poetry became the water to heal my thirst and to keep me strong. In Chinese culture, water is multi-faceted, both vulnerable and invulnerable. I find the same wisdom and complexity in Page's poetry. In "The Crow" [1]:

> By the wave rising, by the wave breaking
> high to low;
> by the wave riding the air, sweeping the high air low
> in a white foam, in suds,
> there
> like a churchwarden, like a stiff
> turn-the-eye-inward old man
> in a cutaway, in the mist
> stand
> the crow. [1]

The images are startling and sharp. Page's *Crow* reminds me that poetry turns me inward to seek peace through dark times.

Page's life was continually in involved with traveling and seeking. With her early years' reading of Virginal Woolf and Katherine Mansfield, she pondered states of consciousness and how to lead life as an artist. In her story "The Sun and the Moon", Page explored, perhaps unconsciously issues later she would face as a woman artist. "There is much we do not know…."[2] but she also acknowledged an unexpected (entrance)/into the door of (her) mind. [2] Fortunately, Page's father recognized her talent in writing and offered her financial support. With it she found some freedom and pursued her dream, and eventually became her own teacher to guide her artistic life.

In her poem "Waking", Page writes, "I lie in the long parentheses of arms / dream of love / and the crying cities of Europe."[3]. I read it as if Page were waking to see her landscape, half psychological, half mythological... And what did she mean *dream of love*? As we know, Pablo Picasso's *Guernica* is full of broken and distorted human and animal bodies. Perhaps Page hoped for love to cure the war's horrible damages.

In 1957, Page moved to Brazil with her husband Arthur Irwin, a diplomat. There she found herself a total foreigner, like an infant, with a new language to learn. She described the process of growing up again: one is a toy at first, then a doll, a child, gradually, an adult again, but a different adult. She asked: Who am I, the one changed by language, what is personality, identity? [4]

When I immigrated to Canada in 1999, I had a similar experience. With a huge cultural shock and new things to learn, especially a new language, I felt lonely and helpless. One night after I read The Emperor's New Clothes to my son, a poem came to me. In the poem, a child turns to me asking "Who are you?", …a sadness hit me… I left China to come to Canada to seek a better life, however I found I was lost. The child awaked me and let me see my lost self. When I read P.K. Page's poem "Single Traveler", I felt it was very familiar:

"What is this love that is my life's companion? / Shape-changer, sometimes faceless, this companion. / Single traveler, I wander a wasting world / awaiting the much anticipated Companion…" [5]

I translated this poem into Chinese long ago, but today I still ponder her questions, "Am I too bound and blinded by coarse wrappings / ever to know true love as my companion? / O Poet, squanderer of time and talents / why do you search for love as your Companion?" [5]

From 1957 to 1959, Page stayed in Brazil and found herself not able to write poetry. Fortunately, she discovered her painting talents. In a wordless world, colors, lines and shapes became her new companions. In her later artistic life and difficult times, both her paintings and her poetry became vehicles for her spiritual journey. Her third poetry collection: *Cry Ararat* was published in 1967. It contained a half-dozen of her drawings. The book jacket used her painting of a bird titled *And You, What Do You Seek?*

Ararat is the traditional name for the mountain where Noah's ark landed. The long title poem, "Cry Ararat" is a dream poem, involving water. It could refer to both the story from the Bible as well as her difficult life journey.

The poem ends with these lines: "Will the grey weather wake us, / toss us twice in the terrible night to tell us / the [dove's] flight is cancelled / and the mountain lost? O, then cry Ararat!"

At the age of 70, Page learnt a new poetry form: the glosa. It is an early Renaissance form of tribute developed by the poets of the Spanish court: each line of the opening quatrain by another poet, becomes the final line of the four following stanzas which "gloss" (or comment on) that opening quatrain, often with the sixth, ninth, and borrowed tenth line rhyming. Page soon mastered the art and became a Glosa Queen.

Her "Love's Pavilion" is a glosa based on four lines of Dylan Thomas's "And Death Shall Have No Dominion". Page reframed Thomas' declarations for her own time and place, her own spiritual yearning. It ends with these lines:

"With the Lord of the Dance we shall form a ring
and there in love's pavilion
hand in hand we shall say Amen
and we shall dance and we shall sing
with Love, with Love for companion.
And death shall have no dominion."[6]

Here again we see love as companion.

Another glosa "Soft Travelers" from Page's book *Coal and Roses Twenty-One Glosas*, borrowed four lines from Dionne Brand: "some words can make you weep, / when they're uttered, the light rap of their / destinations, their thud as if on peace, as if on cloth / on air, they break all places intended and known…"[7]

Page started this glosa with her own line: "There is magic, of course, and among the many magics there are / words-spellbinders…"[7] Then she wove her own life experience and spiritual journey into "all places intended and known," which might refer to Mexico where she studied Sufism –"the transcending of ordinary limitations and higher consciousness to learn 'the very me of me' and destinations".

In fact, Page turning to magic, to mystery that could be traced back to her young age. Her mother Rose used to say, that she, her husband and her daughter had lived together in previous lives, over and over and over again… When Page was 18 and lived with her Aunt Bibbi in England for a year, she found Dante Gabriel Rossetti's painting *How They Met Themselves* and his poem *"Sudden Light"* quite moving: "I have been here before, / But when or how I cannot tell: / I know the grass beyond the door, / The sweet keen smell, / The sighing sound, the lights around the shore." Both the poem and the painting suggested reincarnation-the continuation of life and love through centuries, which linked to Page's Sufism study. Page embraced the concept of man having multiple states of being.

In Page's later essay entitled "Traveler, Conjuror, Journeyman", she said, "I am traveler, I have a destination but no maps."[8] Yet from her poetry and paintings, we can see that she made maps for herself - maps pointing to experiences of nature, experiences of love and experiences of the self.

"Planet Earth" is Page's well-known glosa that develops from a poem by Pablo Neruda; it speaks, in tenderly domestic terms, about how we must learn to love and appreciate the earth. [9]

"It has to be loved the way a laundress loves her linens,
the way she moves her hands caressing the fine muslins
knowing their warp and woof,
like a lover coaxing, or a mother praising."[9]

Page ends the poem with holy hands doing all this work of caring for the world: "Archangels then will attend to its metals / and polish the rods of its rain," and "Seraphim will stop singing hosannas / to shower it with blessings and blisses and praises."[10]

And human beings too should be "newly in love, we must draw it and paint it / our pencils and brushes and loving caresses / smoothing the holy surfaces."[10]

When Page died in 2010, she asked that her ashes be divided -half to go where her husband Arthur was interred, half to be scattered on the sea. With this division, Page might acknowledge the two great loves of her life: Arthur Irwin and Frank Scott. Moreover, she wanted to return to the original source where every life starts and meets again like her poem: "The End"[11]

We are the sea's, and as such we are at its beck,

We are the water within the wave and the wave's form.[11]
Perhaps one day my ashes, too, will return to the sea and we shall meet there.

Here I finish this article with a poem I wrote in 2012.

Purple and Gold *(In memory of P.K. Page)*

Your life is a purple pearl
sent from the old Kingdoms
to the long West Coast.
Your childhood rides on horseback
with iris, bluebells and lavender
all violet in the purple clouds.

Your married life, a lucky star,
glides from one destination to another.
The exotic winds mix
your nostalgia and talents,
open a world of wonders.

But what do I know?
How does
Black and white at midnight glow
This garden of barbed wire and roses?
What is the life in a shell?
What kind of waves are calling?

Yet I do know –
your poetry is the gold
beyond time and space.
It speaks of the color of harvest,
and the weight of life
where you see two *divine moons,*
and the love of Planet Earth.

Extracting from streams of life,
refining through fire of passions,
you crown us with the power
and the beauty of words
where our *third eye sees*:
gold shining from the underground,
roses rising from purple dreams.
Under The Sky Tree,
you find the way home. [12]

July 8, 2020

Notes:

The Crow, from "Journey with No Map -A life of P.K. Page" by Sandra Djwa" page 71
from "Journey with No Map -A life of P.K. Page" by Sandra Djwa" page 67
from "Journey with No Map -A life of P.K. Page" by Sandra Djwa" page 67
from "Journey with No Map -A life of P.K. Page" by Sandra Djwa" page 163
Single Traveler from https://canpoetry.library.utoronto.ca/page/poem5.htm
from https://www.cardus.ca/comment/article/how-to-honour-dead-poets-p-k-page-and-the-glosa-form/
How to Honour Dead Poets: P.K. Page and the Glosa Form by Deborah Bowen
Soft Travelers, from "Coal and Roses Twenty-One Glosas" Page 40
from "Journey with No Map -A life of P.K. Page" by Sandra Djwa" page 177
from "Journey with No Map -A life of P.K. Page" by Sandra Djwa" page 298
from https://www.cardus.ca/comment/article/how-to-honour-dead-poets-p-k-page-and-the-glosa-form/
How to Honour Dead Poets: P.K. Page and the Glosa Form by Deborah Bowen
from "Journey with No Map -A life of P.K. Page" by Sandra Djwa" page 321
Purple and Gold, from Inhaling the Silence by Anna Yin (Mosaic Press 2013)

To Sleep with Stones, by WL Hawkin

BA, BEd Gail M. Murray. Teacher, Writer, Poet, Book Reviewer

W.L. Hawkin is a stand-out author from Vancouver, B.C. writing "edgy urban fantasy with a twist of murder". Her first three novels (LGBT mysteries and thrillers) form a trilogy, yet each stands alone. Her novels include: *To Charm a Killer*, *To Sleep with Stones* and *To Render a Raven*. Hawkin researches all her locales (Ireland, Scotland, the B.C. Coast) to soak up the sensory landscape. In 2017, she climbed Croghan Hill in Ireland to survey the land her king would rule in *To Kill a King* (a time-travel thriller coming in 2021). She is a seeker and mystic, fascinated by language, archaeology, and mythology. Hawkin graduated from Trent University, Ontario and has a background in Indigenous Studies and English literature. She found her voice publishing poetry and Native Rights articles in Canadian news magazines and now is an Indie author/publisher at Blue Haven Press. http://bluehavenpress.com

To Sleep with Stones is an edgy, urban fantasy. For the uninitiated "urban fantasy is a hybrid genre that lives at the crossroads between fantasy, horror, hard-boiled thriller and romance. Every urban fantasy involves supernatural beings and/or beings with magical abilities yet it's rooted in reality." (A. J.Blakemont)

To Sleep with Stones, a virtual smorgasbord has something for everyone: an archaeological dig in Scotland, action, suspense, an intense anti-hero, and a murder mystery to solve. Hawkin's first chapter explodes with the promise of perilous adventure. From the discovery of the priceless Egyptian artifact to the Wiccan solstice; she had me at "Aye".

To Sleep with Stones is *True Blood* meets *Outlander*. Prepare yourself for steamy LGBT love scenes, unique vampires, and a journey through Scotland's Inner Hebrides. Hawkin's edginess shows in the unbridled eroticism of the Wiccan solstice, flame-haired Sorcha's seduction of Dylan McBride, "the sweet peach", Michael Stryker's flirtation with Vampire, and the escapades of sensuous free-spirited Estrada.

Set in Argyll, along the southwest coast of Scotland near Glasgow, it opens with a brilliant find, a jewelled broad collar, worn by the daughter of Queen Nefertiti. After site boss and head archeologist, Sorcha, discovers the gold broad collar she deems her ticket to fame, she takes her crew to an Oban pub to celebrate. On the upstairs pub patio, the feisty beauty seduces young archaeology student Dylan McBride. He is later accosted by Glasgow journalist, Alastair Steele, who caught them in the act on his cell.

Later that night of summer solstice, Dylan goes out to commune with the standing stones.

> *. . . he leaned back against the cool three-thousand-year old rock . . . For thousands of years, humans had worshipped, as he did now, on this sacred landscape . . . When Dylan McBride leaned his palm against a stone it revealed its secrets. Sometimes he heard voices, sometimes he saw visions. (15)*

Dylan can sense memories of people who worshipped there and he sees Egyptian princess, Meritaten, in her gold broad collar. Next, he is arrested, cuffed and dragged from the field at Ballymeanoch—jailed for the murder of Alastair Steele. His grandfather contacts Estrada.

Hawkin introduced Estrada in *To Charm a Killer*. Performer, magician, and High Priest of Hollystone Coven, he flies to Scotland in aid of his friend, Dylan. In leathers astride his Harley we witness the black avenging angel. The image of the angel wings tattooed across his back serves as a brilliant metaphor and serves as the cover for this book.

In evocative mystical scenes, our high priest *becomes* the horned god – Cernunnos (fertility god/adorned in antlers spirit of the hunt) and meets the Celtic Oak King. Later, in the Taynish woods on a quest for an oak branch, he reconnects with Primrose his faerie love and we glimpse his tenderness.

> *Sorcerer. The voice was faint at first, evanescent, a lilting on the breeze, and he thought he'd imagined it. Sorcerer. He heard it again: higher, louder, clearer, the tone teasing and he whirled around, searching for her. There was only one woman who called him by that name, whose cadences were flecked with old Irish. (96)*

Though the second book in the series; this novel stands alone. Hawkin has flawlessly woven in essential background and characters from her first novel as well as introducing new ones: a female detective (Rachel Steele), a half-fey Druid dwarf who deals in Scottish antiquities (Magus Dubh), and a rough Viking (Kai Roskilde) – a rival for Dylan. Though her characters are fictional, her settings are authentic: Argyll, Kilmartin Glen (rife with cairns and stone circles), Ballymeanoch (megaliths), and Her Majesty's prison Greenock.

Hawkin's tight and well-paced writing and knowledge of Celtic myths (Robert Graves, *The White Goddess*) combine with multi-layered characters, lush language and plot twists and turns, to draw the reader in. No spoiler alert – the ending is surprising and satisfying. In fact, the hallmark of this novel is the author's seamless interweaving of myth and reality. She appeals to our intellect and our desire for vicarious adventure.

Author Profile: Inside Jennifer Robson

BA, BEd Gail M. Murray. Teacher, Writer, Poet, Book Reviewer

With a doctorate in British economic and social history, Robson planned to be a professor; instead she found work as a copy editor. With her creativity and talents as editor and historian, little wonder her novels make The Top Ten Lists. Robson is a triple threat in the writing world.

Getting inside an author's process is fascinating. Robson reveals her almost obsessive focus on historical detail, all the meticulous research she completes to produce an authentic setting integral to her story; essential to the Historical Fiction genre. She frequents libraries and archives devouring general histories then specific histories (e.g. to learn about food rationing in WWII). When possible she searches out primary sources such as the women she interviewed in the oral history project she undertook as part of her doctoral thesis. Her advice to writers is to be sure you are fascinated by the time period as you'll be living there.

To flesh out her characters, she answers Proust's questionnaire for primary and secondary characters. Some questions include: Which talent would you most like to have? Which living person do you admire most? What is the quality you most like in a man/woman? What is your greatest regret?

She chooses to write about ordinary people in extraordinary times. I flash back to Helena in *Moonlight Over Paris*, as she leads the reader through Gertrude Stein's salon encountering Picasso, Hadley and Ernest Hemingway. It's not about them. We are privy to Helena's impressions and feelings.

Robson offers "My books turn on women's history." Captivated with women's place in history, her heroines reflect their times but grow in strength. Perhaps their journey to empowerment is what makes her stories so relevant to women today?

Although each novel stands alone, she conceived of her first three novels as a trilogy. Timing is everything. Robson completed her breakout novel, *Somewhere in France*, in 2009, receiving little interest from publishers. After the success of British TV drama series, *Downton Abbey*, on PBS in 2011, she re-submitted her manuscript with the pitch "*Downton Abbey* meets *M.A.S.H*" and the world was her oyster. This reminds me of Canadian icon, L. M. Montgomery taking her novel out of a hat box where it had been stored for 8 years and giving it one more try. Imagine Canadian Literature without *Anne of Green Gables*? There's a lesson here for all writers.

Asked about her favourite character she smiles, "Charlotte in *After the War is Over*; she's like my mom."

Asked about writing love scenes I almost sense a faint blush. She explains that there is an art to it and that she feels uncomfortable when her father, acclaimed historian, Stuart Robson reads them in her novels. He proof reads her final draft, before it is sent out to her editor.

If you have yet to discover this best-selling author, may I suggest…..?

If you are a fan of Downton Abbey, you'll love the drama and intensity of *Somewhere in France*. Our spirited young heroine, Lily, defies her family and the strict restrictions of aristocratic British society to drive an ambulance to clearing stations in war torn France. She follows Jamie, her surgeon sweetheart, to the front lines of WWI.

After the War is Over focuses on the relationship between Charlotte (columnist and symbol of the burgeoning women's movement) and upper class Edward who is suffering PTSD, the psychological wounds of war. Set in post war Britain, the people and the country deal with hardship and economic wounds – the aftermath of war.

Moonlight Over Paris is the perfect time warp to 1920's Paris; a richly detailed journey back in time and rite of passage for Helena who finds her footing as an artist and love with an American journalist. Reminiscent of Woody Allen's film, *Midnight in Paris*, Robson's story is more intriguing and pure.

In *Goodnight from London*, set in 1940's Britain. Budding authors will champion Ruby Sutton's tenacity to report WWII news stories, including a private interview with Eleanor Roosevelt under curious circumstances. Amid the toll of the London Blitz, Ruby grows in stature as a journalist. When Ruby's hotel is bombed, she finds a real home for the first time in her life. She also experiences love with Bennett, a man whose top secret missions involve danger, intrigue and a most tender love letter.

Goodnight from London, is "homage to my grandmother, Nikki Moir." Although their personalities are totally different, it's about the struggle a female journalist faces in a male newsroom. Nikki inspired the character of Ruby Sutton. Nikki began at Vancouver *News-Herald* writing for the women's pages until WWII came along providing opportunity for women journalists. With the men overseas, Nikki was assigned to courthouse and military beats. Later she became a feature writer for Vancouver *Province,* interviewing Eleanor Roosevelt in 1949. "I imagine Grandma's face when I think of Ruby." Hobson's grandfather, Reg Moir, posted to London as an information officer in the R.C.A.F., served as a primary source. I have noticed among my writing colleagues this tendency to draw from their own lives and build with imagination

The Gown set in 1947 London, as Britain struggles with shortages, rationing and rebuilding the country and revolves around the making of Princess Elizabeth's wedding dress. Her characters work for the Queen's designer, Norman Hartnell. Take a look at Robson's face book page to see the results of eight hours she spent at Hand and Lock embroidery studios in London to experience embroidery techniques, first hand.

By perseverance and sheer luck, Robson discovered Betty Foster, now an elderly woman, fourteen at the time of the royal wedding. Having worked on the gown, Betty filled in precious details about attitude, working conditions and how thrilled everyone was when each seamstress was called to place a stitch so they could say they had worked on the magnificent gown.

The story line of the novel follows the lives of Ann, an ordinary working class British girl living in a council house in Essex, and Miriam a French émigré and survivor of Nazi persecution. The third character, Heather Mackenzie, a young Canadian, inherits an exquisite set of hand stitched flowers from her late grandmother and discerns that these motifs match those decorating the queen's stunning wedding dress. Her grandmother had never spoken of her early life in England. Heather sets out to uncover her grandmother's secret, giving the novel a sense of solving a mystery

As we have come to expect, Robson's prose is fluid as she flawlessly transitions between 2016 and 1947. When the elegant gown is completed: "Ann hadn't expected it to be such a bittersweet moment…her part in its creation was over. This was the last time she would touch the flowers she had sewn" (p. 307). In dreary post war London, it had been a bright moment.

Robson's latest novel *Our Darkest Night* is set for release in January 2021. Set in Monta Grappa and Venice, Italy during 1943, it deals with the perils of being an Italian Jew in Nazi occupied Italy. She's seeing the country through her character's eyes. Later she'll move on to Auschwitz in Poland – sure to be intense.

Robson's strength lies in her smooth writing style, authentic settings and making the reader care about her well-developed characters. Though they face struggle, Robson rewards us with personal growth, a sensitive love story, and an uplifting ending.

Rupi Kaur:
South Asian Canadian Poet Phenomenon

BA, BEd Gail M. Murray. Teacher, Writer, Poet, Book Reviewer

Rupi Kaur is a South Asian Canadian poet, and spoken word artist whose first poetry collection *milk and honey* (2014) sold over 2.5 million copies, graced the New York Times best seller list for over a year and has been translated into over 30 languages. Her second poetry collection – *the sun and her flowers* (2017) – continues on the Top Ten lists of fiction, quite unheard of in poetry circles. It has sold over 8 million copies. In terms of book sales, Kaur is one of the most successful living poets and has achieved international success.

As a 21 year old university student, Kaur wrote, illustrated and self-published her first collection – milk and honey. This feminist, millennial writer appeals with her raw, personal poetry. This overnight Instagram sensation sometimes referred to as 'Instapoet' has tapped into the voice of her culture and women everywhere. Ms. Kaur writes on themes of abuse, love, loss, heartbreak, self-image and the immigrant experience.

Rupi's life began in Hoshiapur in the Punjab, India. At age four, her family immigrated to Canada moving a lot until settling in Brampton, Ontario (Canada). Her mother gave her a paint brush, encouraging self-expression through art. Today her spare line drawings illustrate her books. Rupi describes herself as a young South Asian woman growing up in the West doing the dance between cultures. This duality is reflected in several of her pieces.

Rupi does not use capitals or punctuation and rarely titles her work. Her themes appear at the bottom of her poem. Some of her pieces are affirmations. Some are brief – "on the last day of love/my heart cracked inside my body"; others lengthy such as *broken english* – a tribute to her mother and strong, immigrant women everywhere. One wonders if this age of texting and cell phones are responsible for her style or is she trying to be unique like e e cummings? On her website she explains the reason she only uses lower case letters, yet I still think texting has been influential with her generation. Below is her explanation taken directly from her website:

"… although i can read and understand my mother tongue (punjabi) i do not have the skillset to write poetry in it. to write punjabi means to use gurmukhi script. and within this script there are no uppercase or lowercase letters. all letters are treated the same. i enjoy how simple that is. how symmetrical

and how absolutely straightforward. i also feel there is a level of equality this visuality brings to the work. a visual representation of what i want to see more of within the world: equalness. so in order to preserve these small details of my mother language I include them within this language. no case distinction and only periods. a world within a world. which is what i am as an immigrant. as a diasporic punjabi sikh woman. it is less about breaking the rules of English (although that's pretty fun) but more about tying in my own history and heritage within my work."

Rupi states that her poems are meant to be easy for the reader and they are – most accessible. This is a bright light. I find much modern poetry obscure and oblique.

This feminist and millennial writer appeals to young women who identify with her raw personal poems. I can see her appeal to women of color, the downtrodden, new immigrants and women getting over a love affair; but then love and loss are universal themes. When she speaks of love it is dramatic, all-encompassing and out of control.

Rupi began writing to express her fears and feelings as a shy introverted bullied twelve year old, later shared her poems with family then posted on Tumblr and Instagram becoming an almost overnight sensation. We sense the private self in her guttural response and rejoice with her as she taps into self-care, transforming pain into resilience and triumph best illustrated in her long poem – *home* - which she performs during her TED talk – *I'm Taking My Body Back*. This poem is five pages long. It is essentially a story – prose like with line breaks – that contributes to the immediacy. To start - "it began as a typical thursday from what I recall' and he becomes physically abusive:

> while I hid at the back of some
> upstairs closet of my mind as
> you
> kicked the front door in
>
> i was a hundred and ten pounds of fresh meat
> you skinned and gutted with your fingers (p.69)

Gradually the person works through the pain "and after years of rain/the truth comes like sunlight" and like a phoenix she rises from the ashes to "wash yesterday out of my hair/and enjoy…../this typical thursday afternoon." (p.72)

Her poems are so visceral one wonders if they stem from her own life experience. The book is divided into five sections that echo her title: wilting, falling, rooting, rising, blooming. It makes sense to read them in order as they build in intensity with the persona in the poems growing from weakness to strength. When it comes to upbringing and abuse, not all are as fortunate as Rupi to develop her resilience.

Some are not at all pleasant-made me cringe-yet their rhythm and smooth lyrics appeal. *lessons from mama* has an edge and poignancy to it as the daughter has a much easier life then her wise and long suffering mother.

The most graphic poem on the theme of female infanticide or feticide, angered me not only as a woman but as a human being

> 1790
> he takes the newborn girl from his wife
> carries her to the neighboring room
> cradles her head with his left hand
> and gently snaps her neck with his right

The next verse 1990, points out the astounding number of girl babies aborted in rural India-"a hundred baby girls were found buried/behind a doctor's house in a neighboring village".

> 2012
> twelve hospitals in the toronto area
> refuse to reveal a baby's gender to expectant families
> until the thirtieth week of pregnancy
> all twelve hospitals are located in areas with high
> asian immigrant populations (p. 144, 145)

Her respect for her mother shines in the simple first line "she left an entire village to be his wife" (p. 150). When she writes of her mother and mothers it is with a deep respect and love.

Kaur's latest collection, *home body*, has a release date of November 2020. In it she explores the concept of self, and reflects on home, mental health, love and acceptance.

Ms. Kaur who talked very little as a child has found her voice. Perhaps she has tapped into the voice of her culture and women everywhere. The *sun and her flowers* culminates with hope:

> there is
> nothing left
> to worry about
> the sun and her flowers are here.

Lightfoot, by Nicholas Jennings

BA, BEd Gail M. Murray. Teacher, Writer, Poet, Book Reviewer

Although Canadian musician, composer and, superstar Gordon Lightfoot has been making music since the 60s and granting interviews during that time, the 82-year-old has always been shy when it comes to revealing too much, preferring to let his music be the window into his world.

In the last few years, there's been a softening; Canadian author and journalist Nicholas Jennings (who was asked in 1999 to create extensive liner notes for Lightfoot's Songbook Box Set) was invited into Lightfoot's Toronto home and given access to the troubadour's history. The result is a fascinating, informative and well-researched account of Lightfoot's life story. In keeping with Lightfoot's tendency to stay out of the spotlight – except when onstage – this book delves openly into the musician's romantic and family relationships and alcohol abuse.

Pages are spent discussing his song writing, unwavering loyalty, perfectionism and selfless generosity to the people and causes close to his heart. To read this book is to come away with a greater understanding of how a young choirboy from Orillia became one of Canada's most revered songwriters and performers, and beloved among music fans around the world.

Chapter one called By Lake Couchiching deals with his early life, love of nature, singing in the church choir and later barbershop in High School. Serious about a musical career, he attended The Westlake College of Modern Music in Hollywood learning music notation, sight reading, composition and arranging. He and pal Terry Whelan headed to Toronto singing mostly folk ballads. When Gord met Ian & Sylvia at the Riverboat in Yorkville, they were impressed with his song writing and introduced him to their manager, Grossman ,who booked him into New York clubs and folk festivals launching his career. Ian & Sylvia had a big hit with his *song Early Morning Rain.*

His debut album is superbly crafted with quality, depth and range. His baritone voice, mellow sound and poetic lyrics stand out. His ballads are often inspired by real events, the Canadian landscape and the dynamic between men and women.

"Lightfooot's songs always took listeners on a journey, drawing them in to stories rich in emotion…..meticulously crafted, the songs were instantly accessible." (p5) He was influenced by Bob Dylan whom he admired. They shared the common language of music and often jammed together at his Rosedale home when Dylan was in concert in Toronto.

With Canada's Centennial Lightfoot was commissioned by CBC producer Bob Jarvis to write a song to capture the grandeur of Canada. He gave Gord the book by William Van Horne, architect of the first transcontinental railroad. Three days later after much focus, coffee and whisky, he emerged with the iconic *Canadian Railroad Trilogy* which he debuted at Massey Hall. Lightfoots 'appearances there became a yearly ritual. Pierre Berton, author of *The Last Spike* praises him saying "You did more good with your damn song than I did with my entire book on the same subject." (p74)

Gord gives Jennings background to many of his songs. *Bittergreen* (1968) was written for his first wife Brita, his muse, about whom he could romanticize, in spite of booze and women on the road. Drinking helped him socialize and it settled his nerves before a concert. It also took its toll on his body and his relationships.

"If You Could Read My Mind (1970) bares his soul in a bittersweet poetic way capturing the breakdown of a relationship (his marriage breakdown with Brita) showing his vulnerability and guilt with lines like "heroes often fail" and "chains upon my feet". His songs frequently deal with wanderlust, movin' on.

"Canoeing demanded organization and orderliness, two things Lightfoot excelled at. With his disciplined approach to work, he thrived on the challenges of wilderness trips." (p 176) It helped clear his mind and body after being on the concert circuit. Some songs that echo his experiences: *Whispers of the North* (opens and closes with a plaintive loon call*), Christian Island, Knotty Pine, A Winter's Night.* He was also an avid sailor.

Lightfoot is quintessential Canadian. In 1988, who better to open the Olympic Games at Calgary than Gord Lightfoot and Ian Tyson singing Lightfoot's *Alberta Bound* and Tyson's *Four Strong Winds*? Lightfoot also worked with David Suzuki on environmental activism.

Women loved Lightfoot. There were three marriages: (Brita Olaisson/Elizabeth Moon/Kim Hasse) which produced Fred, Ingrid, Miles and Meredith and three cohabitations (Cathy Smith/Cathy Coonley/Joanne Magee) which produced Eric and Galen. Gordon is proud of his six children.

In 1981 at the age of 44, he finally quit drinking. He has emphysema and must take oxygen at intermission while performing. He is happily married to his third wife and takes her touring with him. He's grateful for the success and life he has lived creating music. This also comes across in the 2019 documentary *If You Could Read My Mind* where this author (Jennings) is interviewed along with friends – Murray McLauchlan, Ronnie Hawkins, Ian Tyson, The Good Brothers and more. This accomplished artist and storyteller we claim as our own. This masterful biography of Canadian songwriter legend by fellow Canadian Nicholas Jennings is a superb read. It's authentic and personal giving insights into the man and his music - as Canadians - our music.

Circles in the Spiral: How life offers opportunities for reconnection, recovery, and redemption

PhD, MSc Ronald Mackay

Introduction

Shane Joseph's choice of title for his most recent novel can be understood as a metaphor for a perspective on the nature of life and the fortuitous breaks that it affords us. Redemption lies within our grasp if only we recognise, seize, and act upon these moments.

Circles in the Spiral (Blue Denim Press Inc.) suggests that our lives are not constrained to follow the temporal links in a metaphorical chain in which earlier events restrict subsequent opportunities so that our future is inescapably predetermined. The word *Circles* in the title, conveys the idea that life is structured like a carrousel, returning to us opportunities that we earlier handled badly; that life is cyclical and so offers us a second, even a third, chance to get things right. The word *Spirals* complements *Circles* by adding the potential of upward stirring, of reaching, of the opportunity to strive for and embrace betterment, our own and that of others.

Thesis

In this essay, I argue that *Circles in the Spiral*, despite the failure and demoralization especially in the earlier chapters, offers the reader an ultimately reassuring view of life, one in which we as individuals are afforded the opportunity to review our past, acknowledge our present, amend our ways, forgive those who have trespassed against us, and make the world a better place.

The early chapters of the novel focus on the cyclical nature of lives grown out of deception, neglect, and desecration. In the later chapters, the potential for redemption is revealed. Nevertheless, throughout the entire novel, the author scatters crumbs of hope that suggest, rather than promise, a path to reparation.

Circles in the Spiral tells a story of contemporary life in Canada and the modern world beyond any single country. It is a story of vice but also of virtue. It portrays in the most graphic and immediate of ways the dereliction of moral duty, of self-absorption that extinguishes empathy, of disregard, dishonesty, carelessness, apathy, treachery, malevolence, and despair. It shows a world in which our moral sentiments have been taken over by market value. Nevertheless, true to the title, it ascends – or rather, clambers clumsily – towards the promise, if not the realisation, of what Western classical and Christian culture has always encouraged: a firm disposition to aspire to that which is good through the practise of virtue, in particular the virtues of prudence, justice, temperance, and courage; of faith, hope, and charity.

I support these arguments by revealing some of the ways and means by which Shane Joseph's *Circles in the Spiral* successfully conveys this initially bleak but ultimately affirmative view of life and the redemptive implications it has for the characters and, by extension, for us readers.

Outline

First, I summarise the premise of the novel and the roles the protagonists play in the dramatic plot and some of their circular and spiral movements. Then I discuss the evolving moral perspective demonstrated by the action, and the recurring opportunities for personal and social betterment offered to the main characters. Finally, I draw a broad conclusion about the importance of this book as a work of contemporary Western, and particularly Canadian, fiction.

Synopsis adapted from the novel

Will Smallwood, a writer suffering from the dreaded writer's block as well as tormenting dreams, is plunged into a living nightmare when he is swept up into a misinformation campaign aimed at hijacking the Canadian Federal Election.

On the run, Will is forced to confront his personal demons: his suppressed childhood, his stalled career as a historical fiction writer, his lost love, Jacqueline, and the malaise of his aimlessness. He is offered a second chance to put things right when he is drawn to a yoga retreat and meets the promiscuous painter, Divine Secrets (Dee), along with a motley group of academics, alcoholics, and ascetics. The key to his deliverance lies in his uncovering the identity of the mystery person with the Twitter handle @abandonedchild97 stalking him on social media.

From an idyllic lake to a series of dashes between Ottawa and Toronto, pursued by mobsters and police, Will assembles the pieces of the puzzle while coming to the realization that his dysfunctional past and complicated present are connected, that people and events are re-entering his life for a reason, and that to open his mind and heart without cloaking them in fiction or fake news is his only road to redemption.

Techniques used by the Novelist

Will Smallwood is the sole narrator. Occasionally, he admits to being self-serving in his account of events, suggesting that he is not entirely reliable.

The action takes place cyclically in three locations in chronological time: at Guru Swaminanda's lakeside retreat located in cottage country north of Ottawa; in the National Capital Region of Ottawa; in Canada's most populous region, Greater Toronto; and then back in Ottawa until the dénouement at the guru's retreat once more.

The plot is complex and original. It makes use of recurring events, the apparently random but multiple appearance of the same characters and a sweeping circle through the same places from beginning to end.

The story is told within twelve lucid chapters. Overall, events are shown in chronological order. The principal exception is an account of a crucial period of Will's life when he was married to Jacqueline, like Will himself, a damaged being. Jacqueline committed suicide shortly after giving birth to Roy. The author offers this chapter as a deeply moving piece of reminiscence and introspection on Will's part. From time to time, the principal characters, Will, Dee, and Roy – and the secondary characters: Guru Swaminanda, Professor Darlington, Phil and Marge Davis, and Roy's social worker, Peggy Smithers – provide essential information about their backstories in conversation and flashbacks.

Discussion

Will Smallwood, a twice-divorced novelist whose earlier good fortune and creativity have dried up, spends his few remaining dollars to attend a rural spiritual retreat run by Guru Swaminanda. Swaminanda is "full of secrets and contradictions." He apparently indulges an unseemly appetite for the more attractive women attending his events. Once there, Will meets other souls like himself – lost and damaged individuals seeking serenity, respite, and whatever else they can grasp to make the expense worth their while.

Dee is a commercial artist fatigued by the corporate world, pursuing self-knowledge, sex, and liberation from the material. The widower, Professor Darlington, enjoys viewing naked bodies through his binoculars and casting aspersions on the sincerity of the Guru and everybody else. The Davis couple, Phil and Marge, appear to seek no more than a change of venue where they can vent the resentment they harbour for their ungrateful, dependent, adult children, as well as for each other.

In addition to successfully wooing Dee from the Guru's bed to his, Will experiences a mild epiphany. He recognises the futility of his life as a writer of formulaic historical fiction. He vows to abandon this genre and replace it with more current, penetrating writing about "real people and the things that matter in their lives."

One of the few insights that Guru Swaminanda offers his guests during the retreat is that life is cyclical, the same people and similar circumstances continuously re-present themselves. This, he suggests, foretells future encounters among the members of this small group and the recurring opportunities they offer each other to readjust their lives.

Will Smallwood's sexual affair with Dee continues when they return to Ottawa. However, neither Will nor Dee fulfil the resolutions they made to change their lives. Will had resolved to write novels based on immutable truths and real people; Dee, to abandon the commercial world of decorative art in which she had been successful but frustrated, in favour of more personal and fulfilling creativity.

As if to highlight the repudiation of his resolution, Will accepts an offer to write highly-paid, positive spin for social media on behalf of a department within the office of the Prime Minister of Canada. It turns out that Professor Darlington, he of the binoculars, runs this office for the purpose of preserving and polishing the reputation of the Prime Minister to ensure that he and his party will win the upcoming election and remain in power. Will also toys with writing a commercial blog funded by advertisements.

Equally neglectful of her resolution, Dee accepts a lucrative artistic assignment to decorate the headquarters building of a major corporation in Toronto.

Before Dee leaves for Toronto, it becomes clear that their relationship is more carnal than intellectual, certainly on Will's side. "After all," Will reflects, "Dee and I were just meeting to have sex"; and again, "Sex was our substance." Dee, for her part, tries to get closer to Will by telling him about her own unhappy and abusive childhood. She tells him that she admires him, "for reaching upwards. That's attractive in a man." Dee herself is taking the first steps to rise, to confide in another person and to form a trustful relationship.

Will's hovers on the brink of revealing his past to Dee but is unable to revisit his childhood hell. He fails to reciprocate the confidences she shares with him and reflects to himself, "I knew I was running away from my past…"

Will is merely circling, repeating superficial relationships. Dee, too, is circling but striving, now, to rise into the spiral.

It is at this point that the author uses flashback. In an entire chapter, one of the most important in the novel, Will reflects on his early life as a way of explaining his inability to connect closely with Dee. As a child, he was shunted from one foster home to another. He suffered psychological and physical abuse. As a young adult, he fell in love with Jacqueline, a fractured woman who had herself never recovered from a background of parental rejection that led to social disfunction and mental instability. She becomes pregnant and uses her pregnancy to torture Will by suggesting that he may, or may not, be the father of the child she is carrying. Shortly after the child, Roy, is born, Dee commits suicide. Will, unable to cope, allows Roy to be adopted and washes his hands, though not his conscience, of the entire episode.

Back to the present. In his well-paid government work as a writer of promotional social media, Will is harassed online by a troll whose Twitter handle is @abandonedchild97. The troll's communications suggest that the Prime Minister of

Canada has engaged in duplicitous behaviour, which, if revealed might cost him and his party the election.

Alerted by the evocative title, @abandonedchild97, Will suspects that the troll may be Roy, the child he discarded. With help from Guru Swaminanda who runs an ashram in Ottawa, Will tracks Roy down. They talk. Roy assures Will that his twitter tag was stolen, and that he knows nothing about it being used to harass Will or to threaten a disinformation campaign against the Prime Minister. The swift but frank reunion serves to form the beginnings of a bond between Will and Roy. Will admits that he abandoned Roy and that he may be the boy's father. Indeed, a DNA test later proves them to be father and son. The bond between them is strengthened by their relationship, the abusive childhoods they share, and by Will's desire to make amends.

This represents the crucial point at which Will begins, excruciatingly slowly and against his natural inclination, to spiral out of the cyclical trap within which he has been imprisoned for most of his life: "Deep down inside me," he reflects, "despite my protests, jubilation was gurgling. I had a son."

Meanwhile, Professor Darlington, now Will's boss, turns out to be unsound. He may have assisted in the death of his own wife to inherit her life insurance, his university post has been withdrawn, and he associates unaccountably with a repugnant Russian called Igor. By accident of circularity, Will encounters the two of them together in an Ottawa restaurant. Darlington lacks the capacity – or is it the will? – to manage the department established to ensure the success of the Prime Minister and his party in the upcoming election and shows himself unable – or unwilling? – to counter the false news about the PM's political integrity. Most alarmingly, Darlington encourages the finger of accusation for leaking information that can only help the campaign of false news, to be pointed at Will.

To Darlington's satisfaction, an agent of the Canadian Security Intelligence Service appropriates Will's laptop to search for evidence of collusion with those shadowy characters seeking to influence the election. In panic, Will flees from Ottawa to Toronto where Dee is working temporarily. That Dee welcomes him and offers him sanctuary is another hint that she is in the upward spiral, willing to trust and help take Will with her. However, when Will is alone, the mysterious Russian, Igor, breaks into Dee's suite with two henchmen. They transfer their captive to a motel. Will's captors are so inept that they fail to deprive him of his cell phone. Unwilling to contact the police for fear of being accused of treachery, Will calls the only person he believes may help – his son, Roy. Will is starting to experiment with trust.

Here, the rising spiral effect becomes more prominent. Circumstances are transforming Roy from child abandoned into saviour of the very man who abandoned him – his own father. Roy is developing into a redeemer. These are instances of the circular and spiral essence of the plot sufficient for the purpose of the essay to this point.

Discussion of some of the vices and virtues depicted

In what ways is *Circles in the Spiral* a contemporary story of vice and virtue?

I start with vice since the author gives a great deal more space to demonstrations of self-absorption that extinguishes empathy, neglect, dishonesty, carelessness, apathy, treachery, malevolence, and despair. In the first chapter, at Guru Swaminanda's lakeside retreat, the author presents characters almost entirely devoid of virtue.

Will is bitter at having been jilted by his second wife, Susan, for a lover more capable of providing her with a stable, decent, and comfortable life, and fathering children she can take care of with his financial and emotional help. Will is bitter also about his "achieve nothing life" and about "losing his groove," resulting in his failure to develop as a successful author. Will's motivation for signing up for Guru Swaminanda's retreat is more escapism than a search for spiritual renewal. He is attracted to Dee for "her curvy bottom swaying under the flimsy pastel dress" and wonders if this preliminary encounter "would extend to sex."

After Will and Dee couple, then depart for Ottawa together, their relationship becomes largely devoid of the close, human "I to thou" exchange of equals seeking to know each other, to love, trust, and share. Will appears to be unable to relate to Dee as anything more than a sexual object; Dee appears more willing to view Will as a subject to whom she might connect with as a person. To that end, Dee recounts the neglect and abuse she suffered as a child and asks Will for a reciprocal account of his life. But Will is incapable of mirroring Dee's confidences. He himself admits, "I was also avoiding my own unravelling to Dee. … I knew I was running away from my past, not the one with Susan, but the one that had come before, the one that even Susan knew nothing about." Will has lived most of his life without a trusting relationship.

Will tries to work on the more meaningful novel he had resolved to write, but his efforts diminish as he realises that "after all, Dee and I were just meeting to have sex." Indeed, sexual encounters seem to count for more than communicating profoundly with words. Dee and Will barely know each other, principally because Will cannot find a way of trusting his confidences to another.

Especially in the case of Will, this is a strategy employed by the author to have us appreciate how difficult, even unthinkable, it is for him to revisit the trauma of his youth as an abandoned orphan farmed out to foster homes who cared only about the profit for their efforts and not for the well-being of the subjects entrusted to their safekeeping. Several times, after Dee or Roy has unburdened themselves to Will and sought a like confidence, none is forthcoming. Will has suffered what might be Post-Traumatic Stress Syndrome and copes only by refusing to revisit his past.

The first real person-to-person communication occurs when Will has found Roy but their relationship as father and son has not yet been confirmed by the DNA test. For the very first time, Will is able to reveal the hardship of his own childhood to Roy. This is the low turning point of the story. This is essentially part of the recurring circle but most importantly it is the beginning of the spiral that will allow Will to begin an upward trajectory towards his essential humanity and allow himself to relate to others, Roy and Dee in particular, in meaningful human relationships created out of trust, perhaps even leading, ultimately, to a relationship with the eternal *Thou* of transcendental importance.

Will begins to trust more when he becomes a suspect in the disinformation campaign. His first trusting step is to put his life in Dee's hands by escaping to Toronto and going into hiding in her hotel suite while she is fulfilling her contract. Still too wary of the police, the very institution created to inspire confidence and uphold certainty, to ask for their help when he is kidnapped by the Russian goons, Will takes his second step towards trust when he calls Roy and asks for his help.

Will, like Dee and Roy but with far greater difficulty, is slowly emerging from a repetitious and deleterious circularity into the spiral that may lead to his redemption.

Guru Swaminanda, head of an ashram and host of retreats dedicated to divine aspiration, comes across as a flawed character. On the one hand, he is a shallow imposter as much intent on personal gain – whether it be free sex, money, or ownership if a lakeside resort in which to host his retreats – as on providing spiritual and moral guidance to his paying guests. On the other hand, his rejection of the material life, however pleasurable or painful it may be, in favour of "facilitating spiritual evolution," raises him to the status of guardian angel and liberator, if only in his own eyes.

Roy is one of the most intriguing characters in the novel. Despite all that he has suffered at the hands of his biological parents, his foster parents, and then from the clients who paid for his sexual services, he has retained a certain purity, an improbable integrity. These qualities are at one and the same time both the purity of the blameless child and the purifying wrath of the Angel of the Lord that "stretched out his hand upon Jerusalem to destroy it" in 2 Samuel 24.16. When Roy frees Will by killing the Russian goons, Will marvels: "Why are you doing this for me, Roy? When all I did was abandon you?" At that point, Roy seems to grow to the dimensions of a biblical saviour. He is in the upward spiral.

In the end, the most corrupt character of all turns out to be Professor Darlington. Throughout, he is gradually revealed to be spiralling in a direction opposite to the others. The route he is taking is downwards and away from virtue into the depths of degradation and treachery.

With this contrasting portrayal of Darlington, the author is showing that circles in the spiral have the capacity to move in either direction.

By tracing some of the depictions of vice and virtue through this novel, I have tried to demonstrate how the author has used narrative structure to transform our perception of the characters and of the world they inhabit. We, the readers, change our perception because the characters have been induced to change theirs.

Conclusion

In this essay, I have shown some of the literary techniques and creative ways by which veteran novelist Shane Joseph draws our attention to the fundamental thesis of *Circles in the Spiral* — that the interplay intrinsic to all human relationships are founded upon continuous exchange. If such exchanges are reduced to mere "goods" in "markets" – such as Will's initial preoccupation with the pursuit of sexual satisfaction from whoever could provide it at a cost he could afford; in the purely financial link between the Davis couple and their grown but still dependent children that causes resentment; in Roy viewing his body as a commodity to be offered to whomever for economic rent; in Dee's frustration that her artistic creativity has been hijacked by the highest corporate bidder – then humanity is adrift.

Exchange considered in this narrow way leads inexorably to moral degradation and societal breakdown. On the other hand, exchange can, Joseph shows, be considered more broadly and more in keeping with the expressed intention of Adam Smith, the great 18th century moral philosopher and economist. This broader interpretation incorporates, necessarily, the exchange of communication and mutual respect; communication by means of meaningful conversation and personal regard through the reciprocation of mindful esteem of the other, so establishing trust.

In the novel, Will, Dee, and Roy gradually acquire this appreciation of what true exchange must mean and how they must realise it in practice. On their part, resolution to act on that appreciation will bring them a long-awaited redemption. The author's cunningly slow reveal that this is the direction his protagonists choose, is why the reader can enjoy this novel as a tribute to hope rather than as a condemnation of despair.

Circles in the Spiral demonstrates that our future does not have to be dependent on our past if we choose to replace vicious circles with alternatives more virtuous. In this accomplished novel, Shane Joseph captures the essence of the principle that has shaped and continues to shape the personal, social, and political temper of Canada – the resolve to "get things right".

Making history come alive – an interview with author Morgan Wade

Kimberley Sherman Grove. Poet, Writer, Editor, Lecturer

"Put down that book. It's time for supper." Morgan wanted to obey his mother, but the lion Aslan was in a horrific battle with the White Witch so he couldn't think of eating. This might have been Morgan Wade's childhood scenario because he loved the CS Lewis series of Narnia books when he was a boy. They ignited his imagination. He told his parents that he was going to be an author when he grew up. Living in the small town of Tottenham helped with that dream as he had his favourite teacher, David Anderson, for grades 3, 5 and 6. "He gave us many creative writing projects," said Wade.

Wade lives in Kingston now, a city steeped in history, with constant visual reminders of it in relics like Fort Henry. He decided to do an in-depth study of its history. "There has been a lot of history written about Kingston. It lends itself to storytelling so well. It just cries out for novels."

The power of fiction is that from the safety of one's own couch, a person can really go deeply into the story and ask oneself important questions. When Wade reads he can't help but wonder what the historical figures were thinking. Were they afraid, motivated by conscience to do the right thing, or concerned about patriotism? He imagines their emotions that led them to their actions. It is that questioning that leads to interesting characters for his novels.

Each of his books begin with an in-depth look at history of a specific period. "I hope they [the readers] enjoy it, I hope it is entertaining but for someone who loves history I hope that it transports them to a different time and place and they get the chance to inhabit the lives of some of the characters, to imagine what it was like to be these people." He expects the reader to examine their own life and wonder what they would do if they had been in a given situation.

George Orwell, author of Animal Farm and Nineteen Eighty-four, is Wade's favourite author. Wade thinks he has read everything he wrote. His most admired work is Orwell's essay Politics in the English language. To him, it shows that "Clear prose can help you fight dictatorships and wrong thinking, help you identify truth from fiction. He [Orwell] was a champion of human freedom and dignity in the face of huge institutional challenges."

If the reader thinks of Orwell's essay Why I Write, looking at the four points he makes it is clear that Wade is incorporating some of the same principles.

1) Sheer egoism: Desire to seem clever, to be talked about, to be remembered after death, to get your own back on grown-ups who snubbed you in childhood, etc. Egoism is not to be confused with egotism as Wade is a humble writer. Enjoying his clear writing style, he was asked if he would accept a writers-in-residence position. He modestly answered, "I don't think I have the profile. I think it would be valuable work.

Editing for me, clarifies my own writing." He remembers telling a neighbour that he hoped to be a writer, but the response was not encouraging. "She took the wind out of my sails by saying that I shouldn't bother because they are a dime a dozen." Though Wade has a memory of that comment, it didn't stop him. He studied at the Humber School of Writing where he learned the importance of being ruthless when editing. He is the author of three novels, The Last Stoic, Bottles and Glass and Paper & Rags, published by Hidden Brook Press.

2) Aesthetic enthusiasm: Perception of beauty in the external world, or on the other hand, in words and their right arrangement. "Good prose is like a window pane," wrote George Orwell. Wade has adopted the concept in his writing. His description is that window to the external world at times and his choice of words is the right arrangement as in this passage of The Last Stoic.

"The sun's leading edge dipped behind the low hills ahead and shadows distorted the landscape. Marcus refastened the broach of his tunic against the cooling air. The monotony of the journey had inflamed his imagination and he was aware for the first time of his remoteness from home. A misshapen shrub around the bend resembled, for a moment, a prowling animal. Rustling in the long grasses betrayed sneaking highwaymen.

He crested a slope. Every three hundred feet or so, on either side of the road for as far as he could see, stood crucifixes, one after another, silhouetted black and looming against the reddening sky, with a slumping figure fastened to each one." (The Last Stoic, page 10)

He avoids the clichés. There are no honey melting sunsets, and yet the reader can imagine the scene.

Another example of this vivid writing is when he switches to modern day America and writes, "Mark had camped down at a rest-stop along a stretch of the freeway where the Interstate became the New Jersey turnpike, just past the many rows of hulking 18-wheeler rigs, orange and red running lights like patio lanterns strung along the perimeters of their cargo, idling diesel engines emitting an endless hushed rattle, drivers catatonic in the fold-out bunks of their compact cabs.

A quarter mile away the turnpike roared with a host of travelers finding their way through the darkness. The windscreen glowed softly with the unremitting white lights of the distant sixteen pump service station. Inside the car, dashboard instruments cast a low, blue phosphorescence. He sipped from a can of frigid, metallic-tasting Budweiser. For a moment, he felt intrepid. A stranger amongst strangers. Unburdened. (The Last Stoic, page 17)

In Wade's second novel, Bottles and Glass, he takes the reader into the taverns of old Kingston after the war of 1812. His writing was so genuine to the period that in 2016 a talented theatre director, Brett Christopher (now managing and artistic director of The 1000 Islands Playhouse), in Kingston requested Wade to convert his novel to a play. It was sold out for 5 nights.

As the events in the book took place in the taverns of old Kingston, the play was extended by having the audience visit bars in the city with the actors. "It was a thrill of a life time," said Wade, "to see the characters you have written come to life."

3) Historical impulse: Desire to see things as they are, to find out true facts and store them up for the use of posterity.

Certainly, there is an historical impulse in all of Wade's novels. Too often students have found Canadian history lacking in excitement. By detailing the challenges of characters in various classes in the 1800s, he helps the reader realize what society was like in those times. In that time period, Canada offered an immigrant the chance at starting life again as one character comes from England to escape a scandal, the protagonist is constantly struggling to make a fair wage and a woman is saved from prostitution by becoming a doctor's assistant.

Wade brings out the plight of women in those times, as well as the poverty that was rampant To bring history to life as Wade endeavours to do, demands a great deal of research. Words like grape shot (ammunition for gun or cannon), or quills (pens for writing) or pelisse (a woman's cloak) all help to authenticate the history he is writing about. An example of how he crafts them into his story is in this sample:

"Jeremy laid the quill he had borrowed from Antoine into the narrow trough of the writing box. He dusted a measure of fine pounce over the still damp words, gently vibrated the sheet of paper, and then tipped it, allowing the excess powdered bone to fall to the floor. Once the ink was dry, he folded the letter and sealed it with melted beeswax from the lit candle on the writing desk." (Paper and Rags, Page 224)

One of his characters, Lilac, is shamed as a prostitute and displayed for the towns people to gawk at in the pillory before being sent to jail. His portrayal of her encourages the reader's compassion, rather than disdain.

4) Political purpose: using the word 'political' in the widest possible sense. Desire to push the world in a certain direction, to alter other people's idea of the kind of society that they should strive after.

Wade's book, "The Last Stoic," is a reflection of this idea as his hope is that his reader will see the parallel of Ancient Rome and modern United States. He read a lot about stoicism. He comments that stoicism "seemed to be a fiber that made ancient Rome, when it was great, strong." He fears that the stoicism of the original founders of the US has been lost to the detriment of the country and the world. As Orwell states, "I write it [the book] because there is some lie that I want to expose, some fact to which I want to draw attention, and my initial concern is to get a hearing." Wade has the reader's attention by comparing the two societies.

When the hero of the Ancient Roman story, Marcus, meets an old man in prison he comments on what is happening in Rome. The reader can't help but think of today's society. "Two primary passions afflict us Marcus, Romans no less than any others. Appetite and fear. They are excessive impulses. Disobedient to reason. Ruled by these passions people become slaves to pleasure or distress. It's the easiest thing to do; the passions are always there, beckoning. They can be held in check, but never can be eliminated. It takes a lifetime of study, training, and selfdiscipline to rule oneself. " (The Last Stoic, page 217)

Wade's process for writing is to begin with an overarching concept, sketch out an outline and then fill in the detail. As his books are historical, he does research and then he starts to put plot points down. "With Paper and Rags, I had that last scene in mind and I knew I wanted to get there." He was able to do that in less than the 9 drafts it took on *The Last Stoic.* "

One area that Wade might differ from Orwell is he sees writing as more pleasure than drudgery whereas Orwell said, "Writing a book is a horrible, exhausting struggle, like a long bout of some painful illness."

While Orwell spoke of why he wrote, Wade encourages others to write. He has five points for the wannabe writer.

1) Find books on writing to see how others do it. Two suggestions are Bird by Bird by Anne Lamott and Writing fiction: a guide to narrative craft by Janet Burroway.

2) "Share your work with people you trust who will give you substantial, honest feedback. If you can find somebody like that, that's a real treasure. Friends and family will willingly read your stuff but they probably won't give you complete honesty and you really need that."

3) "Be willing to read others' work and give in-depth feedback for them will always improve your own writing because you will be focusing on what works and what doesn't work."

4) Even with a day job, it's still important to put aside specific writing time. (Wade has organized his work schedule so Fridays are his writing days.)

5) "Write and read as much as you can."

And Wade follows his own advice. He has become so attached to his character, Jeremy Castor, that he plans to write another book that focuses on Jeremy's life and times, and, of course, the setting will be Kingston.

Home Ground: Don Gutteridge's Literary Novels

Kevin Spence

Donald Gutteridge was born on September 30, 1937 in Sarnia Ontario, and shortly after was brought back to Point Edward, where he would live out most of his childhood. It is from this stretch of his early life that Gutteridge draws much of his inspiration and the subject of eight novels. A poet, teacher and a professor, he published several works of verse before the first of his novels *Bus-Ride* was released in 1974. Since then, Gutteridge has authored two dozen works of fiction, creating a substantial body of work.

Writing Style

Don Gutteridge's writing style can best be described as accessible romanticism. He makes use of vivid imagery, poetic phrasing and incisive metaphor to lend emotional impact without the use of overly complex language or metaphor. Gutteridge's portfolio extends through a broad variety of settings and genres, including tragedy, comedy, historical, fantastical, or modern, offering something for most prospective readers. I would contend, however, that Don Gutteridge's novels are best read by those with an active interest in Canadian history and culture. Though a book like *The Perilous Journey of Gavin the Great* offers a witty take on a classic fable structure, the lion's share of Gutteridge's novels breathe life into the days of his boyhood in Point Edward. Gutteridge uses his life experience to explore a people, place and time through his own eyes. It is this unparalleled authenticity that makes Gutteridge's portrayals of his charactersly into something between fact and fiction, an immortalized recreation of the kind of people who once were. The Novels of Lambton County are an exercise in not just writing, but storytelling. Gutteridge shares pieces of himself and his origins through his prose.

Themes and Narrative

Whether ordinary or fantastical, Gutteridge uses three consistent themes and narrative tools in his books: coming of age, the importance of place, and the juxtaposition of innocence and harsh reality. Each work offers a unique perspective on what living and growing in Point Edward was like. Gutteridge's protagonists span both sexes, all ages and occupy over a century of history. There is also a look at the history of more marginalized groups around Point Edward in his largest novel, *Lily's Story.* Through the myriad perspectives involved, the Novels of Lambton County do not shy away from the darker side of its history. The inclusion of the less savoury elements of Canadian village life is connected to Gutteridge's use of juxtaposition. Even in the more comically intended novels of Gutteridge's earlier years, *Bus-Ride* and *All in Good Time,* there are ominous undertones. Through the eyes of boys and provincial village men, Gutteridge highlights not just the passing intolerance and suspicion, but the bleak insecurity of the future that frames their provincial hopes and dreams. A concise and self-contained example of this juxtaposition can be seen in Gutteridge's second novel, *All in Good Time.* In even the innocent context of a piano lesson, the reader cannot escape a reminder of their loss: "'Well, I did bring some Chopin.' He flushed, and again she was reminded of the innocence of his glance. What was she doing? Some field in France, this very moment, might be reclaiming the ripped flesh of her husband." (Gutteridge, 1980, 44) It is in this fashion that Gutteridge's dark sense of humour and tragedy remains ever-present in his novels.

Arguably the most primary theme within Don Gutteridge's novels is the importance of place. There is a single exception in the review section below, but seven of the eight novels covered in this essay are devoted to developing the history and importance of Lambton County. The villagers of The Point are inextricably linked to the land that surrounds them, both conjoining to create the "Village" as Gutteridge wants the reader to see it. The importance of place in his writing is more than a monument or frieze of his childhood, however. Gutteridge explicitly creates the Village as a microcosm of Canada.

A small piece of the gestalt that is the Canada he treasures, The Point serves as memory and metaphor, a tool to share the author's romanticized vision of his beloved childhood home and one used to explore a more universal conception of what connects Canadians. Gutteridge's tone as is that of a storyteller weaving a tale alongside the reader. His tone is one in a long Canadian tradition, both personal and largely informal, displayed prominently in his unorthodox use of pronouns. Stories about The Point, and about Canada are not from the perspective of a passive observer. Rather they are from within, providing the subjectivity that gives each novel its authentic character.

Overview and Analysis

An overview of the novelistic works of Don Gutteridge is best done in three sections: Pre-Point Edward Novels, the Novels of The Point, and the others. Both the Pre-Point Novels and the Novels of The Point feature their geographical location as a matter of chief importance. The themes and narrative through-line are as much about the development of the village itself as any of the individual characters. The Novels of The Point consist of four books: *Bus-Ride, All in Good Time, Summer's Idyll,* and *Winter's Descent..* These books are the most sequential of Gutteridge's works, happening within roughly a decade from 1939 to the late 1940s and feature a recurring and interrelated set of characters. The Pre-Point Novels consist of two books, *How the World Began* and *Lily's Story*, a revised combination of two older works: *St. Vitus' Dance* and *Shaman's Ground.* These two books take place through from the mid-19th century to the early 20th century.

The greater part of these novels takes place before Point Edward exists. Thematically, the Pre-Point novels are distinguished by a generally bleak or tragic tone. They also concern themselves with the formation of Point Edward, Canada's railway and nationhood, and the Anishinaabe/Pottawatomie people in Gutteridge's novels. The novels of The Point are characterized by the setting of the already established village of Point Edward and a tighter time-period. The last two novels covered in this essay, *Bewilderment* and *The Perilous Adventures of Gavin the Great,* do not fit easily in themes or motifs of the other five novels, and ergo are better suited to individual analysis.

How the World Began is a novel following a gentle young farm-boy by the name of Ti-Luc. It begins in the year 1794 on a small farm in the largely unsettled Lambton county. The book follows Ti-Luc's idyllic childhood in the untamed bush of Canada, his transition to adulthood, and his exposure to the unkind realities of the world outside his isolated farm. His journey is inundated with themes of trauma, loss, and purpose. Of all Gutteridge's novels, *How the World Began* might have the bleakest overall tone. It opens with violence: a vengeful Pottawatomie attack on a farmstead as they retreat from the Battle of Fallen Timbers. In one uncharacteristically violent stroke, Gutteridge introduces the reader to a very different Point Edward. He displays the historical unrest in the region, introduces Trill, Ti-Luc's adopted sister, and the parable of Carcajou and Wisakedjak, a recurring duology of First Nations god figures. Within the greater scope of the Lambton County novels, *How the World Began* serves as the prologue. It demonstrates the harshness of life before The Village through Ti-Luc's experience of war, privation, and disease. It is this series of traumas that Gutteridge uses to characterize the early Ontario community. Be it the shattering of tribal nations, the suffering of slaves, or the helplessness of a family succumbing to disease, the Pre-Point is Gutteridge's examination of cultural baggage, personal and societal.

These larger traumas are paralleled by the personal ones experienced by Ti-Luc, interweaving individual and nation through tragedy. Narratively, it is through his small-scale experiences of Canada's national issues that Ti-Luc grows into adulthood and fatherhood. Chief among those coming at the hands of his brother Cal, who dreams of more than the small world beyond The Bend and enlists, finding engagement in the war of 1812. Gentle Ti-Luc, who wished for nothing beyond the borders of his farm-stead, goes out in search of his brother. Through his suffering on his journey, Ti-Luc is tempered into manhood, just as his brother is forced to face the reality of the war he had so lionized. The loss and hardship on the journey reaffirm the value of what he left behind. Ti-Luc's struggle is in the desperate wish to return to the normalcy of the past — having to cope with the tragic reality that it can never be the same, and forging on regardless.

Second in the Pre-Point books is *Lily's Story*, which follows the titular Lily Fairchild from 1845 into the early 1920s. There are two strong thematic narratives at play in *Lily's Story*. The personal story of Lily, which is concerned with loss and the will to overcome grief; and the story of Point Edward, for it is within the pages of *Lily's Story* that Gutteridge details the historical formation of the town. Through the eyes of Lily, the reader can see Point Edward grow from a river-junction shanty town into the modern village that features in later novels. *Lily's Story* can best be described as a sequence of tragic relationships. There are the personal losses of Lily herself, perpetually coming to love someone and finding them torn away by disease, war and old age. There are also the losses that serve as historical commentary on the dark past of Canada and the cost of progress. Lily, growing initially far from the more settled lands near Sarnia and London, offers insight into the lives of runaway slaves, the fading language and culture of the last free tribes, the present day Anishinaabe, and the plight of women without political agency. Just as Lily loses her loved ones, the novel details the losses of the marginalized and the down-trodden, a distinctive feature of the Pre-Point novels. In later writings, the village of Point Edward is relatively peaceful and its tragedies are few. *Lily's Story* is in some sense a monument to the loss of the people who came before. A dedication to the slaves and soldiers and Anishinaabe on whose graves the village was built. Lily's story parallels that motif. Lily, elderly and alone, experiences the final loss of her home, replaced by a literal monument for the losses of the Great War (Gutteridge 2014, 410-411)

Lily's Story is a tragedy, but one that urges an unshakeable optimism. Though she experiences incessant loss and grief, Lily always manages to find the strength and courage to move on. Her story is one of self-admitted suffering, but she explicitly endorses an optimistic philosophy. An indomitable will to keep loving despite the pain of grief:

"Cora, you've told me more about your life and travails than any one man ought to know, and I'll be damned if I can see where you had much choice. Like most women you've been devastated by wars you never started, diseases you can't cure, and children who die on you or run off to lead their own lives without a pennyworth of gratitude. The world cares only for the species, and women bear the brunt of that reality." Cora mulled that over for a while. "May be" she said. "But I chose somethin'. Every time." "And what would that be?" "I chose to love". (Gutteridge, 2014, 502)

Lily embraces the inevitability of loss and the pain that comes with it. In a sense, each of Lily's losses, and her life itself can be interpreted as a series of 'coming of age' tales. Lily has her life torn away by tragic circumstances, and rebuilds it. Lily always chooses to craft a new life, find new things and new people to value. It is a continuum from child to elder, constantly discovering new ways to be, even if it hurts her. Lily's journey is a cyclical one. An inverse of the second narrative through-line of The Point itself. The Village moves ever forward, and the memory of what it used to be fades, save for on the pages of Gutteridge's novels.

The Novels of The Point comprise most of Gutteridge's novelistic works and share many common characteristics. Each book follows a single point of view in the late 1930s or 1940s, features a coming-of-age narrative, and explores how a village reflects the nation. Gutteridge uses perspectives of all different ages and ambitions to depict his vision of The Village, one where the reeve is also a garbage man, there is a single pub, and veterans of the war can live in quiet reprieve. The cast that Gutteridge portrays are emblematic of his broader view, where no matter how fractious or petty they can seem, the villagers adhere to a common sentiment and feeling. In portraying this unified spirit, Gutteridge also makes an explicit connection to the nation. The spirit of the village is reflective of the people, to be identified together.

In *Bus-Ride*, Gutteridge draws on The Point's love of hockey to portray the spirit of the village as representative of the nation:

"'Hello Canada, and hockey fans in the United States!' They, like a million others on this night in March of 1939, would be content to listen, to focus all senses on a single voice, riding outward to the far stretches of the land, carrying in its rhythms and intonations the legends of its generation." (Gutteridge, 2019, 67)

The radio play-by- play serves as a literal and metaphorical device connecting Canadians, framing Point Edward as a single piece in a mosaic. It is through the singular will of the village that Gutteridge turns the individual characters, and by extension each individual Canadian, into the fabric of the whole.

The wreath-laying ceremony in *All in Good Time* is another symbolic and metaphorical connection. A demonstration of a common will for the patchwork villagers: "Many wept, quietly. Others stood, feeling nothing but the awesomeness of the moment as if time itself had stopped to enclose them all in the stunning fusion of a second borrowed from eternity." (Gutteridge, 1980, 159) This theme of commonality, owing to its metaphorical nature, is expressed in a similar manner across the Novels of The Point.

Coming of age, though it is featured in each individual Novel of The Point, is expressed differently each time. There are four separate coming-of-age narratives at play: boyhood identity, sexual awakening, manhood, and middle-aged reinvigoration. The first and youngest stages of this 'coming of age' spectrum are in *Summer's Idyll* and *Winter's Descent*. Gutteridge's only direct prequel/sequel, both follow the protagonist, young Will, through two important transitions in his life. *Summer's Idyll* chronicles Will as he transitions from early childhood into his adolescent years through a journey of self-discovery. The nominal story is about Will and his friends putting on a circus-esque show for their school, while the meta-narrative has the boy experiencing and losing some of his youthful wonder. *Summer's Idyll* has Will come of age through abandoning comforting childhood illusions and fantasies. Gutteridge does so by playing with appearance and reality through several sub-plots: the mysterious 'stranger,' more mundane than Will's childish imagination conjures up, the failure of his parents' marriage, and the subtly-communicated costs of war.

A direct sequel to *Summer's Idyll*, *Winter's Descent* has Will flourishing into youthful manhood. Where *Summer's Idyll* has Will growing past childhood whimsy to see the world for how it really is, *Winter's Descent* is his venture into that world. *Winter's Descent* is a coming of age centered around desire. Will breaks free from his shell with a newfound discovery of love, the opposite sex, and his passion for writing and reading. In embodying his desires, Will undergoes a metamorphosis, defining himself from his peers, who had constituted such an important element of his identity in *Summer's Idyll.*

Bus-Ride is the story of young Will and his transition into independent manhood. It is defined not by soft romantic discovery or self-identity, but by struggle. Bill Underhill is in constant turmoil, stuck between the mountainous expectations of the entire Village and his own unclear future. The villagers view him as their star hockey hopeful, but Bill isn't even certain he wants to play hockey (*Bus-Ride*, 2019, 18). Part of Bill's indecision comes from his powerful resentment for the constrictive, quiet life that Point Edward provides. Bill envies his father, who not only saw the world, but had "Been in the world" (*Bus-Ride*, 2019, 94) and a part of its history. Bill's journey forces him to consider his future and his freedom. In trying to find his way out of the Point, Bill considers what the village means to him as he passes into manhood and confronts an impossible decision at the outbreak of the Second World War.

All in Good Time, following Horace Macintosh, The Point's Reeve (and garbage truck driver), toys with the meaning of a coming-of-age story. Not a boy passing into manhood, the Reeve's coming of age is rather a reinvigoration. As a result of the ups and downs of his going for an ill-considered political gamble, the Reeve discovers new passions and a new purpose, decades past his boyhood. Horace, so unlike Will or Bill, is ambitious and pretentious, but learns to discard old prejudices, make himself anew, and learn to love the old again.

Bewilderment: A Novel of the Great Depression takes place in Point Edward in 1936, but shares few themes with the other Novels of The Point. As a book, *Bewilderment* is a fictionalized history. It is a means of immortalizing the everyday suffering and loss that working class people went through in a period of duress. The story follows the well-intentioned coal worker Gabe Goodfellow as he helps put on a carnival and collect bond money during the height of the Great Depression, all the while trying to care for his own family. *Bewilderment's* aim and achievement is to capture the emotional aspect of history. To see hardship and privation through Gabe's eyes and to humanize what is a matter of historical canon. The tone and themes of *Bewilderment* serve as an absurdist juxtaposition, each page filled with detail on the fallout of economic disaster, clashing against the hope and marvelous excess of a Carnival. Gutteridge reaffirms the struggle that working class families experienced in the depression, and simultaneously the reason for it. In the midst of his hardships and moral compromises, Gabe still finds love and helps bring the village together in wonder at the spectacle of the carnival. More than any of Gutteridge's other works, *Bewilderment* is beholden to its title, providing a window into the inner lives of those living in Point Edward during the Great Depression.

The Perilous Journey of Gavin the Great is Gutteridge's greatest departure from his previous works, being a foray into the genre of fantasy. In the tradition of classic fables, *The Perilous Journey of Gavin the Great* is both whimsical and dark. Set in the forest called Earthwood, it is a world populated by talking and anthropomorphized forest creatures. It follows the story of Gavin, a raccoon, and his two siblings as they flee from a great disaster that threatens to destroy the entirety of their forest home. Thematically, *The Perilous Journey* flirts with biblical allegory, featuring apocalyptic floods, a life-saving and animal-laden raft, and archetypal figures like the wily fox. It is unlike any of Gutteridge's other works in that it has no readily apparent thematic metaphors. Rather, the themes of *The Perilous Journey* are reflective of classical fables and the hero's journey. Gavin and his companions face danger and fear in a grand adventure and must triumph through their cleverness, courage and virtue. Perhaps most remarkable about *The Perilous Journey* is the tone. It combines light-hearted parody and grim danger effortlessly. One moment Gutteridge might humorously draw a comparison to the Arthurian canon when Gavin acquires a "sword" he refers to as Hex-Calibre — in reality a man's discarded hunting knife (*Gavin the Great*, 2012, 252), and in the next he might be describing the simultaneously comical and chilling beasts known as "Squeezels." Gavin's journey exists somewhere in the space of satire and genuine love for fairy-tale stories, with Gutteridge working self-aware mockery into a sincerely told story.

Don Gutteridge's writing, entirely separated from its cultural context, is valuable as a wholly authentic experience. He lived in the land so meticulously and lovingly crafted it into his novels. One can to this day wander the very haunts Gutteridge has written about, and walk in the footsteps of Will, Bill, or Lily. There is a timelessness to the works of Don Gutteridge even as they capture a piece of history.

Bibliography

Gutteridge, D. (1980). *All in Good Time.* Black Moss Press, Windsor.

Gutteridge, D. (1991). *How the World Began.* Moonstone Press, Goderich.

Gutteridge, D. (1993). *Summer's Idyll.* Oberon Press, Ottawa.

Gutteridge, D. (1996). *Winter's Descent.* Oberon Press, Ottawa.

Gutteridge, D. (2000). *Bewilderment.* Borealis Press Ottawa..

Gutteridge, D. (2010). *The Perilous Adventures of Gavin the Great.* Borealis Press, Ottawa.

Gutteridge, D. (2014). *Lily's Story.* Bev Editions. Toronto.

Gutteridge, D. (2019). *Bus Ride.* Bev Editions. Toronto.

Powell, R. (1974, June). Bus-Ride, Don Gutteridge: *Quill & Quire.*

Likeness and Distinction in Building Bicultural Awareness

PhD Adonay Bárbara Pérez Luengo. Full Professor

PhD Manuel de Jesús Velázquez León. Full Professor

Introduction

Bicultural awareness is a necessary capacity of the English teacher as a professional who works across cultural borders. While intimate knowledge of the foreign language and culture is demanded, the Cuban and the Canadian traditions share major similarities. Nevertheless, the way Canadians and Cubans mirror the world has been shaped by distinct historical and cultural experiences. The arduous settlement of the continent left a significant imprint on the Canadian soul, but the Cubans as a people underwent a longer and more excruciating historical ordeal to become what they are. The search for open spaces and for dilated skies, as voiced by Canadian literature, shapes unlike voices to people living in the sea-confined spaces of an island. Margaret Atwood and Fina García Marruz reflect those similarities and differences in their poetry. Both in form and content, these writers share common themes of universal value, dear to both cultural traditions. At the same time, differences in the way each deals with their themes are discernable. Such is Atwood's elegant detachment in her topics in contrast with a somewhat more intimate engagement perceived in Marruz's writing about her country.

This paper synthetizes a class experience in a rather new field of educational studies: bicultural awareness in the study of English as a foreign language. The authors theorize on the pertinence of paying attention to the cultural interstices between Anglophone and Spanish cultures in the learning of English. Starting from praxis, attention is rendered to the particular case of shared visions of the homeland by two leading poets of Canada and Cuba. Differences and similarities are contrasted and practical observations are offered to teachers of English who would like to replicate this experience or emulate it with generalizations towards new bicultural areas in poetry, prose, music and other forms of artistic expression.

Development

Bicultural awareness is related to the processes of acculturation, transculturation and cultural appropriation, in the main. Acculturation refers to cultural characteristics resulting from continues first-hand contact between groups of individuals with different cultural patterns. As a result of acculturation, the original cultural patterns of either or both groups may be altered, but the groups remain culturally distinct.

Transculturation, a term coined by Cuban ethnographer Fernando Ortiz, implies different phases of transition from a culture to another and involves the loss or uprooting of a previous culture (*deculturation*) and the consequent creation of a new culture, *neoculturation.*

Cultural appropriation refers to the assumption of some definite features of one culture by a different cultural group. Like previous terms, it may carry negative connotations when the interaction takes place between a dominant or majority group and another in a position of subordination. The appropriated cultural elements may be forms of dress, music, art, religion language or, simply, cultural behavior.

Bicultural awareness in the teaching learning process of English as a foreign language does not imply relationships of cultural domination or the predominance of cultural assimilation or domination. To begin with, cultural interaction mostly takes place between the student and culture rich texts in the foreign language rather than between groups of individuals with different cultures.

Nevertheless, in the ensuing teaching-learning process there are perceptible changes in the cultural patterns of the students that deserve especial attention. Bicultural awareness does not imply a zero-sum conflict in which one culture is displaced by another, but the enrichment and strengthening of the student's spirituality and personal cultural repository and acumen that result from intercultural aesthetic and ethical conflicts.

Bicultural awareness is a necessary capacity of the English teacher as a professional who works across cultural borders. While close knowledge of the foreign language and culture is demanded, the professional must also master his home culture intimately. Cuban and the Canadian traditions share major similarities. Knowledge of cultural differences also contributes to necessary intercultural work. The way Canadians and Cubans mirror the world has been shaped by distinct historical and cultural experiences. The arduous settlement of the continent left a significant imprint on the Canadian soul, but Cubans as a people underwent a longer and more excruciating historical ordeal to become what we are. The search for open spaces and for dilated skies, as voiced by Canadian literature, shapes unlike voices to people living in the sea-confined spaces of an island.

Margaret Atwood and Fina García Marruz reflect those similarities and differences in their poetry. The work of both poets, in form and content, share common themes of universal value, dear to both cultural traditions. At the same time, differences in the way each deals with their themes are discernable. Such is Atwood's elegant detachment to her topics in contrast with a somewhat more intimate engagement perceived in Marruz's writing about her country. The presence of these two leading poetic voices in our class has been a momentous event in this ongoing cultural dialogue between our countries.

Our class of English as a foreign language, as a platform to Margaret Atwood and Fina García Marruz, allowed them to articulate their views on their nations as "the motherland," their personal vision of their countries as cradle and home.

Margaret's and Fina's voices, in a bilingual duet, helped our students satisfy, in the words of Atwood, "the wish to know and the need to praise" each these cultures and people's realizations. A brief reflection on the poetry of these two leading poets constituted an inevitable glimpse into the universal and the singular in the minds and souls of Canadians and Cubans. Respect comes from praise of the other's heritage and realizations, but also from recognition and acceptance of difference.

"Butterfly" is a poem in which the vision of the homeland rises from the family to the changing landscape of a quickly urbanizing culture, from a Whitmanian, universal revelation to the very personally felt event. The images do not lack deeply felt longing for what is gone, both personally and culturally— despite different shades of intensity in comparison to Fina's poetry.

The first landscape built by Atwood, depicts her father walking through the forest on his way to school. Like Whitman, she sums up objects of value along the "sedgy wetfoot shore/of the brimming eel-filled rush-fringed/peat-brown river," so vivid in her words that one cannot but feel the boy's feet across the grass "leaving a trail of jittering blackflies". Atwood's boy also "goes forth" incorporating everything he sees into his living experience "mushroom and scat, wildbloom,/snail and iris, clubmoss, fern and cone" in an endless breathing in because "between/the wish to know and the need to praise/there was no seam."

Besides this portrayal of Canadian forest scenario, the quest for the transcendent in the common is thus revealed as essential. Unexpectedly for the reader, the exaltation of daily walks among trees and by riverbanks is interrupted by the very personal revival of imagined memories, a sequence so much expressive of the intensely felt that it is worth quoting in length.

> "One day he saw a drenched log floating
> heavily downstream,
> and on it a butterfly, blue as eyes.
> This was the moment (I later heard)
> that shot him off on his tangent
> into the abstruse world
> of microscopes and numbers,
> lapel pins, cars and wanderings,
> away from the ten square miles
> of logged-out bushlots
> he never named as poverty,
> and the brown meandering river
> he was always in some way after that
> trying in vain to get back to."

"The Door" deals with a theme of human generic condition. Detachment in feelings somewhat blur the graphics displayed in pitiless succession. Given its universality, the unfolding drama could have had a Caribbean, Latino scenario, no doubt. If so, purportedly there would be less aloofness. Once more, coincidence and difference mark what Cubans and Canadians have in common.

The door swings open, you look in.
It's dark in there,
most likely spiders
nothing you want.
You feel scared.
The door swings closed.

Like in Martí's simple verses, the supposed simplicity of the lines of this poem hides profound human connotations. Repeated day-after-day events contrast with everlasting occurrences, "The full moon shines," "The sun comes out," while the rush of life prevents your noticing that the door opens and swings closed. Then, life speeds up and while you love your children or read a book, or the snow falls, old age slowly unfolds and you start asking yourself why the door keeps opening into unknown darkness. One by one, children, husband, dog, even much of living memory are gone, until,

"The door swings open:
O god of hinges,
god of long voyages,
you have kept faith.
It's dark in there.
You confide yourself to the darkness.
You step in.
The door swings closed."

It is difficult to define what "the land" means for Cubans. For many, it is more than what we tread upon, paraphrasing the young José Martí. For some, the land is a place to stay for eternity and they want it all upon their grave, in the passionate and definitive demand of Carilda Oliver Labra.

As illustrated by Martí's "Two Homelands," Cuba is at once the dreamed impossible and the bittersweet fruit of the reiterated historical attempts to achieve it, efforts of painful and heroic gestation that have always put independence and justice side by side in the audacious foundational venture. Cintio Vitier, one of Cuba's thinkers who best sees the ethical roots of the nation's historical matrix, wrote that the bloody battles for independence of the Ten Years' War and the angry internal conflicts, showed every Cuban the true face of the homeland, which "furrowed by tears, smeared by blood, was the face of justice and liberty."

In one form or another, this vision of "the land" is portrayed by Cintio's famed wife, Fina García Marruz. Many of her meditative sonnets address themes of essential universality, as Atwood does. But in her writing, the homeland is somewhat portrayed with more personal consequence, viewed perhaps more intimately in its rainbow of cultural and historical drama.

In "The Poor of the Earth" Fina reveals a soul painfully close to her country's realities: honestly, she starts by claiming that "My land touched my heart," a statement in which the dependency of the subject to the act of possession is sadly lost in careful translation: "Me tocó el corazón la tierra mía". See the overemphasis of the possessive at the end, the indiscriminate emotion of a metaphor that Atwood would probably avoid. Then, amidst "innocent palm trees" (the symbolically important national tree), she features the poverty of "little pines" and scorched banana plantation, preferred in contrast to the sumptuous but soft sea. And Fina delights in staying forever where many left; almost celebrating uniformity that, sadly, comes from poverty.

> "My land touched my heart,
> one by one its words fell,
> found gladness in my eyes,
> poor little pines,
> innocent palm trees. [...]
> Ah to remain forever where your
> uniform colour of poverty illuminates..."

"Its Hummingbird Lightness, Iridescence, Wicker" shows Fina at her best. The mature poet's mind nurtures from a life-long experience in her country, from her own poetic reflections, especially her own piece "Oh Cuba, Cuba." In a mostly evocative series of lines, she describes her motherland with passionate anguish and delight. On the one hand, she tells of its hummingbird lightness with an insistent tone: "its living, like the bird, in the instant" "Its kite-like lightness in the blue", probably unacquainted of "the soft wood of its toys and walls". Consequently, "its pollarding the plantations of the secular", "its love for extravagance and personal peculiarity, / its firecrackering and racket, / the shallow depth of its arm waving", in sharp contrast with "the unreachable distance of its eyes."

> Its hummingbird lightness, iridescence, wicker,
> its gentleness of unswerving iron,
> its pollarding the plantations of the secular,
> its living, like the bird, in the instant.
> The soft wood of its toys and walls, [...]
> Its kite-like lightness in the blue, [...]
> its devil with a gold tooth and the enigma
> of what has no enigma and smiles.
> Its fake angels with a wing of truth,

its clove saints in the wardrobe and butterfly membrane, [...]
breeze that swirls into cyclone,
slight gust that later sweeps and leaves the outdoor sun.
the fathomless of its irresponsibility
capable of setting off the spark that would ignite the universe
without any previous plan,
the impossibility of blaming the blame of that face
that smiles at nothingness and speaks of her mother with love."

There is a profound reflection in the poem that results from close knowledge of Cuban history and culture, the soul and its unfolding, praxis that returns to nurture the spiritual fountain of the nation. The inconsistency of understanding, apparent in "its devil with a gold tooth and the enigma/of what has no enigma and smiles," leads to the "breeze that swirls into cyclone/slight gust that later sweeps and leaves the outdoor sun." A daring venture, indeed, which could perhaps be regarded as "the fathomless of its irresponsibility" in an endeavour "capable of setting off the spark that would ignite the universe/without any previous plan. Everything has to be understood, in the end, by the presiding reign of the innocent palm tree, "shadeless in the sun of its royal poverty."

Thus, in love and pain, Cuba, Cuba...

Conclusions

During the class experience, the students realised that the Cuban and the Canadian traditions share major similarities. It was relevant for them to understand that the way Canadians and Cubans mirror the world has been shaped by distinct historical and cultural experiences. Although the arduous settlement of the continent left a significant imprint on the Canadian soul, Cubans as a people underwent a longer and more excruciating historical ordeal to become what they are, something significant for our students to understand. Awareness of cultural differences may be difficult, so it was for students to perceive that the search for open spaces and for dilated skies, as voiced by Canadian literature, shapes unlike voices to people living in the sea-confined spaces of an island.

Margaret Atwood and Fina García Marruz reflect those similarities and differences in their poetry. Both, in form and content, these writers share common themes of universal value, dear to both cultural traditions. At the same time, differences in the way each deals with their themes are discernable. Such is Attwood's elegant detachment in her topics in contrast with a somewhat more intimate engagement perceived in Marruz's writing about her country.

Bibliography

Atwood, M. morning in the burned house: new poems. McLelland & Stewart Ltd. Toronto, 1995.

Atwood, M. The Door. McLelland & Stewart Ltd. Toronto, 2007.

Cubarte. http://www.cubarte.cu/index.php.

García Marruz, F. Antología Poética. Cubaliteraria. http://www.cubaliteraria.cu/

García Marruz, F. Antología Poética. Editorial Letras Cubanas. La Habana. 1997.

The Ambassador. (Spring, 2008) Hiddenbrook Press. Toronto, 2008.

The Ambassador. (Winter, 2008) Hiddenbrook Press. Toronto, 2008.

Velázquez León, M. A Sheaf of Poetry: for the Students. Biblioteca CD-ROM de los estudiantes. Ciudad de la Habana, 2003.

Velázquez León, M. A Sheaf of Poetry: for the Teachers. Biblioteca CD-ROM de los estudiantes. Ciudad de la Habana, 2003.

Velázquez León, M. Beyond Poetry: Experiences in Values Education. Editorial Educación Cubana. Ciudad de la Habana, 2008.

Previously published at the WEFLA-IX International

Seminar on Canadian Studies, 2015

Cuba and Canada: Chosen Places in John B. Lee's Work

PhD Adonay Bárbara Pérez Luengo. Full Professor

PhD Manuel de Jesús Velázquez León. Full Professor

MSc Alison González Cuba. Associate Professor

Introduction

John B. Lee's biography as a poet is impressive. In 2005, he was inducted as Poet Laureate of Brantford in perpetuity and received the distinction of being named Honourary Life Member of The Canadian Poetry Association and The Ontario Poetry Society. In 2007 John was made a member of the Chancellor's Circle of the President's Club of McMaster University and named first recipient of the Souwesto Award for his contribution to literature in Southwestern Ontario.

He was also named winner of the inaugural Black Moss Press Souwesto Award for his contribution to the ethos of writing in this region of Canada. In 2011 he was appointed Poet Laureate of Norfolk County (2011-14) and in 2015 Honourary Poet Laureate of Norfolk County for life. In 2017, John received a Canada 150 Medal from the Federal Government of Canada for "his outstanding contribution to literary development both at home and abroad."

A recipient of over eighty prestigious international awards for his writing, he is winner of the CBC Literary Award for Poetry, the only two-time recipient of the People's Poetry Award, and 2006 winner of the inaugural Souwesto Orison Writing Award (University of Windsor). In 2007, John B. Lee was the winner of the Winston Collins Award for Best Canadian Poem, an award he won again in 2012.

He has well-over seventy books published to date and is the editor of seven anthologies including two best-selling works: That Sign of Perfection: poems and stories on the game of hockey; and Smaller Than God: words of spiritual longing. John co-edited a special issue of Windsor Review—Alice Munro: A Souwesto Celebration published in the fall of 2014.

His work has appeared internationally in over 500 publications, and has been translated into French, Spanish, Korean and Chinese. He has read his work in nations all over the world including South Africa, France, Korea, Cuba, Canada and the United

States. He has received letters of praise from Nelson Mandela, Desmond Tutu, Australian Poet, Les Murray, and Senator Romeo Dallaire. Called "the greatest living poet in English," by poet George Whipple, he lives in Port Dover, Ontario where he works as a full-time author.

Development

Let us begin these lines with the informed words of poet Marilyn Gear Pilling who knows John's poetry intimately:

"Lee's poetry comes from the deepest well of the self, a place of rare depth and beauty fed by omnivorous reading and openhearted living. As well as writing the work he has formally researched and re-imagined, he pours his daily life into poetry every morning, creating a skein that contains the natural and the human worlds, the public as well as the private. Lee has said –in tones of wonder, for he experiences himself as simply a conduit through which an expression of grace becomes manifest– "I could sink the world in poems." (…) Lee's poetry contains and fully engages heart and mind, body and soul. His is an eye that can look at a trucker and see an angel.

He has said, "White contains the entire spectrum and we're primed by the illusion of our separate lives. God would have us all enter into the grand and lovely osmosis of the universe entire." (…)

John B. Lee reveals in his work a germane poetic insight of both his homeland and Cuba. Many of his poems live their normal lives in the open spaces, under Cuban sun and clouds, over the sea, between mountains and beaches, the country we know. There, the island is felt in its move in time, through droughts and hurricanes and flashes of lives, all momently frozen and then thawed by a shrewd hand for the poetry feast. Consequently, there are salty breezes over waves, and rumors of palm fronds, and the reds redder and the greens greener of the Caribbean. Landscapes are peopled by humans of some common sort only revealed uncommon by a scrutiny that comes from the depths of a very personal poetic tradition, already with an old testament. However accurate, this vision is mirrored from the democratic vastness of North American landscapes and history. Cuba is more sensed than seen, intensely sensed, like pain in the marrow, like guiding, unavoidable memories that keep one erect and walking towards life's ever-changing horizons. But felt rather than watched. Consequently, that sense of pending tragedy, of life at the edge of life that permeates some of John's poems on Cuba and that the inhabitants of this island know so well.

In all manners, this is an uncommon glance at Cuba's landscapes and people. In no way an outsider's slanted sight. As the poet concedes in a moving move, the poetic acquisition almost helps him to learn "to remember the meaning of life." Quite a confession for a mind so mature, for these veteran eyes, for the crafty workings of a soul so intensely trained in living a life he chose to live dangerously consciously, as his readers must know well. So is it in this poem written after visiting the Cross Hill, in Holguin:

"So, this is a place of places
for Manuel and Tai
we climb the four hundred steps
to the cross of Holguin
and Manuel says
in recognition
of the importance of our destination
"So, this is a place of places ..."
and we stand
above the city
looking east where the sun
is leaving the neighbourhood
and staining the squares
like the light
lacquering of old wood
for the restoration of a much-loved dollhouse
village
another day
we descend to the west
follow a crumbled trail
down the green stone
pathway knobbed
with bone and broken glass
and ancient coral from the sea
we are coming down
through the nuisance ground
with its frail rust
and tin aromas
its pungent swill of vegetative rot
and paper scuttle sounds
when I see
the gyre of ravens
hovering and circling
over the blackened body
of a bent-ribbed dog
disarticulated by maggot work
and the carrion hunger
of those scavenging shadows
as I pass
I look and take in

the final sneer of canus lupus
many days dead
and I think of the night
with its tongue of stars
and the sorrowful solitude
of that morbid moment
of his passing
that full exhale of his
final lying down
and am sad
not to have been there
to give comfort"
(...)

Sweet Cuba: the Building of a Poetic Tradition: 1608-1958 (Hidden Brook Press, 2010), is a bilingual anthology of Cuban poetry that John B. Lee translated and edited with his friend Manuel de J. Velázquez León and that was intended as an introduction to Cuban poetry for the English-speaking reader. As the editors wrote in the introduction, they offered it as a "vase of fresh flowers at the gate of vast garden."

The complex demands of this anthology brought the poet closer to Cuban soul and, especially, to José Martí, whose work set up the internal structure of the compilation and became that moment in which, all the tones sketched along the protracted configuration of Cuban poetic consciousness take shape in a harmonic and coherent voice. In the opinion of a specialist:

"In José Martí culminated all the Cuban traditions of the word, whose outline and development we witnessed in preceding periods. His personality reminds us of what Oriental mystics call the alibi, capable to create reality out of image. His importance exceeds the limits of our frontiers to become a universal personality in the perspectives that grow from him." (Lezama Lima, J. Opus Cit)

It was in José Martí that John B. Lee found the key to many of Cuba's spiritual mysteries. In his own words:

"If in the voice of José Martí we might find the spirit of Cuba, so too in the spirit of Martí we have sought and found the voice of Cuba. Just as each Cuban poet who predates Martí seems to anticipate his arrival, so too each subsequent poet herein echoes his having lived. With this in mind, we dedicate Sweet Cuba to the memory of Martí. As Manuel and I say in the words of Rubén Martínez Villena, we dedicate our work to "Martí's marble dream." Over the course of translating these works, I have noticed the exiled poet, the tragic nostalgic, the dying soldier, the suffering slave, the grieving widow, the idealistic dreamer, the joyful celebrant, the home-loving and all-too-often disappointed patriot, and of all of these I find an apotheosis in Martí. And so, we have chosen to honour the work by weaving the poems of Martí into the fabric of the entire book so that we create a tapestry using the motif of his poems to gather the entire body of work into one unified whole. Martí's poems frame and thread together this celebration of Cuba's strength and beauty, her triumphs and failures, her land and language, not impoverished here by translations, but rather enriched by new music in the poetry of another language."

John B. Lee's translations of Cuban poetry are notorious for their elegance. Connoisseur of the art of writing, John found ways to portray profoundly Cuban cultural traditions to his poetic versions of Cuban poetry. A piece of natural poetry, close to the island's best peasant tradition, shows John's artistic craftsmanship at its best:

"By the blooming riverside
Of the Yara washing near,
So pleasant, fresh and clear
Slowly the sweet flow glides,
Where the glowing sun resides
In our region of the heat,
A sky beautifully crowned complete
With forest, and meadow, and mountainside,
As a handsome peasant rides
On his gracefully trotting mare."
[…]

According to M. G. Pilling, John was born to write and developed a lyric voice that sings like no other voice heard before in Canada. In her opinion, while his "melody soars and praises, the tenor line is often wistful, poignant, or gently melancholic; there is often a pervasive nostalgia for lost worlds." Recurrent themes in Lee's poetry are the very Canadian topics of family and rural life. John has immortalized his life in the farm where he was born with the vivid portrayal of landscapes and stories of his ancestors.

"The Songbirds of My Father's Mind"
"There is one song
in the chirping summer
my father hears it
from his parlour chair
and marks it
with a life
and we both listen
saying, there it is upon the wind
anonymous among the throng
and I am forty and my father
lists deaths

naming the ghosts he knows
even his sister
drooping in her bed needs water
but we are listening
to that one voice
we cannot fix
unqualified, the sparrow lands in water
fluttering like a lover's heart
the cardinal wounds remembered snow
while Latin poets waste their time
living forever
in a language no one speaks."

Sometimes a natural voice triggers the poets mind and there is a revelation of rural Canada unheard before but so vivid that the presence of the distant and past is actualized into the readers' present.

"The Full Measure"
"There's the voice of the dog in the barn
you can measure his mood
in the mind
take his size
from the weight of his breath
seek his span in the volume of sound
find fear in the blood
of his moon
or loss in his lonesome lament
you can know
both by the girth of his ribs
and the fall of his thought
how his heart
might break over hay
or race like a hare on the lee
where he's home
in the scattering clods
that screed
in the wake of his claws
what wags
on the hinge of a leaf
what sleeps
in a slow-dying snow

where the knots
are like stars
in his world
and the dust shafts
that swirl to be seen
seem angels gone mad
to the floor
what he names
for the car on the road
what he calls
to the yard in the dark
or the sun
if he's held until noon
is this not the shelter
of hope
is this not the lonesome
repair
come close to the lock
and I'll say
what's gathered away
in the windings of time
by the rain and the wind
on the heel that covers the land"

John B. Lee has traveled extensively, from the Caribbean to Europe to the Middle East to Korea to Africa to the Artic, and more. From all corners of the world he has brought poems. With a keen eye for cultural jewels, he has seen the entrails of "the others" with love and compassion, linking their fortunes and tragedies with those close to him at home, in Canada. Thus, in many of his poems love for his ancestors and his land connects with love for timeless generations in the spacetime of our misshaped global village, where national boundaries pretend to be oceans, rivers, roads and newly built walls. Perhaps never is John B. Lee more a Laureate Canadian Poet than when his loving pain for those who suffer transcends geographies and cultures; perhaps he is a better son of the best of Canada when he brings the distant and the different into the broad heart of his poetry.

"No More Need for This Old Man"
"There is a photograph
of a Christmas long ago
when I stood grinning

beside the guest bed
in our farmhouse
in pajamas
my hair, a slash
and I wore a pair of blue
lenses pince-nez, playing doctor
touching the plastic bell
of a toy stethoscope
to my cousin's soundless heart.
Since then
my uncle died.
Since then my father's sister
breathes no more
as sorrow by sorrow
we might name them sadly
under stone.
And yesterday I heard a story
how outside a distant village
a soldier
told a refugee
who walked a weeping road
in a river of human woe
with his ailing father in his arms
"you have no more need
of this old man"
and he
learned grief
how deep it goes
"you have no more need
of this old man"
how light he was, how small of form
how like a wormy branch
his father fell
upon himself
"you have no more need
of this old man"
and I think
I need everyone, I want them all back
those dying uncles
those perishing aunts

those cancerous cousins
that baby sister
those generations of ash and dust
my best friend breathing
in his father's mouth
listening for his heart
like placing his ear to a horseless hill
with the wind in the grass
when the cruel rains come."

Conclusions

These words are brief, too brief. So they have to be when approaching a poet like John B. Lee in the vain attempt to fathom the depth of his poetry, even of one of his poems. John, the conjurer of images and words, the profound intellectual, the man to whom no human experience is alien. To love his poetry is to love what he loves and to love him, dear John, the poet close to a universal heart, if there is one, the simple-complex poet of Canada's cultural and geographical vastness, Cuba's lover, the brother, the friend.

Bibliography

Ducker, Stella (2008). Hola Cuba. Hidden Brook Press, Canada.

Grove, Kimberley (2010). Sí Cuba, a CCLA Cuba Trip Anthology. Hidden Brook Press, Canada.

Lee, John B. (2009). Island on the Wind-Breathed Edge of the Sea. Hidden Brook Press, USA.

Lee, John B. (2010). Dressed in Dead Uncles. Black Moss Press, Canada.

Lee, John B. (2010). In the Muddy Shoes of Morning. Hidden Brook Press, Canada.

Lee, John B. (2011). When the full moon comes. Hidden Brook Press, USA.

Lee, John B. (2015). The Full Measure. Black Moss Press, Canada.

Lee, John B. and Manuel de Jesús Velázquez León (editors) (2012). Beyond the Seventh Morning. SandCrabBooks, USA.

Lee, John B. and Richard M. Grove (2013). In This We Hear the Light. Hidden Brook Press, USA.

Lezama Lima, J. Antología de la poesía cubana. Consejo Nacional de Cultura. Ciudad de la Habana, 1965.

Martí Pérez, José (Eds. Vitier, C., F. García Marruz, E. de Armas). Poesía completa. Edición crítica. Editorial Letras Cubanas. Ciudad de la Habana, 2001.

Velázquez León, Manuel de Jesús and John B. Lee (2010). Sweet Cuba: The Building of a Poetic Tradition: 1608-1958. Hidden Brook Press, Canada.

Previously published at the WEFLA-International Seminar on Canadian Studies

Teaching Gender in Literature Lessons: Why The Handmaid's Tale?

MSc Aylene Rodríguez Sondón. Associate Professor

PhD Marla Vega Romero. Associate Professor

Introduction

Over the last decades, issues that have gained relevancy within contemporary life, have also made their way into the academic field. Gender studies, for example, now have an established place on university syllabuses and on a large number of courses from accredited educational institutions. The official introduction of gender issues in literary studies in the English Language Major greatly enriches the range of topics to be addressed in the lessons, while standing out for its presence and significance in Anglophone literature.

To some degree, since the 1970s, Canadian literature has experienced a widening of its literary canon, now more diverse and inclusive, resulting in more female writers being anthologized and more texts written by women taught in classes. The thematic diversity of the woks of Alice Munro, Anne Michaels and Margaret Atwood, to name some of Canada's literary celebrities, has ensured them international followings.

Atwood's work comprises themes that range from Canadian national identity, relations between Canada and the United States, relations between Canada and Europe, the Canadian wilderness, environmental issues, biotechnology, human rights issues, to feminist issues, a prominent theme throughout her career. Her representations of gender explore the social myths defining femininity, representations of women's bodies in art, the social and economic exploitation of women, as well as women's relations with each other and with men. (Callaway, 2008)

Precisely *The Handmaid's Tale*, a novel by Margaret Atwood and one of the cornerstones of feminism in literature, leads the selection of works to be analyzed in Anglophone Literature lessons from a gender approach.

Development

A best-selling book first published in 1985, *The Handmaid's Tale* takes place in a terrifying image of a dystopian future, often compared to 1984 or even to The Hunger Games. In this future, the author presents a world in which some women are forced into various roles including as child-bearers for infertile, elite couples, as nearly all the women have become infertile, so the few who can still have babies have been brainwashed, and assigned to powerful men in a twisted attempt to restore the human race. (Armstrong, 2018)

According to Armstrong, the novel, conceived as 'speculative fiction', portrays a future that could conceivably happen without any advances in technology from the present and every aspect of the book was inspired by social and political events of the early 1980s, when Atwood wrote it.

Some of what Atwood describes wasn't merely speculation about the end result of the religious right taking power in the US but was based on what was happening elsewhere. Atwood says she was inspired in part by Nicolai Ceausescu's preoccupation with boosting female birth rates in Romania, which led to the policing of pregnant women and the banning of abortion and birth control, not to mention the murders of dissidents by the Ferdinand Marcos regime in the Philippines. (Armstrong, 2018) On the other hand, the idea of 'giving' the offspring of lower classes to the ruling class came from Argentina, where a military junta seized power in 1976, subsequently 'disappearing' up to 500 children and placing them with selected leaders (The New Yorker, 2012).

Readers of dystopian fiction will de able to identify in *The Handmaid's Tale* many of the themes and features of Atwood's novel, namely war, constant surveillance, oppression and lack of freedom, and underground movements and rebellion, and a lot of these issues could be easily traced back to real issues in the world. David Ketterer (1989) writes that it is usually assumed that writers of dystopias are concerned with describing the horrors of life if present trends continue, and that the author may hope that his or her fiction will 'serve as a warning' or call for a rebellion against the current systems. The Tale does this by showing "what might happen if certain attitudes are carried to the extremes" (Miner, 1991, p. 149)

On the other hand, Lois Feuer (1997) writes in her critique of *The Handmaid's Tale* that reviewers of the novel "invariably hailed it as a "feminist 1984" and, like many handy tags, this one conceals a partial truth". While both the Tale and 1984 depict totalitarian regimes, Feuer points to the fact that Atwood brings something new and different into the dystopian tradition, namely the feminist debate over "essentialism". With this she both "participates in and extends the dystopian genre" (Feuer, 1997).

The *Handmaid's Tale* brings forth feminist themes and issues in what is not only a novel, but a social critique. The exploration of the shortcomings of marriage as traditionally envisioned also re-emerges as a theme in *The Handmaid's Tale.* (Callaway, 2008) It is regarded as one of the classics within its genre and was nominated for the Ritz-Paris Hemingway Prize in France and was shortlisted for the Booker Prize. The novel won the Los Angeles Times Prize, the General's Award in Canada, and the first Arthur C. Clarke Award for the best science-fiction work published in Britain in 1986 (Ketterer, 1989, p. 209).

The Handmaid's Tale novel, which differs in some ways from the TV show, was adapted for TV in 2017 by the streaming service Hulu, and remains a sourcebook for gender studies in Canadian literature.

Gender in literature

From a sociological perspective, Wharton (2005) defines gender as a "system of social practices" that creates and maintains gender distinctions, also responsible for organizing relations of inequality based on the distinctions between sexes (Wharton, 2005, p. 7). Therefore, gender involves the creation of differences and inequalities between sexes (7).

At the same time, Wharton highlights the importance of three features of the definition of the term gender, the first being that gender is not a merely fixed state, but a process as well. Such assertion implies that gender is continually being produced and reproduced (7). Second, gender is not only manifested at the individual level, meaning that it occurs "at all levels of the social structure" (7), so it involves institutions, interaction and individuals that, as a whole, "embody and reproduce gender" (7).

Last but not least, gender refers to "its importance in organizing relations of inequality" (7). Nyberg (2018) illustrates the latter through the deeply rooted roles assigned to boys and girls since childhood: "raising boys and girls differently, the former with posters of action figures and fast cars and the latter with posters of Disney princesses that await their Prince Charming to come and swoop them off their feet, will likely result in a more action-minded boy and a more passive girl, features that will influence their adult lives as well".

Both Wharton (2005) and Nyberg (2018) agree on the complexity of gender, as a multilevel system whose effects can be seen at every level of social life. Consequently, one framework is not enough to understand gender inequality and its multiplicity of expressions. To show precisely how this takes form, different episodes of the novel will be analyzed, based on the sociological perspectives on gender proposed by Wharton (the institutional, the interactional and the individual perspective on gender), however emphasizing on the institutional perspective.

Gender inequality in The Handmaid's Tale

The Handmaid's Tale is a novel that contains several aspects that are fruitful to approach from a gender point of view, to show how gender, the forming of gender and the sexual violence in the novel are all interconnected. Gender inequality, which is what leads to the sexual violence, is produced on every level of society, and especially at the institutional level of society, that is, the culture of the society. (Nyberg, 2018)

According to Wharton (2005) sociologists define the term institutional perspective on gender, in the simplest terms, as "an organized, established pattern". The institutional perspective on gender uses the term institution as an abstract and an almost all-encompassing term which permeates the society as a whole, or large institutions within a society, for example organizations such as schools (64). Institutions are those features of society and life that seem so ordinary, so ongoing and so permanent that they are accepted as "the way things are" (65).

As a result of institutional gender inequality persisting without conscious intervention and effort, they do not require coercion to sustain themselves, which makes participation appear voluntary and easily justifiable (Nyberg, 2018, p. 220). Crucially, the "dominant group's vested interest in perpetuating inequality, together with the subordinate group's lack of alternatives, shape the ways both groups make sense of their relationship" (221).

In other words, the focus of this perspective is centered upon how gender is created and maintained in organizations and culture and is thus aimed at examining the practices and policies of cultures, societies and organizations. Nyberg (2018) does not circumscribe these practices and ideas of culture and society to a micro-context but sees them are at a macro-level where they "play a central role in the perpetuation of gender distinctions and inequalities". Thus, beliefs about what men and women are and should be are "conditioned by these institutions" (70).

As women live in an extremely hierarchical and patriarchal society in Gilead, they are treated poorly and have almost no rights all. The Aunts, subjugating characters in the novel, try to convince the Handmaids that Gilead has actually restored respect for women, who are now valued and appreciated because they are "holding the future in their hands" (Callaway, 2008, pp 55).

The patriarchy has institutionalized adultery, under the guise of reproduction. Both Wife and Handmaid/Mistress are required to co-habit the house and must collaborate in the procreative mission of the household, in an act of humiliation for all the female characters involved in the monthly ceremony. The Aunts accomplish their brainwashing mission, till the handmaids are deprived of their own selves and led to ironically be thankful for becoming Mistresses instead of Unwomen.

The fact is that I'm his mistress. Men at the top have always had mistresses, why should things be any different? The arrangements aren't quite the same, granted. The mistress used to be kept in a minor house or apartment of her own, and now they've amalgamated things. But underneath it's the same. More or less. Outside woman, they used to be called in some countries. I am the outside woman. It's my job to provide what is otherwise lacking. (Atwood, 1986, p. 163)

Aunt Lydia tells her Handmaid trainees in Chapter 1, "'There is more than one kind of freedom [...] Freedom to and freedom from. In the days of anarchy, it was freedom to. Now you are being given freedom from. Don't underrate it'" (Atwood, 1986, p. 24). The freedom to choose to marry or not, to choose to work or not, to choose to bear children or not, has been replaced with the freedom from divorce, bankruptcy, and abortion. Thus, by eliminating a need for choice, the state controls individual desires and directs them into socially acceptable channels. Choice is the enemy of social harmony in Gilead. By controlling choice, citizens' freedoms are controlled as well. The Handmaids have also lost control of their bodies, and, therefore, of their identities. (Callaway, 2008)

In Gilead, women are oppressed and forced to occupy a number of rigidly defined subject positions: frustrated house-bound Wives, official substitute wives known as

Handmaids, half-mistress, half-whore, domestic helpers called Marthas, educators and disciplinarian, sadistic propagandists called Aunts and, lastly, unofficial prostitutes who remain on the hidden underside of the régime. (Coad, 2001)

In Chapter 28 Offred recounts how the women who had had careers before the time of the Republic of Gilead are dismissed when the new régime takes over. The director told the female employees that, 'You can't work here any more, it's the law'. Everybody knew this new law was being enforced by the men with machine guns standing at the door. In Gilead, women are no longer allowed bank accounts, or to hold property, unless handed over to the control of a male relative.

However, some women in *The Handmaid's Tale* were actual agents of Gilead. Serena Joy, for instance, was a well-known television personality whose speeches, as Offred remembers, "were about the sanctity of the house, about how women should stay home" (Atwood, 1986, p. 45). Offred found these speeches and Serena's earnestness frightening (46). Throughout the novel Offred observes Serena, the Wife of her posting. She reflects about Serena's promotion of these traditional values and how Serena reacts to the reality of being a Wife in Gilead:

"She doesn't make speeches anymore. She has become speechless. She stays in her home, but it doesn't seem to agree with her. How furious she must be, now that she's been taken at her word" (46).

Although Serena was clearly an agent of Gilead, she, too, has been trapped by its oppression (Callaway, 2008). This brief passage demonstrates the pointed ironies of Atwood's prose throughout *The Handmaid's Tale*. Here and elsewhere, Offred plays with words to describe the suppression of language, and in Gilead, playing with words is a dangerous act of trespass. The fact that Serena makes no more public speeches becomes "speechless"-ness ; the fact that her life at home, the woman's life she formerly advocated, does not "agree" with her suggests the irrelevance of "agreement" in Gilead, and thus the impossibility of dialogue. The final irony is that Serena's dispossession of voice, of the power of words she can no longer use, is the result of having been "taken at her word". (Greene, 1999)

David Coad's Hymens, Lips, and Masks: The Veil in Margaret Atwood's *The Handmaid's Tale*, examines how the veil, worn by all women in Gilead, functions as the crucial tool of subjugation, one element of the politics of dress within the novel. The red dress and the white bonnet, that the Handmaids had to wear compulsory, were also part of the institutionalized standards that somehow labelled the Handmaids by the role they were assigned, much like the scarlet letter in Hawthorne's homonymous play. While Handmaids were forced to wear the red nun-like uniform, Wives and Aunts were soberly dressed and only the whores at the state-owned brothel at Jezebel's continued to wear makeup. (Coad, 2001)

These regressive social roles are determined by a caste system defining standards for behaviour, dress, and social duties, thereby eliminating undesirable cultural trends and beliefs, while controlling a fearful and potentially rebellious populace. (Callaway, 2008)

For example, the fact that the new family structure relies on "the monthly rape 'Ceremony' which follows the scriptural 'and she shall bear upon my knees/ and grotesquely requires the presence of Wife, Handmaid, and Commander, synthesizes the institutionalized humiliation, objectification, and ownership of women in Gilead". (Cavalcanti, 2000, p. 166)

Such family structure is crucial for the shaping of characters in the novel. Perhaps the episode that best explains the perspective of gendered institutions is the ceremony where Offred is forced to have sex with her Commander and his wife Serena.

The culture of society in the shaping of characters

Being a Handmaid, Offred is systematically raped by her Commander once a month. As women have been deprived of their right to work, their society has assigned them roles for nonqualified people since "the power structure refuses to see women as human" (Diemer Llewellyn & Hicks, 2006, p. 52). What does society expect from her, demand from her? She is supposed to give life to a new generation.

Ironic enough is the fact that before the ceremony begins, the Commander reads a passage from the Bible to all the "elements" involved in the "ritual": Offred, his wife Serena and the household's two Aunts, as overseers of the Handmaids. As he reads, Offred recounts that he looks over them "as if taking inventory" (Atwood, p. 86), a sign of how much power the Commander holds over them and an indication of the extend women are victims of the approved societal objectification.

Offred perceives how the Commander reads the Bible as if he were reading them a "bedtime story" (87), but, once again, irony plays the trick: they are not going to sleep; they are going to have sex. Her mind should be elsewhere, her thoughts and consciousness should leave her, in order to bear the ceremony, which further shows that it is a matter of rape, as sex with an unconscious person always is. The Commander, cold and hard, decides the fate of these women. He makes them flinch as he moves and so far, he has given "no evidence of softness" (87).

During the reading, Serena Joy, the Commander's wife, bursts into tears. She cannot help it, she always does so during the ceremony, which reveals that she does not escape suffering and humiliation either. "There seems to be no women in Gilead who does not suffer at the hands of the new regime" (Nyberg, 2018).

Before the ceremony begins, Offred's memories of Moira come to her mind. She recalls the moment when they brought her back from her punishment for misbehaving and not following the female gender standards of Gilead. She did her best to focus on praying, but all the images of her friend distracted her, and were a remainder of what could happen to her in case she disobeyed or could not fulfil the expectations. Finally, the Commander dismisses the women (92), exerting his authority and ready to begin the ceremony.

Offred lies between Serena Joy's legs, Offred's head resting on Serena's stomach, Serena's thighs on either side of Offred, They are both clothed, except for Offred's lack of underwear. Nyberg (2018) refers to this situation as a simulation of "the typical scenario of a woman being grabbed by a man on the street and getting raped". In addition, Serena holds Offred's arms (93), suggesting that she and Serena "are one flesh, one being" (94). However, it can also be understood as Serena being the one in control at the time she becomes accessory to the raping.

Surprisingly, Offred refuses to call the ceremony rape. "Offred thinks that because there are two choices in this oppressive system - forced labor or forced intercourse - that she has some control over her fate, and that she is partly to blame for the violation committed against her" (Dimer Llewellyn & Hicks, 2006, p. 57). She wishes that "he would hurry up" (Atwood, p. 94), and feels the need for therapy so that she "could feel better and this would go away" (94). Furthermore, Serena Joy cuts Offred's finger with her rings, as she holds her hands, which "may or not be revenge" (94). Both Serena and the Commander are inflicting pain on Offred, they are raping Offred, and no affection, no passion, no love is involved in the act, at least not in what to Offred respects.

After the ceremony is over, the Commander leaves, and Offred is supposed to lie and rest for ten minutes to increase the chances of her getting pregnant, but Serena Joy does not let her do it (95), perpetuating the cycle of sexual assault, humiliation and pain.

Offred is aware that the Commander "too, is doing his duty" (95), in a ceremony that was not his creation but the state's: to have sex (no matter if it is against Offred's will) in order to father children. Besides the above mentioned aspects, from an institutional perspective on gender, it should be noted how "Gilead uses religion to disguise the institutionalized rape that occurs monthly between Commanders and Handmaids" (Diemer Llewellyn & Hicks, 2006, p. 57) in the reading before the ceremony.

Why is the Commander more powerful than all the women of the household? He has the support of the state. The patriarchal society established in Gilead changed not only women's statuses but men's. He is no longer the male of the household but the Commander of the household. The institution that empowered men is the same that silenced women by stripping them of their rights and ability to work.

At times, the power of the state seems to be limitless, unquestionable. As it decides who becomes a Handmaid or a Wife, who is given a Handmaid based on one of the pillars of Gillead society: biological reproduction, the fate and dignity of women depend basically on fertility. Thus, the state is the agent that forces Offred into becoming a sex slave and deems Serena useless to society (Nyberg, 2018).

How to explain Serena crying during the lead up to the ceremony, Serena hurting Offred during the ceremony and finally kicking Offred out of the room when the ceremony is over? First, the state if able to assign roles and control behaviour cannot paralyze feelings on a deeper level. Serena's tears are the result of the pain the state causes her by forcing Fred to sleep with another woman, as it is his duty to the state. Powerless and filled with anger and frustration, she takes it out on Offred, hurting her during the ceremony and reducing her chance to get pregnant. In other words, Serena's rebellious behaviour of secretly breaking the rules is an act of endurance.

Finally, Offred's passive attitude during the Ceremony is conditioned by having no choice but becoming a child vessel or face violence or death, like Moira or the women that went to the Colonies did. Diemer Llewellyn and Hicks argue that "Offred does not resist the Commander and Serena Joy; she is held in place by fear of the Colonies" (Diemer Llewellyn & Hicks, 2006, p. 63). Victims also of the institutional language, the Handmaids' bodies limit their vocabulary to what, by habit, they have internalized as their sole function:

We are for breeding purposes: we aren't concubines, geisha girls, courtesans. On the contrary: everything possible has been done to remove us from that category. There is supposed to be nothing entertaining about us, no room is to be permitted for the flowering of secret lusts; no special favours are to be wheedled, by them or us, there are to be no toeholds for love. We are two-legged wombs, that's all: sacred vessels, ambulatory chalices. (Atwood, 1986, p. 146)

In the words of Callaway (2008), the male- dominated power structure relies on women to regulate one another and enforce social standards. The philosophy informing the social structure is not unique to Gilead: "no empire imposed by force or otherwise has ever been without this feature: control of the indigenous by members of their own group" (308). Hence, the institutional perspective on gender is central to the creation and forming of gender in Gilead, and to explain why the rape and sexual violence in the novel occurs.

Conclusions

Well-known for her feminist views and open mind, Margaret Atwood ranks among the leading Canadian writers of all times. It is impossible to read *The Handmaid's Tale* without being aware that issues of gender and aspects of feminism are central to the novel, as they are to the teaching-learning process of Anglophone Literature.

In the world of Gilead, class and gender are the crucial judges of status, demanding fertile women that they either become subjected to systematic rape in a household with a Commander in charge, or be shipped off to die in the colonies, which is no choice at all. To gain a better understanding of the shaping of gender and the sexual violence in Atwood's *The Handmaid's Tale*, the institutional perspective on gender (Wharton, 2005) proved effective. Gender inequality in the novel was approached through the influence of the culture of society on some of the characters, whose choices and behaviour could be explained looking at society as a whole.

Works cited

Armstrong, J.(25 April 2018) Why The Handmaid's Tale is so relevant today. BBC Culture's Stories.

Atwood, M. (1986). The Handmaid's Tale. New York: Penguin Random House LLC.

Callaway, A. (2008). Women disunited: Margaret Atwood's The Handmaid's Tale as a critique of feminism. [Master's Theses. 3505]. http://scholarworks.sjsu.edu/etd_theses/3505

Calvalcanti, I. (2000). Utopias of Language in Contemporary Feminist Literary Dystopias. Utopian Studies. 11.2, 152-181.

Coad, D. (2008) Hymens, Lips and Masks: The Veil in Margaret Atwood's The Handmaid's Tale. Contemporary Literary Criticism. Vol. 246. Originally published in Literature and Psychology. Vol.

47. No. 1, 2, 2001. 54-67.

Diemer Llewellyn, J. and Hicks, J. (2006) Rape in Feminist Utopian and Dystopian Fiction: Joanna Russ's "The Female Man", Margaret Atwood's "The Handmaid's Tale", and Octavia Butler's "The Parable of the Sower" and "The Parable of the Talents". ProQuest Dissertations and Theses 42-75.

Feuer, L. (1997). The Calculus of Love and Nightmare: The Handmaid's Tale and the Dystopian Tradition.

Golman,F.(2012).ChildrenoftheDirtyWar.http://www.newyorker.com/magazine/2012/03/19/children-of-the-dirty-war

Greene, M. (1999). Body/Language in The Handmaid's Tale: Reading Notes. University of British Columbia, Presses Universitaires de Rennes. http://www.openedition.org/6540

Ketterer, D. (1989). Margaret Atwood's The Handmaid's Tale: A Contextual Dystopia. Science Fiction Studies. Vol. 16. N0. 2. 209-217. http://www.jstor.org/stable/4239936

Miner, M. (1991). "Trust Me": Reading the Romance Plot in Margaret Atwood's The Handmaid's Tale . Twentieth Century Literature Vol. 37. No. 2. 148-168. Published by: Duke University Press. http://doi.org/10.2307/441844 http://www.jstor.org/stable/441844

Nyberg, B. (2018). Sociological Perspectives on Gender and Sexual Violence in The Handmaid's Tale. UMEA Universitet.

Wharton, A. (2005) The Sociology of Gender – An Introduction to Theory and Research. Oxford: Blackwell Publishing Ltd.

Towards Gender Neutral Translation: 'O Canada'

MSc Aylene Rodríguez Sondón, Associate Professor
PhD Marla Vega Romero. Associate Professor

Introduction: Gender, Language and Translation

Many translators and translation scholars still remain unaware of the practices, purposes and possibilities of gender in translation. In order to fully discuss the relationship of gender-sensitive language with translation, it may first be considered necessary to define the notion of gender and its importance in the context of translated texts (James 2011).

According to The Oxford Living Dictionaries (2018), the word gender has been used since the 14th century as a grammatical term, referring to classes of noun designated as masculine, feminine, or neuter in some languages. The sense denoting biological sex has also been used since the 14th century, but this did not become common until the mid 20th century. Although the words gender and sex are often used interchangeably, they have slightly different connotations; sex tends to refer to biological differences, while gender more often refers to cultural and social differences and sometimes encompasses a broader range of identities than the binary of male and female.

The evolution of the notion of gender has been explained by von Flotow (1997) as extending upon the simple definition limited to biological sexual difference as a result of the rise of the feminist movement. Authors like James (2011), affirm that definitions of gender are subject to various influences, and in Western society it may be seen to include considerations of sexual preference. According to Chamberlain (1998: 96), "the issues relating to gender in the practice of translation are myriad, varying widely according to the type of text being translated, the language involved, cultural practices and countless other factors".

Romaine (1999) claims that there is evidence for the existence of ideological factors which enter into gender assignment in systems that are supposedly purely formal and arbitrary as well as in systems where gender is supposedly determined by sex. Consequently, as translators translate gender-related materials, they inexorably must face with the ideological load these materials carry with themselves as well as the problem of how to handle them.

In this regard, Talbot (2003) argues that gender stereotypes and thereof social gender assignments are closely linked with and support gender ideologies. Therefore, if we consider gender stereotypes as ideological prescriptions for behavior, then actual individuals have to respond to the stereotypical roles expected of them both in constructing and communicating gender.

Male-dominated speech may be considered as patriarchal language, defined as 'the language forged and used by the institutions in society largely ruled by men' (von Flotow, 1997: 8). Language "is what carries and structures thought"[1].

As Castro, O (2013) puts it, language is a political act of mediation and communication which either perpetuates or challenges existing power structures within wider social and cultural contexts – and the same can be said of translation. Language, gender and translation are thus fundamental aspects of human existence, cultures and nations.

Since the 1980s, definitions of the translation process have insisted on the linguistic and cultural passage from one linguistic and cultural context (source text) to another (target text), underlining how a translator manipulates and re-writes a text in order to make it available to another language reading public (Palusci, O. 2010) This opened the way to the fruitful encounter between feminism and translation, adding a broader perspective on language, sex and power relations.

In this sense, it is worth noting the key role played by Canadian women authors and translators, who reclaimed a more central role in the culture of both translation and women, both underrated throughout the centuries.

Reviewing Canada

Canadian feminist translation

In Canada, Hubertine Auclert underscored the importance of language as a tool for the emancipation of women in 1899 (Baider, Khaznadar, Moreau 2007). Without any doubt, it has been claimed that the rise of feminism in Canada has increased awareness of the influence of male-dominated language in society and in texts. In the 1970's the important wave of feminism that emerged in Quebec, shook the whole country in a short time and some time later reached Europe.

In Canada of the 1980s, von Flotow (2006) explains that at the same time as anthologies of creative and critical work were appearing, academic journals focused on women's writing were being established. Moreover, the political climate in Canada, where government and university support was available for many of the publications and manifestations led to considerable cultural power.

1 **Founding call of the association** ***L'Avenir de la langue française (Web site not available in English), published in*** **Le Monde** ***on July 11, 1992 with the names of its first 300 signatories***

Von Flotow (2006) summarizes this process by acknowledging that bilingual, fragmented materials filled with unpredictable code-switching and ludic forms of translation as a liberatory gesture from «le langage masculin», working mainly from French to English, were the basis upon which the subsequent influential Canadian materials on «gender and translation» were constructed, by a core group of perhaps ten to fifteen women — professors, writers and translators over a period of about twenty years.

There are at least four Canadians known outside Canada for their work on gender in translation, and they have in many ways defined the field. The earliest writer on the topic is Barbara Godard, followed by Susanne de Lotbinière-Harwood, Luise von Flotow, and Sherry Simon. The publication of Luise von Flotow's book *Translation and Gender: Translating in the 'Era of Feminism'*, only a year after Sherry Simon's *Gender in Translation*, confirms the leading role Canadians play in feminist translation studies.

Among the most recognized Canadian women who currently translate into English and French for Canadian audiences are: Arielle Aaronson, Oana Avasilichioaei, Sheila Fischman (a literary translator for almost three decades), Linda Gaboriau (playwright and translator), Katia Grubisic, Catherine Leroux, Erin Mouré (perhaps Canada's most famous poet/translator), Rhonda Mullins, Christelle Morelli and Susan Ouriou, Chantal Ringuet, Sherry Simon, Aimee Wall and Melissa Bull.

However, although faithful to its fundamental nature, 21st century feminism has evolved into a more comprehensive movement, concerning the wide range of scenarios where women's voices are heard nowadays. In the field of translation, according to Brufao, N. (2011), 21st century feminism, which is mirrored by contemporary feminist translation theory and practice, is closely related to cultural and identity issues in an almost political battle to transport the political claims of women and/or minorities. On the other hand, it tries to incorporate the linguistic techniques resulting from the connection between language and power as studied in the last decades of the past century. In this sense, feminist translation does not focus exclusively on words, but also on discourses, ideologies and identities texts can normalize, legitimize or build.

Legitimizing gender-inclusive writing

Women tend "to not feel involved, to see themselves ignored", claims Dumais, H. (1992), when a text does not acknowledge their presence. About thirty years ago, the Canadian Classification and Dictionary of Occupations was feminized[2]. When the Prime Minister of Canada addresses the public, he commonly uses the doublet "*les Canadiens et les*

[2] *La féminisation au gouvernement de l'Ontario*, version corrigée, Government Translation Service, Toronto, 2003

Canadiennes" (masculine and feminine forms of "Canadians"). However, to properly refer to both genders in writing, you have to go even further since it is necessary to express the presence of women throughout the text, and that is the goal of gender-inclusive writing.

According to *Avoir bon genre à l'écrit: guide de rédaction épicène* by Pierrette Vachon-L'Heureux and Louise Guénette (2006), gender-inclusive writing.

> Describes a writing technique or text that equitably highlights the presence of women and men. That presence is expressed through the use of words that refer to women and men alike (i.e. through neutral constructions) or that specifically talk about both women and men

A number of Canadian institutions have gender-inclusive writing policies or guides. In 1995, the Government of Canada, in its Federal Plan for Gender Equality committed to "*adopter une terminologie uniforme sensibilisée au sexisme dans toute l'administration fédérale*". The Government Communications Policy of 1996 went even further by requiring federal institutions to "pursue fair communications practices by avoiding sexual stereotyping in their communications, by ensuring representative depiction of all members of Canadian society". The writing guide published by the Translation Bureau that same year suggested several techniques for feminizing texts, stressing the optional nature of feminization.

However, text feminization cannot be optional, given the goal of gender equality that the Government of Canada has set for itself. There cannot be equality without visibility; in other words, we must ensure that both genders are represented equitably in our writing and can identify themselves[3].

By ensuring that both genders are visible, gender-inclusive writing contributes to gender-based analysis, which the government first undertook to implement in 1995, and for which it renewed its commitment in 2009.

Thus, following inclusive language recommendations does not only imply linguistic challenges but also social ones in a highly politicized context (Brufao, N. 2011). With such developments in one given linguistic community, adequate translation strategy could be seen as necessary in order to transmit this rejection of patriarchal language to all members of an intercultural, bilingual environment such as Canada.

'O Canada': towards gender neutral translation

'O Canada' was originally written in French. Quebecois judge Robert Stanley Weir wrote in 1908 another English version, which is the official and most popular version, one that

---

[3] *Fair Representation of the Genders in French: Gender-inclusive Writing* at Status of Women Canada, 2011

is not a literal translation of the French. As the two languages do not share the same features, a direct transference may be considered problematic, and therefore certain translation strategies might had seemed justified. Weir's lyrics have been revised three times, taking their present form in 2018, but the French lyrics remain unaltered.

Interestingly, 'O Canada' actually started out as a gender-neutral song. According to The New York Times[4], the second line was originally "True patriot love thou dost in us command." In one of the updates that dates back to before World War I, Weir, a poet also, added the line that later brought about so much debate He changed "thou dost in us command" to "in all thy sons command." The French-language version of the anthem, which uses different lyrics than its Anglophonic counterpart, is already gender-neutral, however.

French version	**English version**
O Canada! Terre de nos aïeux,	O Canada!
Ton front est ceint de fleurons glorieux	Our home and native land!
Car ton bras sait porter l'épée,	True patriot love in all thy sons command.
Il sait porter la croix! –	With glowing hearts we see thee rise,
Ton histoire est une epopee	The True North strong and free!
Des plus brillants exploits.	From far and wide,
Et ta valeur, de foi trempée,	O Canada, we stand on guard for thee.
Protégera nos foyers et nos droits.	God keep our land glorious and free!
Protégera nos foyers et nos droits.	O Canada, we stand on guard for thee.
	O Canada, we stand on guard for thee.

According to the CBC[5], "Since 1980, when 'O Canada' officially became the country's anthem, 12 bills have been introduced in the House to strip the gendered reference to 'sons,' which some have argued is discriminatory." In June 1990, the Toronto City Council voted for the same change as C-210. In 2002, Senator Vivienne Poy introduced a bill to change "in all thy sons command" to "in all of us command." In 2010, Governor General Michaelle Jean spoke from the throne and announced a plan to have the parliament review the lyrics, but a poll showed three-quarters of Canadians objected, prompting the Canadian Cabinet to abandon the plan.

---

[4] https://www.nytimes.com/2018/02/01/world/canada/o-canada-lyrics-gender-neutral-.html

[5] http://www.cbc.ca/news/politics/anthem-bill-passes-senate-1.4513317

The idea began to gain traction in 2013 after a group of prominent Canadian women, including author Margaret Atwood[6] and former Prime Minister Kim Campbell, took on the issue. They argued that the anthem had once been gender neutral – using the phrase "thou dost in us command" – but had been changed to include the word sons in 1913. "Restoring these lyrics to gender-neutral is not only an easy fix to make our anthem inclusive for all Canadians, but it's also long overdue," Atwood said at the time, reported The Star[7].

Former member of the Canadian House of Commons Mauril Bélanger first introduced the legislation in 2016. Final passage of the bill came after an emotionally powerful appearance[8] by Mauril Belanger. Belanger was diagnosed with Lou Gehrig's disease shortly after his re-election and his condition rapidly deteriorated. Following Parliamentary rules that require a bill's author to be present ahead of its final vote, Belanger showed up to see it completed. Once in the chamber, he received a standing ovation from his fellow MPs. Bélanger died in 2016, without having seen his dream of a gender neutral Canadian anthem come true.

The Canadian House of Commons overwhelmingly passed Bill C-210 by a vote of 225 to 74, modifying the third line of "O Canada" to incorporate gender-neutral phrasing. Next, the bill headed to the Canadian Senate where senators were expected to approve it, according to CBC News[9].

Shortly after the bill received the approval of the Senate, it also received royal assent on February 7, and was signed into law by the Governor General's secretary, Assunta Di Lorenzo, as Gov.-Gen. Julie Payette was in South Korea ahead of the Olympic opening ceremonies.

In this regard, Heritage Minister Mélanie Joly said that the line "in all thy sons command" had now been officially replaced with "in all of us command." Referring to Mauril Bélanger's dream, she told reporters that "His long advocacy for the subject has actually changed the course of our history. Now, women across this country will be well-reflected in their own national anthem"[10].

Joly also explained that she had instructed officials in her department to change the lyrics on the government's website and alter materials the federal government distributes to schools. Although no new money would be made available to promote the change, existing departmental funds would be repurposed to make the public aware of the new lyrics.

Members of Parliament traditionally sing the national anthem each Wednesday before the start of business, and they broke into applause after singing the updated

[6] https://www.theguardian.com/books/2018/jan/15/margaret-atwood-feminists

[7] https://www.thestar.com/news/canada/2013/10/01/margaret_atwood_joins_call_to_restore-_o_canada_to_genderneutral_version.html

[8] http://www.cbc.ca/news/politics/mauril-belanger-als-c210-report-stage-friday-1.3628655

[9] http://www.cbc.ca/news/politics/belanger-o-canada-gender-lyrics-bill-1.3636348

[10] Ibidem 9

version in the House of Commons a few hours after the bill received royal assent. Canadian Olympians in Pyeongchang also sang the altered version of the song since the flag-raising ceremony at the athletes' village.

Canada's Prime Minister, Justin Trudeau, has made gender inclusivity a focus since he was elected and named an equal number of men and women to his 30-member cabinet[11]. It was the first time gender parity had been achieved by Canada's team of ministers. Trudeau himself voiced his support of the proposed change after it passed the Senate, when he tweeted:

"Mauril's bill to make O Canada gender neutral passed third reading in the Senate tonight – another positive step towards gender equality. #inallofuscommand" [12]

"I'm very, very happy. There's been 30 years plus of activity trying to make our national anthem, this important thing about our country, inclusive of all of us," Ontario Sen. Frances Lankin said, CBC News[13] reported. "I'm proud to be part of the group that made this happen." "This may be small – it's about two words – but it's huge in terms of one of our major national symbols. It's inclusivity and I'm proud", Lankin stated to CBC News. Margaret Atwood also expressed her delight[14] on Twitter over the bill's passage.

Not everyone was happy with the change, however. The Canadian Press reported that the far-right website The Rebel launched a petition to "save 'O Canada'," asking supporters to help it commission a public-opinion poll into whether Canadians approve of the change. Other Conservative senators and lawmakers don't think Canada's Parliament should be allowed to alter a song whose words were written many years ago and whose author has been dead for so long.

Lawmakers were angry that Sen. Don Plett, who was a long time critic of the measure, didn't have an opportunity to speak against the motion. Conservative Manitoba Sen. Don Plett, thought the new lyrics should have been put to the people in a referendum.

At the same time, Conservative Member of Parliament Bob Saroya argued that some things just shouldn't change, referring to the national anthem, while Conservative Leader Andrew Scheer speaking to reporters said he was "disappointed" by how the government went about changing the lyrics to 'O Canada'. Scheer voted against Bélanger's bill in the House of Commons. Other Tory senators like Leo Housakos showed his discontent with the news and called for a more democratic Parliament, open to debate.

A text, be it an original or a translation, which has been written using inclusive language can be approved or rejected by readers due to the direct link to a specific political ideology, in addition to being classified according to what the general public

[11] https://www.theguardian.com/world/2015/nov/04/canada-cabinet-gender-diversity-justin-trudeau

[12] Ibidem 5

[13] Ibidem 5

[14] https://twitter.com/MargaretAtwood/status/958979864345923584

thinks of feminism in that particular moment. (Brufao, N. 2011) Notwithstanding opposition, Canada's national anthem no longer excludes half the country's population.

Conclusions

Gender is without doubt a cultural construction, but first of all it is conveyed through language. The social and political circumstances supporting the intense focus both on gender and on translation in Canada in the 1970s and the 1980s consolidated the sector of women's writing/feminist writing and translation, both sharing areas of mutual interest.

In a democratic framework, only policies aimed at the inclusion and participation of all citizens are guarantees of social cohesion, lasting peace and the vitality of civil society. Parallel to the gradual process of legitimization of gender-inclusive writing, the moves to make Canada's national anthem gender neutral had been in the works for more than two decades.

Through the introduction of twelve bills in the House and public campaigning, Canadians tried to change the English version of 'O Canada', in order to remove the words "in all thy sons command" and replace them with "in all of us command". Last February, when Canada's national anthem finally became gender neutral, decades of long push to ensure the English language version reflects all Canadians were brought to an end.

References

— *(2018) Gender-Neutral Writing: The Pronoun Problem. Public Works and Government Services Canada, The Government of Canada's terminology and linguistic data bank. Writing tools –Peck's English Pointers*

— Government Communications Policy (1996) Treasury Board Secretariat, Canada. Accessed at http://www.tbs-sct.gc.ca/archives/sipubs/communication/1996/commun01-eng.asp on 4/02/18

— *Oxford Living Dictionaries (2018) Oxford University Press*

— Status of Women Canada (1995). À l'aube du XXIe siècle: Plan fédéral pour l'égalité entre les sexes (Web site not available in English), Ottawa. Published in English under the title Setting the Stage for the Next Century: The Federal Plan for Gender Equality. Accessed at http://publications.gc.ca/collections/Collection/SW21-15-1995F.pdf on 10/02/18

Baider F., Khaznadar, E., Moreau, T. (2007) "Les enjeux de la parité linguistique" , in Nouvelles questions féministes

Brufau, N. (2011) Translation and Gender: The State of the Art in Spain. University Alfonso X el Sabio

Castro, O. (2013) Introduction: Gender, language and translation at the crossroads of disciplines. EQUINOX PUBLISHING

Chamberlain, L. *(1998). Gender Metaphorics in Translation. In M. backer (Ed.) Encyclopedia of Translation Studies (pp. 93-96). London: Routledge*

Dumais, H. (1992) Pour un genre à part entière (Web site not available in English), Recherches féministes, vol. 5, n° 1. Accessed at http://www.erudit.org/reuve/rf/1992/v5/n1/057679ar.pdf on 8/02/18

Flotow, *L von (2011) Contested Gender in Translation: Intersectionality and Metramorphics , Palimpsestes Accessed at http://journals.openedition.org/palimpsestes/211 on 8/02/18*

Flotow, L. von (1991) 'Feminist Translation: Contexts, Practices, Theories', TTR 4(2): 69-84

Flotow, L. von (1997) Translation and Gender: Translating in the 'Era of Feminism', Manchester: St Jerome Publishing

Flotow, L. von (2006) Feminism in Translation: the Canadian Factor Quaderns. Revista de traducción 13

Godard, B. (1990) 'Theorizing Feminist Discourse/Translation' in Bassnett, S. & Lefevere, A. (eds) Translation, History, Culture, London: Pinter Publishers. Cited in Flotow, L. von (1999) 'Genders and the translated text: Developments in 'transformance'', Textus n°2, 1999. Accessed at: http://www.tilgher.it/textusart_flotow.html on 10/02/18

James, K. (2011) 'Speaking in the Feminine':Considerations for Gender-Sensitive Translation .Translation Journal and the Author Accessed at: http://translationjournal.net/journal/56feminine.htm on 4/02/18

Karoubi, B. ( ) Gender and Translation. Islamic Azad University, Tafresh, Iran.

Palusci, O. ed., (2010) Traduttrici. Questioni di gender nella letteratura in lingua inglese, Napoli: Liguori

Romaine, S. (1999) Communicating Gender. London: Lawrence Erlbaum Associates, Publishers

Talbot, M. (2003). Gender Stereotypes: Reproduction and challenge. In J. Holmes & M. Meyerhoff (Ed.) The Handbook of Language and Gender. (pp. 468-86). Oxford: Blackwell Publishing

Vachon-L'Heureux, P., Guénette, L. (2006) Avoir bon genre à l'écrit: guide de rédaction epicene. Office québécois de la langue française, Québec, Les Publications du Québec

Invincibility of Poetry.
A Review on Don Gutteridge's
Invincible Ink (Hidden Brook Press, 2020)

MSc Miguel Ángel Olivé Iglesias. Associate Professor, Author, Poet, Editor, Reviewer

We said goodbye to 2020 with one more Hidden Brook Press publication, Don Gutteridge´s *Invincible Ink*. This is a 111-poem volume loyal to the themes and style that have made Gutteride one of the best poets in the Canadian poetdom.

The first poem, "Litmus," honors the craft of composing a poem. The poet states fluently, tastefully, what poetry writing is all about. I do not see an attempt to limit its definition; it is rather a preamble, comprehensive one, to what each individual may feel. It gives us open territory to roam free after "*the brink of begetting.*"

Nonetheless, there is a statement in the poem which may well be a definitive reference when it comes to declaring the urges, aesthetics and boundless realms of poetry, "*for a poem, ancient / or newly honed, is really / a surging of the soul towards / the litmus of light or the mind.*"

These are epigrammatic lines. Whatever we pursue poetically can be sparked by reading them. Let´s enjoy excerpts:

> The urge to pen a poem
> is as old as the lullaby sung
> to ease the sleep of a fretting
> child…
> or a
> soliciting psalm to the setting
> sun, for a poem…
> is really
> a surging of the soul towards
> the litmus of light or the mind
> on the brink of begetting: words
> stirred afoot, seasoned
> with invincible ink.

Nature will never part from Canadian poets. The next poem I present bathes in it, finds nourishment in beauty and the cycle of seasons, motifs we discern in all five gems I have discussed in this book. "Wintering" is a seasonal passage as the poet moves slowly, in detail, across seasons. Nothing escapes him. Even in the leaf´s grief, "*Bereaved of its leaves, this / maple in my fallen yard / stares bare-boned / into a sky,*" Gutteridge acknowledges the power of nature, of the earth´s renovating magic. This faith can only endure in the poet´s reassurance of life´s constant renewal *(excerpt)*:

… and in this time
of fallowed fields and the fringing
of frosts, we trust in the Earth's
rebirth, when bulbs bulge
with soon-to-be blooms
and robins throb with the nurturing
need and April rains
seize the sleeping seed
and waken it whole to the world…

The same feeling pulsates in "Wings," the poet´s necessary shelter in tomorrow:

Outside my window
the trees are de-leafing,
there is an autumnal hum
to the wind and all things
summer come undone,
and though I have no heart
for what Winter brings,
I remain steadfast
in my belief that Spring will glide
into bloom on welcoming wings.

The elegance and tenderness we enjoy in Gutteridge´s heartfelt poems overwhelms us when we read "Furious Felicity." The title hints two expressive means of the language, alliteration and oxymoron. Gutteridge has been showing his skilled employment of these and other means throughout his work. The repetition of the consonant "f" echoes classic poems of yore (Poe´s "The Raven," for example, "*For the rare and radiant maiden…*" (the "r" recurrence).

But the title also carries a basic opposition of meaning between the noun-modifier, "Furious," and the noun "Felicity." This semantic-stylistic clash is noticeable in the poem´s mood. Above all, we sigh with the profound sensitiveness and melancholy the poet words in his oniric dialogue with his beloved one. While we perceive grief and bits of irony, they never outshine the intimacy and love flowing across the lines. Let´s have fragments from this heart-touching piece:

> I wake in your arms once
> Again…
> and even though I know
> I'm dreaming, I hug you
> … and I want to tell you
> there are gods that keep us
> from harm's way…
> and that love
> with its furious felicity redeems
> us all, but that would be
> a luxurious lie, for such
> deities let me love
> and you, die.

As I have said about poetry reading, for feedback and spirituality we must always go to the classics. Don Gutteridge is one of them. *Invincible Ink* is indelible.

A Memorable Encounter with Three Poems by A.F. Moritz in *The Sparrow*. House of Anansi Press Inc. (2018)

MSc Miguel Ángel Olivé Iglesias. Associate Professor, Author, Poet, Editor, Reviewer

The significance of poetry and poets has been defined by many authors and scholars. Shakespeare told us in his Sonnet XVIII that what we pour down on a sheet of paper remains eternal: "When in eternal lines to time thou grow'st, / So long as men can breathe, or eyes can see, / So long lives this, and this gives life to thee." *(Taken from Complete Works of William Shakespeare, Volume XVIII, Philadelphia David McKay, Publisher, no year)*. Pablo Neruda, the great Latin American icon, saw the duties of poetry in the form of feeling for and with others: "Mis deberes caminan con mi canto: / soy y no soy: es ése mi destino. / No soy si no acompaño los dolores / de los que sufren: son dolores míos. / Porque no puedo ser sin ser de todos, / de todos los callados y oprimidos, / vengo del pueblo y canto para el pueblo: / mi poesía es cántico y castigo. *(Taken from Neruda, 2004) ("My duties tread side by side with my song: / I am and I am not: such is my destiny. / I am not if I don't walk beside the pain / of the suffering: that is my pain too. / Because I cannot be if I do not belong to them all, / the silent and the downtrodden, / I come from the people and sing for the people: / my poetry is canticle and punishment.")*

Canadian poet Hugh Hazelton "believes that poetry should bite, caress, laugh at, confront, lament, name, envision, remember, invoke, oppose, and reflect." *(Taken from Bridges Series Book II, Concave Mirrors. SandCrab Books, 2013)* Sainte-Marie energetically states "The job of a poet is to get information across in a way that's effective in making change." *(Taken from Tamaracks: Canadian Poetry for the 21st Century, Lummox Press, 2018. Introduction by the Editor. The Editor refers the reader to Reader's Digest Volume 191 Number 1,144 (November 2017). Page 38. Print).*

Eva Kolacz in her poem Life, Part 1 *(Taken from What We Are. Hidden Brook Press, 2019)* tells us poets can define and change time, life: "Change becomes us—someone said. / The beginning leaves time behind. / This is what poet & mystic can define / effortlessly." Don Gutteridge in his poem "Letters" *(Taken from Point Taken. Hidden Brook Press, 2019)* speaks of transcendence through poetry, seconding Shakespeare in their approach: "I try again to catch / that fleeting face in the prism / of a poem / in the serendipity of a simile, // knowing that he will survive / as long as these letters / linger and thrive."

Malca Litovitz said: "… the human soul needs poetry and that it will always be around and that it serves a real function in our psyche." *(Taken from Slow Dancing, Guernica Editions, 2008)*. Elana Wolff has said that "a poem is not only a form of self-expression, it is the writer's way of bearing witness to the world in which he or she lives…" *(Taken from Implicate me, Guernica Editions, 2010)*

John B. Lee has said: "I want the heart to feel true sentiment… the body to come alive… the soul to thrill… and the spirit to surround and be surrounded." *(Quoted from memory)*

James Deahl posits: "Poetry was something that could not only speak to the issues and concerns of one's own life but could operate as a tool to allow the poet to discover an organizing principle outside of day-to-day human life…" *(Taken from Under the Watchful Eye, Broken Jaw Press, 1995)*, Wilfred Owen, cited by Terry Barker, states: "All a poet can do today is warn… That is why the true poets must be truthful." *(Taken from After Acorn. Meditations on the Message of Canada's People's Poet. Mekler and Deahl Publishers, 1999)*, and Michael Ondaatje stated: "… most crucial duties of a poet: to map and to name" *(Taken from The Ambassador 015, 2018)*

I have traveled across all these names and quotations paving the way to write about Canadian poet A. F. Moritz. He referred to a poet's "job" in an interview as "To write well: creatively, authentically, powerfully, beautifully…. poetry is partly self-development… is duty, belonging to a community… poetry's role is as the guardian and developer of language." *(Taken from an interview on the Web)*

In talks with Richard Grove (Tai) and James Deahl, they have always been emphatic on my approaching Moritz. Both have said he is a figure I cannot overlook in a review book. James has stressed on the fact that any poetry anthology must have his poems. Therefore, I chose to search in his latest book, *The Sparrow*, for some especially appealing poems to my humble reviewer eyes.

A. F. Moritz has been called "one of the best poets of his generation" by John Hollander and "a true poet" by Harold Bloom. He has received numerous awards and honors in North America: the Award in Literature of the American Academy of Arts and Letters, the Guggenheim Fellowship, Poetry magazine's Beth Hokin Prize, the Ingram Merrill Fellowship, and the Griffin Poetry Prize.

One of the book's back-cover comments refers to *The Sparrow: Selected Poems of A. F. Moritz* as a book that "surveys forty-five years of Moritz's published poems, from earlier, lesser-known pieces to the widely acclaimed works of the last twenty years. Here are poems of mystery and imagination; of identification with the other; of compassion, judgement, and rage; of love and eroticism; of mature philosophical, sociological, and political analysis; of history and current events; of contemplation of nature; of exaltation and ennui, fullness and emptiness, and the pure succession and splendour of earthly nights and days… *The Sparrow* is more than a selected poems; it is also a single vast poem, in which the individual pieces can be read as facets of an ever-moving whole. This is the world of A. F. Moritz — a unique combination of lyrical fire and meditative depth, and an imaginative renewal of style and never-ending discovery of form."

In this context of highly valued appreciation of the acclaimed author, I assumed a huge undertaking: selecting poems that would embody – from my perspective – Moritz's powerful style and make me vibrate. Reducing the analysis to a few poems seemed a futile challenge for a mentally-deranged reviewer; his work is vast and classic in many respects.

However, when I started reading, it fortunately dawned on me that *any* poem I picked would suffice to illustrate the poet's greatness. That is how I came to "Shade," "Morning Fragments" and "In the Dead of Night Only."

On the book's back cover, John Ashbury says that "we seem to hear shattered echoes from the Bible…" I was also privileged to hear other voices. I began my review by quoting Shakespeare. How serendipitous I was initially drawn to "Shade," our first piece. Moritz's technique flies, like a sparrow, in a polished range of multi-styles held in *his* concentrated style. The Toronto Star recognizes it as "polished turns of phrase and fluid cadences." *(Taken from the book's back cover)*; integrating an encompassing gamut of influences and flowing trajectories.

Here the poet introduces the reader into beauty and fantasy, hazy realms and visual-mental explorations: "Before you were born, summer's beauty died. / Now at times it brushes you / with its abstract wing." I pick a brave, ingenious variation from Shakespeare's Sonnet XVIII, "Shall I compare thee to a summer's day? / Thou art more lovely and more temperate… / And summer's lease hath all too short a date… / But thy eternal summer shall not fade…" *(Taken from Complete Works of William Shakespeare, Volume XVIII, Philadelphia David McKay, Publisher, no year)*

Moritz creatively eases from a second stanza describing metaphorical-concrete realities altogether: "The sounds of the beautiful ideas… / sit looking down through mist / at leaves... / and on both sides of the window the water / slowly condenses and rolls earthward" into the third one, where more figurative, imaginary proposals are unleashed: "… a thought of time dwelling in a timeless place / will fall, if a tree dares to dash across the sun. / A blow of shadow strikes your sleep in whitened light."

The next stanza is the meditative poet, caught up in the endless, fathomless well of time, asking the questions so many poets ask themselves *(Read, for example, my analyses on Eva Kolacz in this review book, or about Al Purdy's and Milton Acorn's musings on the same theme, in my previous review book In a Fragile Moment: A Landscape of Canadian Poetry, Hidden Brook Press, 2020. You can also read Henry Beissel's Fugitive Horizons, Guernica Editions, 2013)*, inquiring about existence, this enigma we were headlong-born to: "Again the image: days passing beneath oaks / to nothing but further days, further knowledge / of the sky held in fingered leaves: / it empties you into confusion." Is it a poet lanced by pessimism? Or should we rather discern an inquisitive man probing the entrails of living? His wise choice of language remains unaltered, metaphor-charged: "days passing beneath oaks," "sky held in fingered leaves."

The finale tends towards a possible calibration of events and states of mind, of attempts at charting one's cosmic bearings, physically and mentally – bodily and psychologically: "And that ancient being, you, sole citizen / of the shadow, waits, echoing with muted light; / alone, cannot pronounce itself alone / expecting someone, expecting pleasure…"

The last line reminds us of Shakespeare's Sonnet XVIII, "Nor shall death brag thou wander'st in his shade" again *(Taken from Complete Works of William Shakespeare, Volume XVIII, Philadelphia David McKay Publisher, no year)*, to give us a Moritz whose resourcefulness renders an imaginative deflection in his own poem: "nor shall you brag it wanders in death's shade." Two transcendental poets addressing similar issues.

Still focused on the marvel of life and time, Moritz displays more captivating images in his poem "Morning Fragments." This particularly philosophical poem brought to me the work of another iconic contemporary poet, John B. Lee, his poem "Morning Expectation": "hope's expectations of longer days / birds will soon return / insects waking / life's cycle renewed / in this morning of change…" *(Taken from Two Thousand Seventeen, Sanbun Publishers, 2018, New Delhi)*

In his poem, Moritz targets morning in *tropeful* insinuations of how it slowly glides in, the morning theme being an excuse to ponder over deeper questions: "And the morning fragments, / growing visible, seem to rebuild themselves / out of twilight, mildew, and melancholy / towards an edifice still darkened in you…" Somehow the poet invites to the search for answers, or provides them after posing firstly rhetorical questions: "And were you here yesterday already?... were you following / faint prints of a day before?"

Then the answers, cosmic, as I said before, delving into and out of doubt, a point made by the use of the conditional *if* (there is no *absolute* certainty): "You will know at last if the sun ages / or is created every dawn / out of nothing at the surface of the sea. / You will know if this dayspring is eternal / or lies on a heap of others, / a page just turned, reversing all."

Through his poetry, Moritz leads the reader to a fumbling limp towards an ultimate truth – if there is one. He places layer *after* layer, layer *beside* layer, layer *against* layer, of denotations and connotations of meanings that flit among syntactically engineered word-loops. Take this example: "And meanwhile night has sunk as a hedge / sinks into distance as you walk away. / Voices were making explanation behind it, / something you might have understood, some secret / of a former life…"

You stumble from your present into "a former life" and fall back into uncertainty: "… so that now you will never know what was being said, / if something is lost forever, / or if much, happily, / is put behind you and forgotten." As much as poetry is an act of solitude, the final product evolves into a dialogue in this poem. The use of "you" very much assists in this.

The third poem I chose is "In the Dead of Night Only." The poem is a substantial, sustained metaphor, overlapping with another expressive means, personification. The first stanza's last line is illustrative of this: "… night exhausted, dawn not yet." The poet puts together the idea of color with the idea of feeling; he equates them with an accomplished symbolic treatment: "… a darkness blacker than the young night's / beautiful colour, known at last / now in nostalgia."

The last stanza is definitely surrealistic, a detail worthy of a Magritte or a Dali easel: "Then you recognize / the journey in which your bed is an evening's pause: / it's the house of this moment / in which the journey is a dream."

P. K. Page commented that "Some of [his] poems are… full of portent, with the gravity and power of myth." *(Read the book's back cover)* and the Toronto Star deemed them "… subtle, far-reaching… spiritually revitalizing." *(Idem previous reference)*. I will finish by returning to Moritz's own criterion on how poems must be written: creatively, authentically, powerfully, beautifully." His forty-five-year fertility in poetic production has honored that principle and made the poet transcend in content and form, in time and space. Quite a contribution.

An Essay on Elana Wolff's Poem "Sidewise" in *Swoon* Guernica Editions (2020)

MSc Miguel Ángel Olivé Iglesias. Associate Professor, Author, Poet, Editor, Reviewer

You can know and get to admire poets reading one single poem, or you can follow up on their evolution and maturity when you are privileged to have a collection of their craft spanning decades. In Elana Wolff I enjoy all privileges: her first-step poetry, with *Birdheart* from 2001, her progression, and her latest book, *Swoon*, which will be published in 2020: almost two decades of fine poems. Today I would like to talk about "Sidewise," one of the poems from *Swoon.*

I have pleasantly seen Elana remain faithful to a syntactical arrangement, sometimes longer, sometimes shorter proposals, which has become her signature and object of interest for the reader's attention. The way she handles sentences, allowing enjambment, stanza breaks or continuity to pause/flow creating stylistic effects – plus visual amusement once you ease into it – tells us we are witnessing a sustained poetic style evidential of the map of thoughts, involvement, insights, meanings, feelings, subtleties, pain, fears, teachings – and learning – urging the poet's turmoil of visualization: observant, keen poet eyes and active mind in full poetic labour.

Formidable succinctness of expression is captured in her poem. Heiress of Emily Dickinson, Elana juggles with detached construction, cliff-hanging sentence structure, variation, conciseness and precision, elliptical explorations, meanings and messages veiled and demanding. In a review of her poetry, I said her poems "have a superbly distinct Emily Dickinson flavor in brevity and compactness, both in the rendering of the full poem and in the closing lines. In her capacity to pour out so much swirling inside her and do it with graceful briefness, lies one of Elana's many gifts as a poet." "Sidewise" is no exception to those elements – to rhythms, sudden turns, vertigo, shortcuts and sleight-of-hand skills she displays so comfortably when writing. Let's read below:

"Parts of a poem kept knocking along
my thoughts

            like a cart on a slope. Spinning,
quiv'ring, veering over"

The act of creation is apparent in the poet's disposition of the first sentence. It is not her thoughts shaping up poetry; it is the other way around: "Parts of a poem… knocking along (her) thoughts": reality troops in, the poet is but the vessel that tries to contain it, but it overflows in a million codes. Then the rest of the psychological sentence with the break in sentences appealing to the senses and serving the meanings she wants to convey.

Notice the abrupt halt after "my thoughts," a full blank-space line down – a void – conjuring a sensation of falling, unsteadiness anticipatory to the precipitous "like a cart on a slope." The poet accentuates this notion through words denoting spiral-like meanings: Spinning, / quiv'ring, veering over." Here we have a truly engaged poet who sees beauty (a leitmotif in her pieces) and inspiration in what exists outside her but connects to her trains of thought. How Elana beholds a particular, everyday object and elevates it to a transcendental status transpires in the poem: "Remarkable yet ordinary— / glass in a wooden casement. / One I have in mind is sitting, looking inside out…"

The first sentence provides the significance of the object for her ("the glass"). However "ordinary" – placed second in the sentence – it may be; its "Remarkable" impression appears foremost. That is how the poet sees it, how the poet *sees* things from her gifted perspective. Lines three and four fan out for us the poet's mental bearings and a class-one metaphor: "lapidary shadows." The poet moves to lines five and six, introducing touch ("Handy how it let itself be tapped") to enter the realm of sound: "… the clarion quality glass has," and metaphorically contributory (personification) in empowering glass with will ("let itself be tapped").

After this comes the creative upsurge discussed in the lines analyzed at the beginning; later we are offered the likening of object and bird (nature always present in her poetry), gravitas implied in both, and finally a proclamation dénouement, "Only a poet can pen like this: // heart & hand commanding contradiction. / I'm trembling before such sweetness & disruption; I touch them…" This last sentence builds on the idea of touch: gentle/passionate/enigmatic, as a poem can be; deep and utter, as an implication can sweep her away and make her quiver.

Stylistically speaking, the line "I'm trembling before such sweetness & disruption" is worth looking at, as antithesis clinks in it – or flaps wings! The two words put together strike me as a feeling of both wish to approach (sweetness) and step away from (disruption). That seems to be, indeed, the poet's state of mind, that ambivalence she is experiencing yet cannot shake off.

Carried away by the torrent of excitement overwhelming her, a throbbing Elana plunges into the act of writing the poem with "heart & hand commanding contradiction." Such heart-hand conflict cautions her to be wary not to let her poet brittleness overshow, or her sensitiveness trespass: "I touch them // with as little fondness as possible. Not to seem too see-through, / too invested." One element to bring to analysis is that glass does reflect – might the poet see herself (and her life) mirrored in the window, being such torrential harvest a result of that impression? After all, it all happens *sidewise*… Enjoy the poem. It will positively tilt your world-view.

A Review of

Kimberley Sherman Grove's Poetics

MSc Miguel Ángel Olivé Iglesias. Associate Professor, Author, Poet, Editor, Reviewer

One read of Kimberley Sherman Grove´s poetry was all it took to captivate me and stir clear-cut images in my mind. I instantly called her "The Lady of the Video-words." Talking to her was also an experience to cherish. The woman and the poet are one. She has an aura of sweetness and calmness that envelops you. I said: "*Kim is a gentle Canadian flower, sweet, calm, knowledgeable. She pays attention to your words with committed, welcoming eyes that give you peace and make you feel so comfortable.*"

She lives with her husband, Richard Marvin Grove (Tai) on the shore of Lake Ontario in Presqu'ile Provincial Park, where they run a bed and breakfast for artists, writers and birders. The park is a great influence on her perception of the Canadian landscape. She walks out her back door into her poetry. I was lucky to read a collection of her poems, *The Poetry of Kim Grove*, compiled for the Canada Cuba Literary Alliance Cultural Festival in Santiago de Cuba in January-February 2010.

What I perceived was poetry as an extension of Kim's sensitive heart. She chooses her words carefully and holds them as a painter does with a brush: images spark out of it, flooding the reader's eyes. She is in love with nature, a theme deeply rooted in Canadian writers, but there is also the human presence as a beholder, or as a component of the picture.

When you read Kim's poetry you can feel a serene pat on your shoulder that registers in your brain thanks to what she offers: snowflakes of silence and quiet or white-vapor scurry-offs, or muffled hoof and paw sounds. We watch idyllic landscape movies she gives birth to and gently taps into computer video-words.

In "Nature's Needlepoint" she plays with images and sounds: "*As the rumbling thunder like distant fireworks.*" Further below, Kim goes beyond by activating all senses: "*Bright yellow daffodils worship the sun, while lilacs perfume the air. Roses, lilies and tulips sew more colour into the fabric.*" Spring is personified, in an intimate harmony of poet and nature: "*She adds the hundreds of leaves that will crumple underfoot like worn paper bags. She applies some final touches, blowing away unnecessary edges or redoing ugly patches.*"

Nature is the protagonist. We also see the perfectionist in Kim Grove, the dreamer who can gild the view to ultimate exquisiteness. "Like worn paper bags" is a simile the poet handles so the reader, a stranger maybe, understands the natural wonders using a more "social" acoustic explanation, that of paper bags. Yet, Kim is not a stranger to her scenes; she is the messenger, the bridge that brings together nature and society. The tools are in her hands: she applies dabs across the canvas laid out before her: light slaps, gentle taps, fluorescent strokes that unfold the landscape for us, mesmerized "viewers."

In "White Menagerie," the poet takes pictures or videos the scenes: menagerie swaying with the gentle icicle breeze or posing photographically vulnerable to the poet's sensitiveness and sharp eye.

There are oozing shadows and damp fleeting noises in the movies that she wondrously edits and reedits so winter is no longer unknown to one's eyes. Kim has collected it in cozy glass igloos tenderly allowing the sleet to shower them with tidbits of frost that the reader feels. She marvels at the place she describes, and we marvel at the way she introduces her "explorer." She reaches up to kiss the man amidst a glorious setting, again the simile to fuse nature and society, "*Creaking like Styrofoam under our feet*," this time accompanied by onomatopoeia, "*creaking*."

"His Creativity" opens and closes with excellent lines. It is the apparently simple description of an intimate moment. It speaks between the lines of a gentle, sentient, valuing heart. "*His creativity was in a fragile moment*" is a euphemism that reveals the poet's state of mind.

The intricate, sometimes infinite paths of love are explored in "Falling in Love." The poet knows she will "*slip off this thing*" that is the red balloon of love, and complains she "*should have got off a long time ago*." But there she is, clinging to hope, to the experience, even in the dark notion that it all might take her to "*have to live on a far-off planet alone*." She is willing to take the risk anyway, so it seems.

Questions pop up: How and why did she get on the balloon in the first place? Isn't falling in love a human thing we must never give up, must strive for as many times as is necessary, and are entitled to?

In "Snow" the writer refocuses on one of her favorite motifs, nature. The poem stands on a simile: "*like huge eiderdown pillows*." I had already mentioned that Kim is able to translate into images what winter is. This poem continues the "didactic" endeavor of the poet, successfully. The "*illusion of sugar covering the earth*" reinforces my assumption of the sweetness in the poet´s heart and her penmanship to find the right words for the best of comparisons.

"The Challenge" is the endless battle of the mind and the physical part, the race against oneself, the test of natural instinct versus human psyche. Among the resources the poet wisely exploits are the expressive means of the language, turned into powerful stylistic devices: understatement ("*a small thumbnail of a toad*") repetition ("*I´d*" and "*Of how…*") skillfully handled to poke the readers´ capacity for patience, placing them in the poet's situation.

The poet defends the tranquility of the scene, the patience of the animal, as opposed to the "*rush of the city*," her own impatience, and leaves it to us readers to estimate how long she could really stand the test and check how many would turn and walk away.

One of the traits of Canadian literature is the observation of nature as a divine force that comes to us in splendid manners. Kim catches these manners and gives us a handful of images in motion.

Kimberley Grove sings to her Canada, that white Canada she sees from her cottage with an artist's eye. It is an array of images neatly, slowly, gently sketched; superb choice of words, divine success. The Lady of the Video-words has left us a gallery of images as impressive as the wondrous Canadian landscape they represent.

Comments on John Di Leonardo's *Conditions of Desire.* Hidden Brook Press (2018)

MSc Miguel Ángel Olivé Iglesias. Associate Professor, Author, Poet, Editor, Reviewer

In the weeks before the pandemic expansion of the virus scourging the world, the Canada Cuba Literary Alliance (CCLA) Founding President, Richard Grove, forwarded me a stock of first-rate books published by Hidden Brook Press (HBP), some of them under the John B. Lee Signature Series. To my honor and delight, many of the authors are poets I reviewed in my book *In a Fragile Moment: A Landscape of Canadian Poetry* (HBP, 2020) and in this second volume we are presenting now.

I wrote a new essay about one who was not in my previous book, John Tyndall, and proceeded to read John Di Leonardo, who was not either, drawn by the profound meaningfulness of their poetry. The more I read Di Leonardo, the more I saw distinct elements in the poet in manners that motivated me to review his book. John B. Lee´s introductory words to it were helpful in many points I will try to reveal here. In a sad context of sickness and death, culture comes to us to soothe our bodies, bring a bit of comfort to our souls and necessary hope to our lives.

I remember now, amidst so much pain and so many deaths, what I wrote for The Envoy 84 (CCLA digital newsletter), a month after the tragic airplane crash in Havana where many Cubans and foreigners lost their lives, "… we seek peace and enlightenment reading… poetry and prose… The deep riddles of life and death must be decrypted by looking for and holding on to spiritual healing, and sheltering in human sympathies and love… let´s try to turn then to less rending realms." *(Taken from The Envoy 084, June 2018).* Spiritual healing, human sympathy, hope and love is what we need. Faith, fortitude and *love in times of virus* (paraphrasing García Márquez´s book title, *Amor en los tiempos del cólera (Love in Times of Cholera)*) – is what we must find today to overcome this dark hour.

Di Leonardo offers his spirituality and aesthetics by exploring and evoking, unveiling and *connecting* in that sentient human drive to build, either with words or with images – or with the overlapping produce that results from blending both, as we have enjoyed in the works of John B. Lee and Richard Grove *(A Small Payback, Ode to Victoria Lake (Poetry and*

Photography) (2016) Hidden Brook Press, Canada), James Deahl and Richard Grove *(North of Belleville (Haiku and Photography) (2011) Hidden Brook Press, Canada)*, Stella Body and Robert Bateman *(Keeping the Earth Alive (Poetry and Art) (2005) Hidden Brook Press, Canada)*, the Bridges Series Books I, II, III, IV (Poetry and Art) (2011, 2013, 2017, 2018) by SandCrab Books, an imprint of Hidden Brook Press, etc.

However, Di Leonardo takes a novel step up: many poets do include in their poetry pieces inspired by paintings or other works of art but I had never read an entire book of poems dedicated to – or stemming from – them. He writes inspired by images, he turns into poetics *what was already poetry*, as he lets us know opening his book with a quotation from Simonides of Ceos: "Painting is silent poetry; poetry is painting that speaks."

Well-known Canadian poet and professor, Antony Di Nardo, has wisely looked into and shed light on this notion too: "I often consider poetry as a form of visual art painted with words. As varied as that world of art can be with paintings ranging from the representational to the abstract, so too poetry encompasses such variety. The surreal and the absurd in poetry can be as intellectually effective as a Dali or painting by Frida Kahlo. In my mind, Picasso's *Guernica* is an epic poem like no other, and there are poems by Ashbery I consider echoes of the finest cubist paintings. Such parallels are endless. The image often dominates a poem's aesthetics." *(Taken from Di Nardo´s review on a work-in-progress poetry book of mine, This Pulse of Life, These Words I Found)*

Thus Di Leonardo re-paints, in word form, the works of art he so admires. He engages in ingenious labor and materializes a second "reading" – that is, a re-construal of a reality that had been interpreted before by a visual artist – this time with words. While I read his poetry book, I was crossing readings of Joseph Gold´s *The Story Species*, where this author voices concerns clearly spelling for me that Di Leonardo grants an "extra salvation" to the paintings he writes about. Consider Gold´s question in his book: "Why is it that if a painting is burned, it is gone forever, but a poem… can be memorized intact, unaltered and transmittable as long as a human brain retains it?" *(Taken from Joseph Gold´s The Story Species, 2002, Fitzhenry and Whiteside. Canada)* I couldn't help thinking about K. V. Skene´s evocations of "all things beautiful and old / and otherworldly…" in her poem "Notre Dame de Paris Brûle" *(Published in The Envoy 088, June 2019 after the Notre Dame fire)*. I couldn't help thinking about the Alexandria Library fire…

Therefore, through highly emotional (the poet has been touched by the paintings) information transfer (visual/pictorial/graphic), Di Leonardo "saves" them via a re-perpetuation process. He is more than experienced to do so because he is a graduate of McMaster University, where he earned an Honorary BA in Fine Arts, taught Visual Arts for thirty years, and is an artist who divides his time between writing, painting, and travel. Being an artist *and* a poet, he becomes, fortunately for us, perfect vessel and "medium" enraptured by beauty/meaning/impact, aesthetic-cognitive-affective stimuli, absorbing a painting and returning it to us in another code.

His fascination is best measured when we read comments by Canadian poets Malca Litovitz and Elana Wolff: "You can only write from the depth of an emotion if you've been there." *(Taken from an interview made by Elana Wolff to her friend and poet Malca Litovitz, included in their book Slow Dancing (section Duologue). Guernica Editions, 2008)* and their competent decoding of what happens when we read/write poetry: "Malca Litovitz said: "… the human soul needs poetry and that it will always be around and that it serves a real function in our psyche." *(Taken from Slow Dancing, Guernica Editions, 2008).* Elana Wolff stated that "a poem is not only a form of self-expression, it is the writer's way of bearing witness to the world in which he or she lives…" *(Taken from Implicate me, Guernica Editions, 2010)*

Litovitz and Wolff stress on the role of emotions, of those emotions felt deeply by the individual, and how poetry is a necessary spiritual repository and "exhaust valve." Di Leonardo writes *after* the paintings with heartfelt surrender to their aesthetic and nurturing worth.

Ponder John B. Lee´s introductory words to Di Leonardo´s *Conditions of Desire*: "For what we experience, what we remember, what we dream, what we imagine, there is a language that reifies and makes real and true both original experience and the secondary experience of the poem as written," or Di Leonardo´s Preface to his own book citing Henry David Thoreau: "It is not what you look at, but what you see."

Yes, Di Leonardo saw word-stories streaming from the paintings he was looking at. He creatively re-transformed them into reified written text, not only letting us see through his own eyes the paintings we don´t have before ours but also unfolding the endless story-telling possibilities each art piece evokes and waxes as a new *dual* result.

At this point, let´s examine two poems by Di Leonardo for exemplification. "Conditions of Desire" (which entitles the book too), inspired by Alex Colville's "Refrigerator," acrylic, 1977, shows that duality of result I referred to earlier: we see the painting and the ensuing story Di Leonardo skillfully knits out of it. A fragment will suffice:

"When you are gone
I pace kitchen tiles, roam living room walls
hunger for the stars in your eyes
nibble self pity in the blue flicker of a fridge door.
Among cold things, I whisper your name
in the sweetness of morning jams, evening fruits
and the Atlantic that draws me towards you.
When you are away
I stalk the cell under cuticle moons
until its notes ring me a moonlight sonata.
I sleepwalk horizons, tip-toe a collage
of love's smallest details."

We also notice it in "Reproduction", inspired by Sandro Botticelli's "Birth of Venus," tempera, 1486:

"You linger
like a milk-skin model
on the largest shell
my best lit wall… //
… Your placid glaze will end
when the classical toes
step on shore
turn to good wife
The glow
below your torrent of hair
rose shower
makes us ashamed
for not making beds
clearing dishes
sipping morning coffee…"

John B. Lee asks in his introduction: "And how then might a poet hope to express something of the original in a parallel text when the medium of the original is paint and canvas and the medium of the poem is language written for contemplation on the page?" Of course Lee is not questioning the probability of attaining such feat (in fact, Di Leonardo did find the *expression fulcrum*); Lee is quite aware of that and is walking more on the wonder-thread he wishes to rhetorically make us see and walk on. I believe that the key word in Lee´s question is *contemplation.*

In both cases, painting and written poem, we pause for contemplation – defined in the dictionary in what is for me, more than just an enumeration of meanings, a sequence of brain processes: "looking at; thinking about; meditation, deep thought." *(Taken from Babylon, Digital Dictionary)* – in which hedonic-intellectual nexuses are sparkled through the eyes.

Yet the key answer lies probably in Di Leonardo´s own explanation in his Preface: "… elaborate description of the artwork… interpret, confront, inhabit, mediate, or simply use the visual elements as a springboard for the poet's imagination to take flight." Let´s cry *Eureka!* for Di Leonardo, who has succeeded in finding the "tools" needed to make the transference, tools which are duly sharpened by factors such as the poet´s preparation and sensitivity, the painting´s – and the painter´s – unique significance to him, and, voilà, the "conditions of desire" ignited to prompt the poet to write all these jewels.

The poems in the book transcend beyond the poet´s urge to put in words what was so indelibly suggestive and substantial to him, logical trigger and outcome if we consider his formative years as a visual artist and his poetic flair as well. They are in their own right fine pieces of poetry, superbly signed with well-thought-out expressive means and stylistic carvings.

Let´s visit four of them, beginning with the end lines of the previous poem, "Reproduction," where Di Leonardo embraces his acknowledgement of life´s richness and sighs about the mixed sensations stirred sentimentally, olfactorily – and figuratively in the end phrase, "the scent of land."

"… our lives reflecting
living warmth, the scent
of land"

"Tangoing," inspired by Fernando Botero's "Dancing Couple," oil, 1982, where we are swept by the exquisite depiction of "tango mood" and the atmosphere, elegantly heightened by metaphorical phrases. Enjoy the last stanza:

"… Should you smile
with every breathy pause
I will inhale such pirouettes of scented hair
our shadows swirl of daily cares
to measure time in scattered blooms
your moonlit eyes entranced
as each rose in bud awaits an autumn rain."

"Breakup," inspired by Salvador Dali's "Girl at Window," oil, 1925, where more imagery engulfs us and invites, sensually, through between-the-lines insinuations; word-stories hinted and masterfully elaborated upon by the poet, impressively reminiscent, as we read the whole poem, of Dali´s surrealistic brush:

"Stillness
leaning on a sill.
Your tousled hair
vocal with love
learns to wait
across a muted sea
where stirrings
aloud with song
are not depicted… //
… muzzy eyes
the palest stars //
yearn the moan
of a tender kiss
if not to live, at least
to whiten your silence"

"Nude," inspired by A. Maillol's "Île -de France," sculpture/Bronze, 1925, in which the poet innovatively gives us a pre-existing time, a pre-condition – a pre-story!, something/somewhere *that step comes from*! – by simply starting with "Then."

Let´s keep in mind that this particular poem comes not from a painting but from a sculpture, which adds a more "realistic" sensation, being a sculpture tridimensional. He magically blends two seemingly different, distant realities: human ("the softness of her step") and natural ("autumn leaves"). To work this out, he resorts to a simile: "transient *as* autumn leaves" (Italics are mine). The distant realities perception is sensed in the closing lines: "autumn leaves on sullen passersby." Let´s read the full poem:

"Then the softness of her step
turned bronze
transient as
autumn leaves
on sullen passersby"

Imbued with Di Leonardo´s mesmeric, accomplished poems I go back to my initial tenet in these comments, the distinct elements marking his work. The poet is able to intensely explore and passionately evoke, imaginatively unveil and concretely connect; he becomes a *double mediator* (from painting to poem, from poem to reader/indirect "spectator"); he confirms Ceos´s adage; he responds Lee´s questions; and he stands as a *sui generis* convinced curator of art by re-framing it into a new format as a symbolically salvaging act that reinforces the old say, *Ars Longa*, for poetry *too* is art represented in a parallel code system.

Furthermore, Di Leonardo brings us relief for Joseph Gold´s unsettling worries about paintings and poems, and bequeaths to us his legacy/understanding of painting from a broader perspective, which will last – allow me to cite Shakespeare´s Sonnet XVIII, "When in eternal lines to time thou grow'st, / So long as men can breathe, or eyes can see, / So long lives this, and this gives life to thee." – as we have now two versions of one reality, a visual and a written one.

One last comment on the broad spectrum of paintings (and sculpture) Di Leonardo has included in his homage. Ranging from the 15th to our 21st century – notably outstanding 19th and 20th century works – the paintings mirrored in the poems "at our disposal" evidence the poet´s thorough voyage through the plastic arts´ world and his connoisseurship. We must thank him for "poetically collecting" the pieces in one book.

The eternalizing quality and value of what Di Leonardo has done in writing these poems inspired by paintings is, nonetheless, best worded lyrically by William Wordsworth: "Poetry is the first and last of all knowledge – it is as immortal as the heart of man." *(Taken from Joseph Gold´s The Story Species, 2002, Fitzhenry and Whiteside. Canada).*

That is why I quoted Margaret Atwood to begin this book: ""“The arts”–as we’ve come to term them–are not a frill. They are the heart of the matter, because they are about our hearts… A society without poetry and other arts would have broken its mirror and cut out its heart.”

This is Di Leonardo´s contribution. Poetry *is* “the heart of the matter,” it *is* eternal; it immortalizes us and what it depicts.

Antony Di Nardo's *Gone/Missng*

Hidden Brook Press. (2020)

MSc Miguel Ángel Olivé Iglesias. Associate Professor, Author, Poet, Editor, Reviewer

In early 2020, I published my review book *In a Fragile Moment: A Landscape of Canadian Poetry* with Hidden Brook Press. It was a compilation of thirty-five essays on thirty-one fine Canadian poets and prose writers. One of them was well-known poet Antony Di Nardo and his book *Skylight* (Ronsdale Press, 2018). I was fortunate to have feedback from the poet when I sent him what I had written. His response to my emails and our exchange for a period of time was heart-warming and edifying for me as an essay writer.

In January 2020 I met the poet and his wife, Ann Nadin Di Nardo, a professional photographer. They came to Cuba with some of the Canada Cuba Literary Alliance (CCLA) members who visit Holguín every year, invited by its Founding President, Richard Marvin Grove (Tai), and his wife, Kim Grove, and were accompanied by Canadian painter and poet Eva Kolacz, poet and professor Laurence Hutchman and writer Donna Wootton.

Meeting Antony Di Nardo is an act of pleasure and learning, a lesson of life. He has the ability – blessing – to intoxicate you with his high spirits, his cultivation, his word and winning style in reading poetry for a public, his friendliness and kindness, his joviality and deportment. He was a professor too, and it surfaces when he stands up, holds a poem in his hand – his or someone else´s – and rather than just read it he acts it out. Words sound magically different in his readings.

When he was about to leave he left me a manuscript with poems he was working on and was meaning to publish. He asked me if I would have some free time to go over them and give him my opinion. That is how *Gone/Missng* fell on my hands. The first bait was the title itself, the *i* missing in *Missng.* Apart from the interesting conjugation of Gone and Missing, I instantly found it attention-grabbing, at least for me, that the letter he chose was *i*; not any other. Was it because the "I" (the poet) in the poems takes a step backwards and recedes into the darkness of the gone and missing? Was it because Di Nardo poured himself out entirely leaving no word unsaid, no stone unturned to pay tribute to Susan Briscoe, whom he calls "a formidable poet and friend," thus remaining – seemingly – in the background and shifting highlights towards her?

Gone/Missng is an impressive book, one of homage to friendship and poetry, from the multi-visionary world-view of a poet who knows his craft and opens up here with a varied yet well-structured bandwidth of styles I noticed as I moved across the sixty-eight poems therein grouped in three sections.

A poet who lives fully and action-immersed, whose feelings and sensations bubble in and around him, explodes in and explores sentiments we humans cannot avoid: loneliness, deference, social criticism. Above all, he embarks on a righteous journey of singing to life – even in the lines dedicated to death, as in writing to his friend he keeps her memory alive for posterity. We would have to remember Shakespeare´s Sonnet XVIII, "When in eternal lines to time thou grow'st, / So long as men can breathe, or eyes can see, / So long lives this, and this gives life to thee." This is what Di Nardo has done: memorialize through his poetry, for poetry will be read in years to come.

I remember one of his most intriguing phrases in his poem "I Write and Write" from *Skylight*, which I commented in my review book, *In A Fragile Moment.* I said: "I Write and Write" is a pause in Di Nardo's river of poems. I disagree with him saying that "I write and write and nothing happens." *(Taken from "Letting the Light In. A review of Antony Di Nardo´s Skylight" (Poetry) (2018) Ronsdale Press. Canada)* When we discussed these lines in Gibara, I discovered that I was in the presence of a committed poet. Di Nardo complains that he writes his poems yet nothing still changes the negative side of things, and that is why he continues his poetic crusade towards a change.

However, as he complains so he soldiers on to fight causes worth fighting for, noble duties he follows because it is in his nature to leave an imprint. In his transcending anthology *Tamaracks: Canadian Poetry for the 21st Century (Lummox Press, 2018)*, James Deahl cites: "Sainte-Marie has recently said, "The job of a poet is to get information across in a way that's effective in making change."" *(Quoted by Deahl from Reader's Digest Volume 191, Number 1,144 (November 2017). Page 38. Print).* Thus we see a Di Nardo inbued in effecting a change, the environmentalist, the engaged observer who clicks in and bleeds emotive words, the grieving friend who realizes some things are gone/missing and seeks out for them in his new book to secure them immortality.

Wide-ranging in tessitura and technique, we walk along poems like "Missng," for example, which speaks of absence, an absence suggesting this surreal impression in me both in time and space. The poem confirms my early assumptions about the lack of "i" as a letter and a first-person singular pronoun in the title, a skilled, purposeful maneouver by the poet. We encounter also "Bay of Quinte," with play on words, social criticism and a clearcut ecological approach.

The poet observes. He unveils sights, describes them in both direct and figurative dabs, as happens in "Hiding Places," where personification is achieved. The poet is an explorer, as we mentioned before, of the physical world but also of a world an ordinary eye cannot see – Di Nardo does, using metaphorical keys.

The meditative poet is felt in "She Was By Herself." Like he does in the line "and flit between two thoughts," the poem skips from thought to thought, from mental swirling to a bustling outdoor life both flowing irreversibly towards a "beyond my sight." Further in the book we come across "Missing," now with the "i," that speaks sadly of emptiness, sense of loss yet does not fail to address social issues and be critical in doing so.

The environmentalist is also appreciated in "A Tree Is Missing." With his direct criticism, Di Nardo stands as a concerned poet and a nature lover. His preoccupation about writing and writing and nothing is happening vibrates in this poem, and many others. One deep source for writing is quite evocative in "one more poem." It is a piece on death and absence, central leitmotifs in Di Nardo´s *Missng.* The poem "Gone" reminded me of a Latinamerican classic, Pablo Neruda. Wording and syntax brought the Chilean giant to me.

"graveside, exit" leaves for us the heavy gravitas of a distinctively heartrending moment. Particularly stylistic is the use of the Latin word *Exeunt.* A few pages ahead, we read "graveside, grim," with its message of an awareness of death, maybe fear or calmness before what is inevitable. Awe-inspiring phrases are "… a gaping hole stares back / ghosts and threads of past events re-appear // yet it´s the grimace of an afterlife that steals the show / in thrall that I can see myself in there"

A poet concerned with the premises of life amidst so much loss and pain arises in "Autumn Colours." We are told of how much we do and lose and wonder "When it´s in our nature to name a leaf and watch it fall."

"Dead Waste" is a highly ekphrastic kind of poem. It is naturalistic and direct, to get to the reader so the message strikes home. "Family Portraits" gives us one of Canadian poets´ most revered themes for writing, family remembrances. Di Nardo travels in time and reminisces to offer this tender piece we welcome. "First Draft" is a brilliant short piece, almost haiku-like, of a writer and his bond with a straight representation of things. The last words, "and copy the clouds / the way nature / intended," speak of a keen poet, connected with nature.

"It Takes an Owl to Make an Owl" is an example of the professor Di Nardo is, where he "teaches" jocosely and leaves for us this intensely "didactic" poem. Finally, we find a poem of reflection in "Moonlandings." Age comes as a realization to the poet. The idea has landed on him that he is old, that he can no longer conquer the moon – it rather "crushes" and urges him to write this poem.

I have handguided the readers through some examples of Di Nardo´s proposal in *Gone/Missng.* At the beginning of my comments I stated that the book shows a diverse Di Nardo mode in his writing. Nevertheless, there is a solid cohesion that unifies thought and pen in poetry forging, an individual input of mastery and passion, of creativity that is put to the service of mankind and, above all, of hope, because Antony Di Nardo writes, writes and many good things will happen.

Reading Collected Poems of Raymond Souster (Ten-volume Collection). Ottawa: Oberon Press. (2004)

MSc Miguel Ángel Olivé Iglesias. Associate Professor, Author, Poet, Editor, Reviewer

Poet and friend, Richard Marvin Grove, Tai, Founding President of the Canada Cuba Literary Alliance (CCLA), forwarded me some poems from the *Collected Poems of Raymond Souster*, on the eve of the year 2020. He and James Deahl had praised my reviews on Margaret Atwood, Milton Acorn and Al Purdy *(In my first review book, In a Fragile Moment: A Landscape of Canadian Poetry. Hidden Brook Press, 2020)* and were encouraging me to write about other iconic figures of Canadian literature.

This second review book includes my analyses on Leonard Cohen, Pauline Johnson, Bliss Carman, and now Raymond Souster; a must read, an unavoidable name in the Canadian poetdom, deemed by James Deahl as one of the most important poets in the Canadian 20th century.

Deahl's words I read about Souster might at first discourage anyone attempting at approaching this poet, "No anthology can come close to celebrating the life and work of such an important, indeed essential, figure in the history of Canadian literature; several large books would be required." *(Taken from Under the Mulberry Tree: Poems for & about Raymond Souster. Quattro Books Inc. 2014. Edited by James Deahl, his introductory words: "Simply Ray: An Introduction") (Unless otherwise noted in-text by the essayist, all non-post-bracketed, non-referenced quotations of James Deahl were taken from his introduction to the book cited).*

As I moved down his discourse I realized the intention was quite the opposite of my initial perception: "… But my publisher and I will do our best." What Deahl did was put sheer stress on the greatness of the poet. I join then publisher and editor in trying to condense in a few, always insufficient, pages my understanding of one of the seminal authors of Canada, a worthy representative of the Great Generation Poets.

It was a promising coincidence to learn of Grove's appreciation of Souster and his decision to send me the collection, and Deahl's admiration for him in his explicit allusion to *Collected Poems of Raymond Souster* as "… essential reading for anyone interested in fine poetry." Hence, I devoted my end-of-year days off from work to read and comment some of Souster's poems.

Souster's concerns about social affairs are reflected in "Four Girls at a Corner." (Volume 3) Deahl tells us that the poet pointed at "… social/political issues… Poverty, oppression, violence, racism, anti-Semitism, avarice, and human degeneration were all targets of his poetry." There are deeply critical lines in the poem, "four girls at the corner, / three about eighteen, / the fourth not more / than thirteen, I swear, / Not one day more…," which bring to the surface scenes like the one Souster presents in descriptive style, no embellishment for the crude reality he depicts *(Fragments from all the poems taken from Collected Poems of Raymond Souster. Ottawa: Oberon Press. 2004).*

The poet pokes deeper at the issue by saying: "… waiting for the Man / to come and take them / for a few short hours / out of misery…" It stands to sad reason that the misery he describes too hits the streets and is commonplace. Such plights do not escape the poet's committed pen. However, if the reader thought it was it, Souster becomes sarcastic and inquisitive in the last lines: "… God, the taxi-driver said, / but He hadn't come along yet either."

The seemingly strong descriptions read in the previous poem pale when you move to the next, "Girl at the Corner of Dundas & Elizabeth." (Volume 1) Straightforward and incisive, the poem lashes again at social scourges. Souster introduces slang and direct dialogue – no circumlocutions – to reinforce the realistic character of the situation: "You want it / or you don't / I'm twenty-one / I ain't / got any time / to waste…"

In terms of language use, Deahl states: "What appealed to Ray was the mixture of image-based poetry with realism. Such poems would utilize plain speech, and avoid Classical or academic references. This poetry could easily embrace both urban and rural themes, both social-political issues and nature."

"Mister / make up your mind" is the poem's last line. It brought to me scenes from the movie *Pretty Woman*, to mention a lightly-treated reference, where Roberts and her "partner" engage in similar exchanges with "potential customers."

One of Souster's themes is love. I cannot think of one poet – there are, perhaps – who has not written love poems, at least – not necessarily – during his/her early writing stages. "Night on the Uplands" (Volume 2) is a brief, intense, humorous one. Nature commingles with love, opens the poem as a fitting preamble: "A fire on such a warm night? / Crazy, wasn't it, but then / the mosquitoes wanted our flesh / as much as we wanted each other…"

The subordination of end-lines "… and as I remember / won out in the end!" to the previous line, "as much as we wanted each other," and the absence of "they" or "we" – I am positive there is intentionality in this – before "won out," really makes me pleasurably wonder whether Souster refers to the insects or themselves – or he *purposefully* made me feel that. It endows the short piece with a gentle sensuousness I value as a reader.

In his poem "Raymond Souster," Laurence Hutchman summarizes what "Night on the Uplands" stirs in me as a reader: "Your poems drawn subtlety / of the desire of lovers / uncovering their shy naked bodies." In the same poem, Hutchman also acknowledges Souter's mastery to "size up" his city, as I explained in the poems "Four Girls at a Corner" and "Girl at the Corner of Dundas & Elizabeth": "No one has painted this city as you have, / made its history our own." *(Taken from the contributors´ poems included in the anthology Under the Mulberry Tree: Poems for & about Raymond Souster. Quattro Books Inc. 2014).*

Another sweet piece is the indeed to-the-point four-line poem, "Short Short Song," (Volume 7) dedicated to Susi, his wife Rosalia. In my opinion, the fact that Souster uses rhyme here, final rhyme in lines two and four, no rhyme in one and three, enhances the message of the poem and its warmth, and assists in rhythm. By extension, these elements foster musicality, which is the poet's declared intention in his title. In simple but resolute words, Souster praises his relationship with his wife: "When Susi smiles I'm happy, / when Susi's sad I'm sad…" Deahl commented that "In fact, the romance of Ray and Rosalia is a love story for the ages."

"Night on the Uplands" is a fleeting hint at nature, deriving into a love composition. Nature poetry was very emotional in Souster, as Deahl tells: "… nature images appear in Ray's poetry from the very beginning… The natural world is used… to remind the reader of beauty in poems… and… poems directly about the joy… of… nature."

A breathtaking, tender example that blends the beauty and the joy elements and brings nature to the full forefront of the beholder is "Queen Anne's Lace." (Volume 3) In his substantial essay "Archibald Lampman: Poet on the Cusp of Modernism," James Deahl clarifies: "This emphasis on the natural landscape of Canada and on nature poetry, so visible in the work of Confederation Poets, continued into the Great Generation Poets like Milton Acorn… and Raymond Souster… became leading nature poets during the last half of the 20th century." *(Taken from Canadian Stories magazine, Volume 22, Number 129, Year 2019).*

As a "leading nature poet," Souster crafted this poem that sings to beauty and delicacy and makes human eyes turn to them: "It's a kind of flower / that if you didn't know it / you'd pass by the rest of your life. / But once it's been pointed out / you'll look for it always…" Souster's passion goes as far as letting the reader know that "You'll never tire / of bending over to examine, / of marvelling at this / shyest filigree of wonder / born among grasses…" Finally, he forecasts: "You'll imagine poems // so natural with themselves / as to take your breath away."

The book I have taken most of the quotations from in my essay (chiefly from James Deahl's introduction) was a tribute to Raymond Souster. Thirty-five contributors sent their material to produce the book. I will illustrate how profoundly impactful and transcendental Souster's poetry and life are with only three examples of phrases used in their poems. *(Taken from the contributors´ poems included in the anthology Under the Mulberry Tree: Poems for & about Raymond Souster. Quattro Books Inc. 2014).*

James Deahl, editor, friend of Souster's, impassioned reader and inveterate advocate of poetry, said in "Japanese Maple": "You, true master / of the backyard poem…" Terry Ann Carter showed her high regard with much similar direct, colloquial language Souster uses: "… for better, or worse, / Raymond — I'm hooked…" And in "The shy man was absent," Chis Faiers devotedly said: "But tonight the shy man's legacy connects / a tribal gathering of poets his tribute / **not one empty chair.**" Impressive.

When I read about Souster's blindness, I shivered with Henry Beissel's proclamation in his poem "Others Are Writing this Poem" *(Fugitive Horizons. Guernica Editions, 2013)*: "Sight / was never a necessary condition of existence," and re-read, moved, Deahl's words about Souster's resolute, brave attitude: "Ray went blind, and despite becoming blind, which he expected to happen, he kept on with his usual daily life as long as possible. He wrote hundreds of poems after he lost his sight. Every time I visited him, Ray was in a good mood. He accepted his condition, and did not allow it to depress or define him."

It is a lesson of life and rock-solid determination. Deahl summarized it with his assertion: "He was a rare and true example of how to fully *live* a life." I do not have better words to finish this essay. All I can come up with is that I am grateful to Grove and Deahl for pointing me in the direction of Souster. I feel I have rounded off my second essay book with his name among so many other fine poets and prose writers. I'm hooked too, I'll follow the beacon.

Gail Murray. Holding a Handful of her Poems

MSc Miguel Ángel Olivé Iglesias. Associate Professor, Author, Poet, Editor, Reviewer

Canadian, Gail M. Murray B.A. B. ED. was an English teacher and teacher-librarian. After retiring Gail has become a free-lance writer. Like Keats, seeks to capture the essence of the moment. Gail's writing is a response to her natural and emotional environment. Her poems have been published in *Written Tenfold*, *Blank Spaces*, *Wordscape*, *Arborealis*, *The Banister*, and on *CommuterLit.com*. Her creative non-fiction has appeared in *The Globe and Mail*, *Trellis*, *Heartbeats*, *Renaissance*, *The Ontario Gardener*, *NOW Magazine*, *Blank Spaces*, *Just Words Volume 2*, *Stony Bridges*, *Ottawa Review of Books*, *Historical Fiction Magazine*, *Our Canada*, *More of Our Canada and Our Canada, Our Country, Our Stories.* She is a Writer, Poet, Book Reviewer.

Won over by beauty and the lure of words, her style remains captivatingly simple. Almost any line from her poems can be copied and pasted as an epigram: such is the compactness she achieves. From her piece "Poetry" we can pick "*a way of seeing within, responding without*" or "*beyond this world / of clocks and appointments / simple, true beauty exists.*"

Simplicity goes beyond semantics, it enters the poem´s sinews, takes hold of them and returns in fresh, brief stanzas; a happy reminder of Emily Dickinson. Sentences are short, direct within the rich interplay of metaphors. Themes skip and vary, as much as life skips and varies. From the elegant definition of poetry to evocations of champagne, sparkling in the reader´s eyes in the poem "Romance." Therefrom, the great questions about love in "Romantics" and the endless quest for perfection sketched in the poem. Economy in syntax, concise enumeration as an effective expressive means, contributes to the sensations we feel:

Romantics
flit about butterflies
afraid to settle
seek that great love
in love with love
illusion of perfection
beginnings, excitement, promise
Do they miss out on being loved?

Then, the refreshing turn to nature, beauty vibrating in Murray´s "Beach Time" that she shares with us, "*lines of blue on blue / hard sand ripples beneath my toes…*" Here Murray toys with the senses (sight, touch), capitalizing on the beauty of the monarch: "*migrating monarchs fly low / mineral boost from the wet sand / on their long journey*" No period after "*journey*," as if to insist on duration.

Sweetly delivered poetry in the "*wings of angels*" is what we feel in "Poet." Notions approached by many other poets, likening writing poems to painting, are portrayed by Murray in this piece. Filled with tropes, she defines the role of poets, exquisitely put in the last lines: "*a poet is destined to create / poems / delivered on the wings of angels.*"

"Valentine Promise" is soft and inviting, intimate and provocative. The narrative leads the reader through the experience with key cues, "*my martini bright red*," "*bodies touching*," "*we come alive*," "*your pelvic rhythmic*," "*you lead I follow*," "*the vodka hitting me*," "*next morning the bond is gentle*" and "*we sip tea under the sheets.*" The poem´s mood cascades into a last-stanza dénouement, last line: "*as sunlight fills the room.*" It spells ecstasy.

This is Gail Murray to me. She is an acute observer of nature, of social convention, of life. She sails swiftly across the events that prompt her to write and we partake in her will to pass on to us that "*intuitive knowledge*" she told us about in "Poetry."

Calling a Spade a Spade. Comments on Gail Murray's poem "Remember how….."

MSc Miguel Ángel Olivé Iglesias. Associate Professor, Author, Poet, Editor, Reviewer

BEd Jorge Alberto Pérez Hernández. Author, Editor, Poet

Life has given women fortitude and wits to push further from Adam´s rib and rise. From their housewife, non-voting position years ago they have fought, taken off and conquered every field in society. Outdoors and indoors, women have proved themselves to be worthy, intelligent, creative, resilient, capable, independent and courageous, qualities quite a few men lack.

In Cuba, women have been given the place they rightfully deserve and we men have learned to respect and facilitate it stays that way. Even today, we still need to understand the female heart and mind, explore deeper, redeem ourselves from all the injustice done to them and recognize their value and values. Women are stronger than we are and much more sensitive. They are open to feelings and experiences denied to them in the past. They are entitled to demand and to decide, even judge after centuries of being "defendants" in the social court and being constantly relegated, rejected, used and judged.

Women love flowers, holding hands, a poem, a walk down memory lane and along the seaside. Women deserve our full devotion and comprehension for who they are and for what they have given up, given and contributed. Have we, husbands, ever paused to consider the wrongs we do? Have we stopped to think how much we have missed in giving to our wives? How much we have hurt them, cheated on them and disregarded them? How much we have neglected them? We remember a friend´s motto, "*Happy wife, happy life!*" Let´s try to see what we can do to remedy our faults by honoring this motto.

The poem we are commenting today holds many of the answers to – and causes of – a woman´s hurting heart. It is her right to tell, to stand up and change her life for the better. "Remember how….." starts by enumerating what was good in the relation, what kept it alive and necessary:

Remember how you kissed me awake…
Remember how we ordered eggs benedict…
dream out loud about our next trip / Italy, Barbados, Istanbul?...
Remember how we stayed up half the night…

The poet enumerates and states facts that colored the relation. We read of physical-spiritual remembrances:

Remember how you…
held me in your arms
brought tea, a prelude to making love?...
Holding hands, walk the boardwalk
sunset sea…
Remember how we stayed up half the night
kissing, talking, touching?

In the "list," even the every-day (every-night) things had a place, a significance, "*we ordered eggs benedict,*" "*our favourite bistro Sunday mornings / meandered into book stores?*" the deeper ones reverberating strongly in reminiscences and plans:

sky a Monet print
stop at Thai House for dinner
dream out loud about our next trip
Italy, Barbados, Istanbul?

We are witnesses to a woman´s illusion and yearning appeals: things they had, things she deserves to have kept and to have been offered as a woman in her individuality, and those she claims must have been an unfading component of their relation. How complete she felt as a woman is epitomized in the line, "*All new; we couldn't get enough.*" Interestingly, in an interview years ago, Dr. Liebowitz, from Columbia University, explained that what is intense in a relationship is the newness. For the poet there was newness in them, there was exploration and endless enjoyment. That changed: now the poet speaks with a touch of sadness-nostalgia, mixed with a veiled yet stern request-protest we could not avoid picking.

The next stanzas burst, as do the poet´s feelings, restrained perhaps in the calmer, rather aide-memoire previous stanza. A question, irony and directness accompanying it: "*Are you growing old?*" From here, a new type of enumeration, now charged with a different type of claim in each sentence, floods the page:

We don't go for long walks anymore,
you nod off mid conversation
go to bed early
can't decide if you want to go anywhere.
We've fallen into a pattern,
comfortable, predictable
Saturday night stir fry; Sunday steak
Omelettes and asparagus for brunch
once around the park.

Murray made us remember Henry Ibsen´s *A Doll´s House* (Nora´s line "*Sit down. It will take some time; I have much to talk over with you.*") *(https://en.wikipedia.org/wiki/A_Doll%27s_House).* She confronts, objectively, maturely – poetically – the man and the relation, the what-we-had-and-now-it´s-all-gone-where situation. She sees his indifference and is able to detect the evident signs of his apathy, his boredom, his attitude: "*you nod off mid conversation / go to bed early / can't decide if you want to go anywhere.*" She is pointing at the problems, calling a spade a spade.

We are reading the words-emotions of a woman who reminds us of another Ibsen line in the afore-mentioned play: "*You don't understand me; and I have never understood you–till to-night. No, don´t" interrupt. Only listen to what I say. We must come to a final settlement…*" *(ibidem)*

One stanza clearly reveals what Murray craves and does not hesitate to bring up:

I want the beginning
yearn for intimacy
melt when I hear your voice.

The last stanza, deriving from the previous one, is definitive:

From the admission of your affair
you long for it too,
Just not with me.

This is a resolute woman, who has collected herself and laid out facts and factors to her couple. She is certain of the current state of affairs – and her couple´s affair. That the poem ends like that may allow free interpretation but her determination shows. There is finality in the last line. The poem has echoed in us as it has surely done in every reader: it may happen to anyone.

The moral we surmise from it is what we said at the beginning: Women are entitled to demand and to decide, even to judge after centuries of being the "defendants" in the social scenario. Women deserve our full devotion and comprehension for who they are and for what they have given up, given and contributed. The poet is intent on getting there, on proving her points. She wants attention. In another research, Doctor Chernus, from New York, introduced thought-provoking ideas about how husbands too often do not express their feelings for their wives. He insisted a man has "*to learn to tell his wife how he feels.*"

Leaving the stage open for reflection with that prior quote, we close our comments with fragments from Barbra Streisand´s song "You don´t Bring me Flowers Anymore," which resounds in almost every line of Murray´s poem: "*You don't bring me flowers / And you don't sing me love songs… / You hardly talk to me anymore… I remember when you couldn't wait to love me / you used to hate to leave me… / Well you just roll over and turn out the light… / It used to be so natural to talk about forever / But used to be's don't count anymore… / You don't say you need me / You don't sing me love songs / You don't bring me flowers anymore…*" *(https://www.google.com.cu/search)*

Song and poem cannot be more connected. Murray´s intense poem is an eye-opener. Let´s learn to let our women have their say, respect and hear them when they call a spade a spade in any topic. Most of all, let´s try to prevent such moments by loving them the way they deserve, or sincerely parting before we bring uncertainty or pain to them. Let´s not *get too old* or too lazy when it comes to romancing and lovingly filling voids in a woman´s soul.

A Review of John B. Lee's *Into a Land of Strangers* Mosaic Press. (2019)

MSc Miguel Ángel Olivé Iglesias. Associate Professor, Author, Poet, Editor, Reviewer

One of the longest, yet most captivating journeys is about us. It includes a time ride to our ancestors and to lands beyond our borders and imagination. A friend said that to me when I was maybe twenty and was reading a manuscript about the history of my surname, which had reached my father and he gave to me: "You must know where our name comes from," my father told me.

More than thirty-five years later, John B. Lee makes me remember that. He does it with an impressive journey to a millenary nation we look at with feelings of intrigue, distance, curiosity and respect for its greatness and its contribution to culture. Into the prevailing Chinese contextual vortex, Lee pulls other occurrences, characters, settings and situations.

Lee's writing gift has made him a recipient of as many awards as it is humanly possible. He has tirelessly crafted piece after piece in his long, prolific career. He has written nearly about everything with unique perspective and penmanship. He has memorialized his travelling experiences in books about his own and other countries; one that particularly stays with me is *An Almost Silent Drumming: the South Africa poems*, Cranberry Tree Press, Windsor, Ontario, 2001.

Lee's own words are explanatory enough of his aspirations as a writer: "I want, in poems… the soul to thrill to a commingling of temporal and extra-temporal things… I want the past alive, the present reified and the future remembered in words so perfect they sing alone and in chorus the name of names." *(Taken from John B. Lee's essay "Even at the Worst of Times" in And Left a Place to Stand On, Hidden Brook Press, 2009).*

Into a Land of Strangers is about "temporal and extra-temporal things." It sings to family roots, life, sacrifice and honor. Lee takes words, touches them and – like King Midas turning things into gold – waxes them into indelible witnesses, and erects them as mementoes of events and lives past. Lee tells us he was "born into a family of bibliophiles." Let's toast to that: it planted on him that unquenchable thirst for the poetic, and led him to his wondrous encounter with muses, who have never since then abandoned him. The poet embarks on a discovery epic "into a land of strangers." Even though it remains true that place, people and events are foreign to many, what is depicted in Lee´s own early experiences ("Chinese characters displaying the exotic logograms of the realm of the Han") is now masterfully decoded for us from the very outset and through both prose and poetry.

As he accurately expands on the idea, I quote Roger Bell in reference to Lee's manifold abilities: "Wherever John Lee takes us… be it China, Thailand, Korea, Baffin Island… or the shores of our great lakes, readers must be aware of the archetype of his journey. Yes, the physical voyage has weight, but it is really the interior journey, the progress of the soul, that counts. While he so fluently details the world around him, Lee is more deeply in search of the ch´i, the vital force… something just beyond the circle of light." *(Taken from Roger Bell's Foreword to John B. Lee's book This is How We See the World, Hidden Brook Press, 2017).*

The book is a stunning chronicle, as overwhelming as the nation being portrayed, of Lee's great-aunt, a missionary in China. It took him time, "It would involve another fifteen years of maturing as a writer before it occurred to me to return to that fertile ground and to tell the story of grandma's aunt Ida," to finally give shape to the book. As a reader, I could not avoid being involved in the historic and bibliographical facts Lee exposes with a magnifying glass that crosses time and territories.

In a previous review about James Deahl I stated: "Poets have a gift: they provide light, a different one. They craft words and images in ways no one else can and lay them down for us to marvel at a world that had been there but we hadn't noticed." This is what John B. Lee does over and over again unfalteringly, magically. He has uncovered a strangers´ land; but when you finish "visiting" it through Lee's genuine vision and artistry, you realize the land is no longer that far, nor is it just strangers what you have in mind. Lee's is essentially a poetry book – and more – conceived in love and serious research. It is a tribute that highlights, in polished harmony with himself and the universe, the meticulous researcher, the caring nephew, the formidable prose writer and poet.

He has emphasized that "I want, in poems… the spirit to surround and be surrounded by an interplay between the deep wells of the self and the stars beyond the farthest stars we might dream…" *(Taken from John B. Lee's essay "Even at the Worst of Times" in And Left a Place to Stand On, Hidden Brook Press, 2009).* To me it is an in-depth poetic treatise of Chinese lifestyles and epochs, one that flows with textual merging yet grants each part its self-standing worth. It surpasses Chinese frontiers connecting allusions to the rest of the world, to conflicts, misfortunes, etc.

Suffice it to read Lee's initial words on how much he studied to give birth to this work: "In doing research for this book, in addition to reading and gleaning important details from my cousin Dorothy's genealogical records, I read dozens of books on China including revisiting Chinese poetry in translation through several anthologies…"

The poetry section presents facts, carved by Lee with the hand of a master. He is able to narrate history and fate, beginnings and ramifications, sorrows and consolation, catalyst tragedies and sequels, marked by gender-signed, individual plights framed in the unreceptive end-of-19th-century "interesting times": "when your papa died / after an accident in the forest / your mother widowed / you and your sister / suddenly fatherless / as you lived there then sorrowing on the cusp / of first menses / three women / in a manless house / you mourned the loss / though the consolation / of faith / gave sorrow meaning."

Lee stands philosophical amidst all this unfurling of lives and happenings. He holds invisible threads that poetry weaves and surrenders to him, thus he becomes a traveler who explains: "the past must disappear / as warmth through mist / becomes a clarifying blur / of cooling light… / the present / burns like sunlit chrome / a brilliant / blindness flashing / in the mind / too bright to see / or seen as fire / sees its fuel in flame… / the future's / like a water moon / where light lies / twice removed / in mysteries of deep / refraction / tilted by a shaded stone / transfixed in motion / like white-washed granite in the sky."

In a feat of conceptual consistency, Lee has posited this before: "… I want the past alive, the present reified and the future remembered in words so perfect they sing alone and in chorus the name of names." *(Taken from John B. Lee's essay "Even at the Worst of Times" in And Left a Place to Stand On, Hidden Brook Press, 2009).*

From its factual-experiential basis, Lee's poetry is aware of the dynamics of times and the role of motion; but it also regales us with – as in all his books, Bernice Lever reminds us: "John B. Lee's lines flow smoothly from one fresh metaphor to the next." *(Taken from This is How We See the World's back-cover comment by Lever)* – superb literary expertise in exceptional similes: "the future's / like a water moon… like white-washed granite in the sky."

One feature I appreciate is that Lee addresses his aunt, there is a conversation between nephew and aunt. He creates a bond with the past, not an empty or impersonal or futile one, but a significant, transcendent, face-to-face tale-telling. Somewhere in mid storytelling Lee does shift to third-person narrative, still honoring his genealogy, Chinese culture and history, and he solidly sets his poetry foundation on quotes by great Chinese men and the Bible.

At the center of it all stays Lee's aunt. His constant returns to her life, the impressions she left on him, either by stories he heard, material he read, or a picture, tell us of how relevant she is to him and to the book. His poem "At Least for Now" gives us a woman in all her particulars, physique and costume ("a lean woman / her long-boned body / draped in a black silk dress / she is seated / in a stiff-spined rocker / her well-shod feet crossed / at the ankles / adorned in high-top shoes / laced almost to the knee / like greaves"), along with existential, mental, even theological attitudes and projections: "she grips the arms of the chair / as though at any moment she means to rise / or rather resist / the weightless phantom / that floats her spectral complexion / from the white collar / of this pale-fleshed visage / she, with the self-assured / physiognomy of the righteous / certain of the purity of her Christian soul / with the rectitude / of a widowed woman / bearing the carriage and posture of / her place in time." A complete delineation of her fortitude and endurance is skillfully revealed by the poet in the closing lines: "she poses / in her parlour in China / and she means / to be herself forever / at least for now."

Well-informed, tender, natural, historical, biographical, direct, cultivated, freshly lyrical are some of the adjectives I can use to talk about John B. Lee's homage book. I can safely say as well that I felt it is slightly different from Lee's other works I have read: a mixture of biographical work, poetry types, prose and verse co-existing in finely distributed order and pertinence. It is also mesmerizing, enlightening and monumental. This latter attribute was originally propounded by George Elliott Clarke who, in his introduction to another book by Lee (John B. Lee's Bread, Water, Love in *These Are the Words*, by George Elliott Clarke and John B. Lee. Hidden Brook Press, 2018) stressed the poet's natural talent to make what is elemental a constituent of the monumental. Both elemental and monumental fit in this new book´s theme and scope.

If you want to plunge into a rapid's broad turmoil of love, calamity, personal and world history, hopes and sketches of human/social/universal significance told with scrutinizing solemnity, come to Lee's *Into a Land of Strangers*. Roger Bell validates my invitation in saying: "I encountered a writer of greater scope, and poetry even more profound and wide-ranging, than I was accustomed to… John Lee's wide and deep observations of this wondrous life… the gravitas he brings to his visions of this world." *(Taken from Roger Bell's Foreword to John B. Lee's book This is How We See the World, Hidden Brook Press, 2017).*

If you are willing to know of China's splendid cultural mosaic, I strongly suggest you start with this book before you venture into further readings about a land and a family tree that are by now more familiar to me. Enter Lee's travels, thorough findings, dreams and poetics flooding this book: "when I see / the moon / over China / I cannot help / but recall… how lonesome the light / without us / how dark / those brilliant beams." Do rejoice in those "brilliant beams," and glow with anticipation: there will be more, as Lee himself has said that his favorite poem will always be the one he is about to write! *(Reference taken from John B. Lee's words in his book This is How We See the World, Hidden Brook Press, 2017).*

A Comment on Four Poems by James Deahl in *Travelling The Lost Highway* Guernica Editions. (2019)

MSc Miguel Ángel Olivé Iglesias. Associate Professor, Author, Poet, Editor, Reviewer

Travelling the Lost Highway (Guernica Editions, 2019) is a superb compilation of poems, written from 2011 to 2018, which presents us a mature poet who is always growing, whose acumen in observing, noticing, decoding realities and souls and penning all those experiences with fresh imagery and level-headed layout, ranks him among the most representative Canadian poet-chroniclers of love, life, society and nature.

The book is a man's story told in poetic form. He offers his vision of things, his insights based not on supposition or instinct but on his determination to gain knowledge of his themes while traveling. In his words: "One got to know the nation… one got to know the people." He is primordially interested in finding ways that "might recapture the values that once animated the American and Canadian people." *(Both quotations taken from the book's introductory words by Deahl)* You get a taste of all that in the book.

David Haskins said that "There are meditations, eulogies and laments contained here, passionate love poems, poems that call upon national and generational history…" *(Taken from the book's back-cover comments by Haskins).*

With these assertions in mind we read his opening poem, "A Music Innocent Of Time And Sound." A somber pun comes in the first line, where Deahl seriously plays with the overlapping meanings of "dead": "No Jews visit their dead during the dead / of winter." Solemnity in wording and intention envelops this piece, with a full-grown visualization of death.

The last two lines struck a biblical passage in me, my hypothesis leaping back to Jesus´ lesson about a first stone being cast only by those without sin. In a way, Deahl's variation, "We, the living, are never so innocent / as to fearlessly watch that casket down," is evocative of the teachings and truth in that scene.

In the poem, innocence and fearlessness of the living must bow while they "watch that casket down." In my view, "casket" does not mean only the coffin. Contextually, it develops into extended metonymical shades referring to death or even final judgment of our acts in life.

A hymn to death and life – natural, human and societal – is heard in "Woodlot." The poet has no choice but to seek refuge in nature, elicit hope from eager line-wishes: "buds proclaim / spring might be near at hand," where spring is hope and buds are the slowly blooming evidence that hope will eventually crystallize.

Even when "All is born anew in this woodlot," the second stanza pierces hope with a crude reality: "Last month the remains / of the young teacher were dumped, / whatever life remained / leaking from her forty wounds." If in the first stanza we read of "plague-struck elms," the second bares another kind of plague, a sadly social one.

The closing lines are ominously vibrant, "her blood, / as if to claim this land her own, / tried, but failed, to penetrate / this frozen soil," sending a message of a posthumous symbolic will of the teacher to claim a life that was prematurely stolen from her.

Another poem I want to comment briefly is "Bells That Beat Against The Heart." Metaphors surprise us in this piece, like the one emerging from the title and retaken in the lines: "trees stand frozen where / water will pool in spring; / they are bells beating / against a fragile heart."

The way the poem is structured, the poet returns "through darkness" from nature, depicted in stanzas one and two. Then his "fragile heart" leads him to refuge in his salvation, "the woman I love." He had previously emphasized her relevance in the line "This is my only life," where "only" does not cage the man; it voices a choice, a preference of being within nature and with his woman.

That was stanza three and line one in the next. Stanza four goes back to nature, and metaphors ("dawn summons heavy clouds"), as if he felt safe between stanzas and right in the middle with his beloved.

"A Book Of Snow" is actually a poem filled with warmth, beauty, passion and high-style imagery. We rejoice in Deahl's "… miles of buried fields awaiting spring's touch. / The sky's a cathedral of light, a place / where only the impossible happens." The poet speaks in wonder of nature's might: "What strength do we have before implacable / nature? Even the green thought of April / grows ever more distant, exiled by / winter's fierce grip, by snow's vast solitude."

He runs to his lover's arms and shivers at "… the sudden shock of your beauty, / of pleasure beyond all expectation." He knits a grand finale, breathtaking and unforgettable, "Waking beside you after our night of love, / I want to give you the gift of my life / and February's book of snow."

For my comments on "Sarnia By Starlight" and "Quince-bush In Winter" the reader may go to my essay "Architects and Epitomes. A Word about Three Canadian Poets: Richard Marvin Grove (Tai), John B. Lee and James Deahl. Comments on poetry they have published in The Envoy, the CCLA newsletter (Poetry) (2019)," in my review book *A Shower of Warm Light Upon this Land and Us.*

For my brief characterization of the significance of the poem "After Coming To The North," the reader may consult my essay "My College Canada; My Sentimental Canada. A Brief Reflection on Canada and its Influence on Canadians and Cubans," also in the above-mentioned book.

James Deahl once more strums the strings of feeling and stirs diverse emotions. He has been doing that in the fifteen books to his name I have in my bookshelf. No wonder he is one of my favorites.

A Review of J. Graham Ducker's *Metamorphosis and other Short Stories* Hidden Brook Press. (2019)

MSc Miguel Ángel Olivé Iglesias. Associate Professor, Author, Poet, Editor, Reviewer

I grew up in a home of avid readers and constantly-supplied/replenished bookshelves. Novels, poetry, historical documents, biographies and of course short stories, decorated my childhood, youth and adult years. They made me feel like I was the hero of so many tales or the protagonist of a variety of themes. Poetry and short stories, for their usual brevity, were my favorite read. Asimov, Bradbury, Poe, Lovecraft, Hemingway, O´Henry, Oscar Wilde are just a few authors that I remember from those years.

In more recent years I delved into Canadian short-story writers: Alice Munro, Shane Joseph, Richard Grove, Norma West, Graham Ducker, Kim Grove, among many other fine authors who visited my reading hours. Today I am modestly commenting about, *Metamorphosis and other Short Stories*, by J. Graham Ducker, a well-known and accomplished Canadian writer, teacher and poet. My acquaintance with this author was chiefly through poetry published via the Canada Cuba Literary Alliance formats (*The Ambassador* magazine, Bridges Series Books), but when this collection of stories came to me and I read the opening story, I decided I should say a few words about how I liked his style.

I recall my own attempts at short story writing. It is difficult and tricky, for you must condense ideas, hook the readers, lead them into and through the plot and hand over a sweeping, intriguing dénouement. Graham attains all of this. *Metamorphosis* is part of the title of the book and one of the stories inside this riveting collection. I could not avoid feeling a Kafkanesk appeal as my interest crystallized the instant I saw the title.

The second reader-catcher was his Foreword. I am a teacher, like Graham, and I know well what he means by "no fluff and fill," putting "new twists" and "possible continuation to the narrative." These are as much ingredients of a good short story as they are of good teaching, and Graham Ducker does a good job on all accounts.

It is not my intention to cover all the stories in this review so I will just talk about two of them, which will serve as "bait" for the reader to pick up this book. "Another Time,

Another Place" is the first story Graham chose to offer the readers to showcase this fine collection. I was trapped. I absolutely love stories with the mystery Graham weaves so neatly from the onset. In a succession of rapid, short but precise sentences, the author introduces us into the atmosphere of the place. Well-crafted descriptions, separated into distinct paragraphs and clear-cut wording present a structural arrangement contributing to the desolation and solitude of the place in physical and temporal terms: "old farm house," "uncut grass," "long unused areas," "sealed well," "weather-beaten barn," "shutters, some of which dangled from one hinge."

After that introduction, the author presents the rationale behind the man in the story wanting to purchase the place. Then without pausing, the author introduces glimpses of the plot: haunted house, alleged murder. In what sounds like a ball being hit from one side of the tennis court to the other, fast and without a break, the two characters engage in a realistic, short-sentence dialogue of what-ifs and probabilities.

One of the best moments in the story is when the character enters the house and "The veranda boards groaned as he walked to the door. The hinges whined as the heavy carved door swung back and thumped against the wall. The foyer floor-boards also creaked." This suspense builds up and bursts one page later in the character's inner thoughts: "Why don't the boards squeak when she walks on them? She's probably too light." Confusion and alarm fills the reader.

Graham's narration overlaps with Jeremy's thoughts and face-to-face encounters with two portraits on the wall of the old house. The man in one painting is presented as "austere" and Jeremy decides he will "get rid of that painting." The woman in the other is "a beautiful lady… smiling... her eyes were not."

From this point, a new frame in the story: that of the facts veiled by time and rumor of what had happened there now being revealed. The first twist in the story is when Graham broaches a taboo topic in society – but I will leave that for the readers to find out.

The end of the story is as quick and simple as it is superb. No need for superfluous entanglement. It is an unexpected twist too, which I won't tell either, but certainly worth your reading. "Metamorphosis" is very aptly the eponymous title for one of the stories as well as the book. Beyond the uncomplicated configuration and presentation of the plot, Graham has been able to compose an extraordinary piece. It unfolds from an apparently basic every-day domestic husband-wife situation and personal predicament of a man in the first lines out to a "treatise" that explores social-psychological, philosophical and even anthropological musings in the mind and words of the character.

Prose writers, poets, artists have always wondered at the why of things, why nature, why us – why is this happening to me? Graham brilliantly turns the story into reflection, learning, evidence of the need to pause and think and be human so as to find our place under the sun. There is a moral in the story, outstanding, well-conceived and transcendent. We take delight along the way in the comparison of the butterfly's cycle of life, her metamorphosis, and that of Henry Walker's own change as he ponders and lets off steam and is finally flooded by an understanding that places him back where he belongs, socially, psychologically, personally. The answers he was looking for were inside him; he just needed to find inspiration on the outside first.

I could not avoid noticing that the character's surname is "Walker." Did Graham name him like that on purpose? Was his "walker" status a condition to grow in and outwards towards a mature insight of his world?

As in the other stories, Graham honors the foundation of his style: unexpected twists, sense of continuity passed to the reader, suspense, fiction, mystery, humor, delicately knitted in amusing turns of the story and of our own minds. I enjoyed this almost 300-page book.

A Review on Don Gutteridge's *Lily Fairchild* Hidden Brook Press. (2019)

MSc Miguel Ángel Olivé Iglesias. Associate Professor, Author, Poet, Editor, Reviewer

An unquestionably outstanding and well-established poet, Don Gutteridge shows the rich tessiture of his writing in this superb, heart-touching piece of prose, *Lily Fairchild*. The novel is an ode to sacrifice and endurance, to determination and courage, to freedom of thought and act, to faith magnificently worded in one of the book's final meditations: "… belief is a hard flame to extinguish…"

As a reader I don't need a more suitable way to connect with a book than the one chosen by the author, as he starts by describing Lily's childhood settings, packed with family details: "Lily was glad to be in the comfort of the trees' canopy. It was cozy here, like the cabin with Papa's fire blazing… While outside, heard only by her, the snow sang to the wind and no one in the world was lonely… She would surprise Papa at his work, celebrate another tree felled, and laugh when he swept her up and twirled her around, saying ´Lady Fair Child, may I have the pleasure of this dance?´"

The opening line in the book, "Something stirred in the darkness ahead," can be considered premonitory of what would befall Lily prefaced in her Mama being sick. I value the allusions to Old Samuels´ mumbled stories, a thoughtfully depicted character in both personality and language, an element that is appreciated in Gutteridge´s choice of all dialogues, idioms, turns, graphic representation of speech, etc., which speaks highly of his meticulous studies to write the novel.

Furthermore, at the threshold of Chapter 6 Gutteridge displays still another ominous act, "I'm...Lily… Papa sent me… Sensing the bewilderment in the woman's face, Lil's heart sank. She fought against the faintness and vertigo as best she could, but it felt as if her bones had melted outright in a treacherous sun."

Exploiting these factors, Gutteridge prepares the reader for the avalanche of events unfurling from his pen. In many ways those early chores and experiences Lily, seven years old, had to assume and learn from molded her charisma, and may have given her strength to face the hardships and setbacks she would encounter along the way.

Two especially tender-sad moments come to us with the mother's "Let's-have-tea,-little-one" instant when she tells Lily of her and Papa's previous life and how they came to a new country, and the scene with the cameo pendant with a silver chain that Lily's mother showed her: "With a start, Lily recognized her own eyes. "Your grandmother." Mama's eyes filled with tears. She reached into the box again. "I saved this, out of the storm." She held up a gold chain on the end of which dangled a slender cross no more than half an inch long. Instinctively Lily leaned forward and the crucifix settled on her throat as if it had always expected to be there." Auspiciously, this moving minute comes back to us at the end.

Lily Fairchild finely chronicles, in its status as historical fiction, a period – rather a succession of periods – in the Canadian past that approaches natives´ life – stylishly accompanied by the use of words coming from their languages, what brings the reader closer to the textual atmosphere – and sketches crisscrossing seeds that grew into the Canada we have today.

Alongside, Gutteridge remains loyal, and constantly refers to one of the central motifs in Canadian writers, nature. He is faithful as well to his excellent treatment of family themes – skillfully addressed too in his poetry – placed either in the 1850s or in more contemporary contexts.

Another welcome virtue in the book is place references constantly being made – a tribute to Al Purdy's devotion to Canadian geography? – which play an important role throughout the novel, not just spatially but also from a historic-contextual perspective. More significantly, Gutteridge´s accounts are the result of deep research to recreate locations and situations accurately.

Despite Lily's misfortunes and hard times, Gutteridge does stimulate the reader with some high peaks in her life in the form of her Aunt Bridie – family – "Bridie wanted to be severe but couldn't manage it… (Her Aunt enrolled Lily in Common School, giving Lily up as help around the house), and "Don't you fret about it, child," Bridie soothed. "Not much learnin' goes on in schools anyway. Come September, we'll teach you to read proper." She was looking at Lily now. "Remember this: We're not gonna spend all our life chewin' dirt." (Bridie gave Lily consolation after humiliation in school). Once more, Gutteridge leans confidently on family ties to channel these two emotional instances in the novel.

A most delicate matter becomes the centerpiece in the story when Lily gets pregnant. Such occurrence in the late 19th century would certainly be critical for a woman, given the epoch, which I won't advance here, of course. From this incident up to the dénouement, readers will be taken on a carrousel ride, going up, going down with Lily's predicaments. Were it not enough, Gutteridge gives us a soul-rending scene in Chapter 12: "I do love you, Tom." "Then you'll marry me?" Lily looked away, then back. "I can't," she said. "But why?" She felt the full weight of his hurt and her own. "I can't marry a soldier."

This is *Lily Fairchild.* The book is masterfully filled with wise dialogue and monologue, with profound reflections, introspective and clear intentions to teach and leave an imprint on the reader. I have enjoyed Gutteridge´s way to deal with history in the making blended with memories and an intensely personal story. These ingredients will please the most demanding of readers.

A Review of Donna Wootton's Novel *What Shirley Missed* Hidden Brook Press. (2019)

MSc Miguel Ángel Olivé Iglesias. Associate Professor, Author, Poet, Editor, Reviewer

"A celebration of life involves stories." This is the first line of the book's last chapter. This is what Donna Wootton's book is about. Family issues, secrets and stories are inevitable and ideal for authors to explore. There are delicate themes, but worth writing about. Everyone has a family, everyone weaves through the "slings and arrows" of family conflicts. What Shirley Missed gives us a taste of what we know well, of what many of us have experienced. The author does it in a fast-moving, snow-balling unfolding of events from the very beginning.

The characters are wonderfully credible. Wootton paints a picture of their behavior with a confident hand. She exploits their predicaments letting mini-plots in the conversations rise and shock me. These fuel the crescendo of the main plot when Pamela, Shirley's daughter, bursts into the room: "How could you?" Pamela barged past her mother. "What were you thinking?" she said as she stomped into the hallway without hugging her mother." Once the conversation starts, it is one discovery after another. Wootton provides surprise turns that create suspense and interest.

To my delight, I detected nuances of humor as well, despite the tense situations, in Shirley's thoughts trailing off to her many precautions ("Shirley kept her hands folded, thinking how clever she'd been wearing that hat. Not only did it hide her face from the dealers, it also hid her from any road cameras they passed.") and arrangements for what she had done that upset her daughter and the family then to her comments about her pregnancy. Such feeling remained with me throughout the book. On page sixteen I was already determined to go all the way to the end.

Another example of the author's skills is her time interplay with scenes, the overlapping of events that shift from the family conversation to Shirley's thoughts, both to the far past and to the moment her husband and daughter are pressing her to talk. The author succeeds in charging the atmosphere with more and more questions, which give Chapter 1 material enough to fill the next 200 pages.

What follows turns into an excellent meditation about immigration, doubt, faith, human values, vanity, old age, etc. As if this were not enough, she covers the philosophical ideas of how life unfurls, people's lives, dreams and sacrifices, and of course finally, death. This confers Wootton's style a plasticity that I enjoyed as a reader. There are social-psychological ramifications at play throughout the book. Wootton handles them chapter by chapter, through the characters´ reflections and aspirations.

The author moves on different themes, touches upon them or develops them, but they pivot on the main plot, as I argued before: the human sketches and circumstances described by Wootton are understandable and believable, a quality I appreciate as a reader.

The story, the plot, the characters and the message are valid for those like me who have accumulated anecdotes and memories with the years. It is helpful too for younger generations experiencing life. The book is a welcome voyage into people like us, no overdoing in its proposal, no superfluous lines or unnecessary characters.

Wootton writes with ease and insight, showing ins and outs, ups and downs in the scenes, the inner lacking and desires bubbling in Shirley, which affect those around her. Wootton also unveils society's multi-cultural fabric and traditions; objectivity, elegance and poise in her seasoned pen, and looks at the gentle threads of family interaction, chiefly the intergenerational one.

I could notice the fineness with which Wootton outlines people's hopes and subjects of conversation. Solidly based on family values and synergy, the author achieves in painting, beyond words, the cultural input brought in by a diverse inflow of immigrants, exceptionally harmonized alongside the existing one. Family is the core, the forge and springboard to venture into the world or come seeking warmth and love.

Wootton also does well in displaying for the reader a variety of events, customs, and musts in social attachments. She knits the chapters together not only on a temporal plane of space, place and concrete names but also blends with the ethereal construct of time.

I was pleased by the author's dedication to the prom. In Cuba, one important date in the life of a teenage girl is the "*quince* party." In Cuban culture this party is held for a girl when she turns fifteen. It is a celebratory day with joyful rituals and ceremonies. It includes a convertible car parade for the birthday girl, photo sessions, new clothes, party with friends, etc. The author's intention to give the reader all the details of the prom stroke home with me.

The prom, the bridge game, the market, the beach, home, the golf tournament, the demonstration, the police station, funerals, etc. are the author's socially-projected "alibi" to ripen the novel's plot. They are the contexts where human thoughts are ignited and acts performed and made visible by Wootton.

Enjoy this new book by Donna Wootton. Readers should not miss it, as they should not miss the author's graceful depiction of people and places, of circumstances and fate. Wootton has celebrated lives, starting with Shirley's, and in doing so she has left us a story that deserves to be read and pondered.

Exploring an Indefatigable Explorer: Robert Sward's *All That I Have Not Made.* Hidden Brook Press. (2020)

MSc Miguel Ángel Olivé Iglesias. Associate Professor, Author, Poet, Editor, Reviewer

It was a delight to read the poetic works by Robert Sward. His book entitled All That I Have Not Made is a gem of a book. Iconic Canadian poet A. F. Moritz referred to a poet's "job" in an interview as "To write well: creatively, authentically, powerfully, beautifully.... poetry is partly self-development… is duty, belonging to a community…" This description applies to many Canadian poets I have read during my years of reviewing Canadian poetry. Such is the exceptional case of Robert Sward, an American-Canadian who has been prolifically, systematically writing and publishing poetry since before I was born.

In a Hidden Brook Press release a blurb reads: "Robert Sward´s life´s work has been and continues to be poetry." There are many ways to honor a man´s work but that statement caught my eye for its overwhelming, simple truth and that is how I took an interest in Sward´s poetry collection, All That I Have Not Made (Hidden Brook Press, 2020).

On the book´s back-cover you will find Earle Birney´s valuation: "Robert Sward proves himself to be one of this country's finest poets…" In a nation producing poets from coast to coast; where literature, including poetry, is deemed as a national treasure and its poets are deeply appreciated, the fact of being considered one of the finest among the fine, unquestionably speaks highly of the man and his talent. Poet Laureate (2016-2018) and recipient of many awards, Sward has published thirty books. He is, as Carolyn Kizer puts it, "still fresh, ingenuous, and funnier than ever…"

The title Sward chose for a collection that brings together his decades-long career of crafting poetry comes from his poem "All for a Day." It is noteworthy that Sward offers a formidable book proving he has indeed contributed so much to what I call "poetdom" yet still focuses on what he has not made. But, that is Sward, an endless seeker, an unstoppable human being on the go, a trespasser of the cobweb into what Foley refers to in the book´s Afterword: "Sward's poems are the result of a plunge into a never fully ironized, often hilarious sense of mysticism: they are the product of a restless, spiritually adventuresome sensibility..."

This is the Sward we read and perceive in his poems. Foley describes him: "At once a Canadian and American poet, one with a foot in both worlds, Sward also inhabits an enormous in-between. It will come as no surprise to readers to find that his poems get at the moment of truth by being deeply unsettled, by refusing to rest in any particular other than the cosmic ambiguity of the wholly visionary and the wholly sensual. Past, present and future—and their tenses—assail him equally" (we will revisit this in our last poem under analysis).

Sward said of himself, "All I am really hungry for is everything". He opened his book with the breathtaking quotation, "I eat the words that remain, and am eaten. By nothing, by all that I have not made." In more than one manner, this is the poet I am revealing today from my perspective. His self-definition, his attitude before the world and his bearings in it will be with us through an understanding of his poems.

Robert Sward is, in my view, a chronicler of both his life and life around him. Canadian poet James Deahl postulated that "Poetry was something that could not only speak to the issues and concerns of one's own life but could operate as a tool to allow the poet to discover an organizing principle outside of day-to-day human life..." (Quoted from Under the Watchful Eye, Broken Jaw Press, 1995). Sward has done that too; he has attempted to look into the issues and concerns of his life to discover how the "outside" operates.

Foley quoted Sward saying that "many of his poems have to do with love, divorce, multiple marriage, aging, loss, and the challenge of bringing up children in a highly unstable world ... What is sought in all this work is liberation, illumination—it. The joy of his writing is the joy of the quest." Such a quest has hand-guided Sward across his writing, where many poems reflect what he sees in a story-telling style, overlapping thoughts and experiences penciled with a conversational, oftentimes informal surrender in poems filled with polysyndeton, interjections, curse words, etc.

In reference to Sward´s work, Foley says it is "Outwardly "zany" and fanciful... inwardly serious, troubled and questioning. As well, the heaviness we might trek into in some of his poems is lightened by the funny component, a marked feature in his pieces. We are in the presence of live poetry that mirrors the poet´s states of mind and the extended anecdotes/urges he needs to burst out on his path to liberating his soul.

Thus, we begin our journey with "The Kite," a heartfelt piece opening the book. Superbly metaphorical, the poem deals with death coupled to flying a kite. Touching, premonitory lines like "I still heard Auntie Blue / after she did not want to come down / again," prepare us, if we are ever able to prepare ourselves for this, for the sadly wonderful integration of realities the poet achieves: "And the string fell down / slowly for a long time. I was afraid to pull it / down. Auntie Blue / was in the sky, / just like God. It was not my birthday / anymore." The poem ends with the insertion of an expressive means called detached construction (after the semicolon): "And it was too bad

/ it was so hard to pull her down; and flowers," which aims at connecting two lines of thought, the former being the way he assumed Auntie Blue´s demise and the latter the image of a burial place.

"A Walk in the Scenery" is very much the story-telling trait I mentioned earlier. The narrative takes the reader along the events being lived by the viewers. Descriptions, senses aroused, the sensation of entering and first-hand experience: "It is there. And we are there. In it. / Walking in it, talking, holding hands. / The nickel postcard—the glossy trees; / the waterfalls, the unsuspecting / deer." In addition, a Sward who honors the deeply-rooted Canadian tradition of contemplating and admiring nature: "The deer / we are watching, at the same time / (through cameras, binoculars, eyes…) / so perfectly wild, and concerned / —with the scene they are, their glossy fate / silence, Nature, their rotogravure pose— / that they remain, not watching; rather, / staring away from us, into the / earnest, green and inoffensive trees."

"Hello Poem" is a hilarious-serious piece where the poet, from an open, broad-view stance, looks at his life, the "feats" done, what was not done. Sward embraces everything trying to cover as much as he can using effective expressive means, enumeration ("Hello wife, hello world, hello God, / I love you. Hello certain monsters, / ghosts, office buildings, I love you. Dog, / dog-dogs, cat, cat-cats, I love you") and repetition ("I love you"). As readers we pick his satisfied attitude, his frankness and peace with all surrounding him, all happened – or not – to him.

I found "Chicago's Waldheim Cemetery" appealing. It reminded me of a poem I wrote, "So we can move on" ("The iron-gate looks gloomy / it knows well where it leads to / what it holds inside: / all those stolen from us / silence weighs heavily / suspended in time, / stagnant / shackled to tombstones…"), as the boy´s words hung over me: "We are at the stone beneath which lies / my father's mother. / There is embedded in it a pearl-shaped portrait. / I do not know this woman. / I never saw her…." The poem carries gravitas in silence only broken by the insistent weeping of the father.

A pinch of irony-humor engulfs the poem too, a resource to hint the divide between father and son; at least in feelings towards a person the boy does not know, but which might be a sign of future decision-making moments in his own life: "My father weeps. / He is Russian. He weeps with / conviction, sincerity, enthusiasm. / I am attentive. / I stand there listening beside him. / After a while, a little bored, / but moved, / I decide myself to make the effort. / I have paid strict attention. / I have listened carefully. / Now, I too will attempt tears. / They are like song. / They are like flight. / I fail."

Of the many themes Sward has written about, sex stands out. One of such poems is "Nightgown, Wife´s Gown" with a sensuousness that rolls on and overleaps the lines. A husband´s claim elegantly voiced, extremely evocative line, "There is no reply," and the end phrase, "I caress her wings": "I knock on their shoulder blades / ask to be let in. It is forbidden. / But you're my wife, I say. There is no reply. / Arms around her, I caress her wings." I saw points of coincidence between this poem and one of mine, "wings of desire" ("all she has on / are wings of desire / we fly…") in which I proudly quoted Sward´s "I caress her wings."

A poem I particularly liked, and also quoted a line from for one of my poems, is "All for a Day." This piece seems to follow Robert Sward everywhere. He quotes the poem often, and it is also quoted by others. Having baptized the book with a line from this poem as we mentioned before, I see a poet who holds it as a banner. The poem defines him from beginning to end: "All day I have written words… // A poem remains. / But in the words, in the words, / in the fire that / is now words. / I eat the words that remain, / and am eaten. By nothing, / by all that I have not / made."

The pleasure of being a poet and writing poetry has been expressed by many poets. I remember Glen Sorestad, for example: "I like the state I´m in when a poem takes hold / and won´t let go," Don Gutteridge: "The unstoppable urge to write" or Richard Grove: "Poetry and I found each other." This is what I felt with "Iowa." While still a chronicle of Sward´s "exploits," it turns out to be, from where I stand, an ode to poets and poetry writing. Its epigrammatic closing is self-explanatory: "What is the point in this? / Someone scrawls six lines and says them. / What a strange happiness." Slightly – apparently – oxymoronic, the words strange (adjective) and happiness (noun) harmonize in the cozy-itchy feel when we have to write. Well-accomplished piece.

I wish to end my comments on Sward talking about one more poem. Being a university professor myself (English as a foreign language), I do know how central grammar is in the learning of a language (I am part of "the vast chorus / of the lovers of English" Sward mentions in our next poem). I even shared the idea with Canadian poet friend, and professor, Antony Di Nardo, who generously offered me grammar books I will find precious use for in my English lessons. Now I have read Sward´s "Grammar as Hymnal" and his first-class "class" on grammar. I loved the poem. One particular stanza I enjoyed was "We sing of grammar which is our compass / providing, as it does, clues as to how / we might navigate the future, / at the same time it / illuminates the past." *Navigate* and *illuminates* strike me as key words not only in-context but also as a compass Sward has pursued his entire life.

Practically impossible to encompass all of Sward´s poems (or his poetics as a whole) in one review, I have briefly attempted to present my insight of his work both by making specific allusions to some of his pieces – those I felt more drawn to if you will – then making generalizations of his craftsmanship and the meaningfulness of his poetry. His input to literature is remarkable. I enjoyed many of his poems in All That I Have Not Made; however, the fact that Sward is published by Hidden Brook Press under the esteemed John B. Lee Signature Series is credit enough.

Nevertheless, there is more. I will end with quotes from what authors and critics have said about Robert Sward:

> "...fierce, new-minted and convincing... he has voice and a range..." The New York Times Book Review on *Kissing The Dancer.*

> "I like the wide sweep of it. There are many mysteries between father and son that people don't talk about… There's much leaping, but each line, so to speak, steps firmly on something solid. The father figure comes through consistently, there's a lot of buoyancy, and the son is consistent and fine too." Robert Bly. Author of *Rosicrucian in the Basement.*
>
> "Comic juxtapositions and startling wordplay heighten immediacy and expectation. [Sward's] larger-than-life [podiatrist] father dominates Rosicrucian in the Basement: 'Feet don't lie/don't cheat, don't kiss ass. Truth is/peoples' feet are too good for them.'" ["One-Stop Foot Shop"] Sylvia Adams, Canadian Bookseller.
>
> And the most passionate of all: "Here is Robert Sward, still fresh, ingenuous, and funnier than ever. His life–and what a life–is an open book. You can read all about it here. What's more, you will want to call your friends and read poems to them over the phone. I know, I've done it." Carolyn Kizer, Pulitzer Prize Winner on *Four Incarnations.*

Anything else to say? Yes, Robert Sward has made and done so much in his long life. And there is much to make and do, much to explore to be "at the service of an essentially visionary impulse" as Foley says. Sward confessed he "saw two worlds interpenetrating… // World "A" and World "B"… // world like a skyful of blue suns…" (Taken from his poem "The Biggest Party Animal of Them All"). Let´s trust he will go on seeing worlds. Let´s toast to that.

A Review on John B. Lee and Richard M. Grove's *In This We Hear The Light* Hidden Brook Press. (2013) (Poetry and Photography)

MSc Miguel Ángel Olivé Iglesias. Associate Professor, Author, Poet, Editor, Reviewer

This is a book of poems and photographs produced by two Canadian doyens in both writing and photography, recipients of myriad awards and titles almost everywhere. The first thing that called my attention was the title, a warm play on metaphors and senses: the light that can be heard. Not any light, probably not falling anywhere but on special places the authors know firsthand and were mesmerized by. Then the "This": you'd have to read the book to discern what This is. The second thing was the infrequent, at least for me, black color of the pages contrasting with the white letters.

The authors´ caprice? A trick to catch the reader's eye? I consider it had to do more with the very heart of the book: the spirit of love, friendship, life, hope and optimism against the gloom. Notice that white pages do open and close the book, a signal of hope and optimism and light that will embrace and protect. Then came my "criticism" of the poems and my "appraisal" of the photographs. In This We Hear the Light is a brochure filled with poetic, cultural, social and human discernment. The poetry within is committed and carefully thought out; the photographs are exquisite and well chosen, well labored upon: two great aesthetic minds at work. One artistic manifestation can replace the other, and the reader will accept the swap: the poems are images, the photographs are poetry.

Both are X-rays of an island and her people taken by pleased, yet insightful and concerned-with-reality artists. Both are a repository of feelings: joy, hope, sadness, nostalgia, endurance, grief captured by the authors, who cannot escape the allurement of the country they depict, and do not wish to veil their way of expressing themselves from a very personal and outsider-who-has-been-inside perspective, which is raw sometimes, but never irreverent, in my view.

Let's visit some of the poems. Both Grove and Lee appeal to the senses, the treading into that light so they – and the reader – can "hear" it better. In the poem "In This We Hear the Light," they resort to verbs like see, hear, smell, touch, and make reference to eating and food. Their words emphasize brightness as opposed to the "crumbs of day," and regale us with the power of sharing and the spiritual magnetism of simple things and simple people. They also move across other poems in the book alongside tall, revered figures in Cuban history: Martí, Ché, Fidel, Raúl.

In "The Urge," the use of polysyndeton carries the reader on waves that move and break on the shore, granting them life and multi-colored appeals to the senses through images in the verbs: shoal, curl, swell, fall, course, and caress.

"And for All of That" is a two-plane poem of cross-cultural significance. One can feel the strong imagery that calls to the senses through colors: crimson, blood-spattered, dark rose. It reflects the poets´ open mind, appreciation for and concern with religious syncretism and life in Cuba, combined with the individual glimpses of people they know.

The book threw light on me. It brought to the surface a different angle of the Cuban mosaic of culture, life, time, death, nature, society and people. It was a snapshot of what visiting friends think of us Cubans and how they see us amidst our social processes. The poems and the photographs sing to the simplicity and beauty of everyday things. They freeze great instances of small and grand things across the island.

Language – both written and pictorial, technical and creative, inquisitive and admiring – offers the reader a book to read again and again. Most of all, it is the people Lee and Grove refer to, the love and the friendship found in Cuba and nurtured through the years, who opened the path towards the light that we can hear in the book.

John B. Lee and Richard M. Grove feel at home. They fell in love with Cuba, its landscape and seascape, its people and the light that comes from them. That is the "This" made words and images in this book.

A Review of Richard Marvin Grove and John B. Lee's *Two Thousand Seventeen* Sanbun Publishers. New Delhi. India (2018)

MSc Miguel Ángel Olivé Iglesias. Associate Professor, Author, Poet, Editor, Reviewer

India is a wondrous land of mystique to the outsider's eyes, a nation of reverence and love to its people. Richard Marvin Grove and John B. Lee are lucky to see their book published in that country as well as translated into Hindi – the book is fully in English and Hindi. There is no doubt that the Indian reader will be fascinated by their poetry in return. They will touch many hearts and nourish many minds with the power of their unique voices. Their poetry sings of the every-day things that pulse in the lives and minds above culture, language or creed: family, friends, love, respect, places and memories.

These motifs are served to the reader with delicate, humorous, intimate and honoring tidbits of nostalgia. Mr. Grove's and Mr. Lee's masterly and generously mold their distinctive style. Universal themes and subjects are recreated in their lines, bringing their lives to us, their remembrances of special locations that are special because their next of kin, their ancestors and their offspring, colored them with their presence through the years. Homeland is at the center of their writing, so are their families and many others whom they have met in their friendship-packed, ever-blessed journeys towards the timeless slumber.

There is kindness fluttering from Grove´s very first poem, "thank you gentle friend," which introduces the tone of the book. Intimacy and description of personal contexts flow from line to line in the book easing the Hindu reader into his world. The descriptive feature is masterfully evident in the poem *"Bike ride was cold to iced edge": "sunsets over lake / grey pink quivers / in February breeze."*

A conversational mode characterizes Grove's poems, involving the reader, as an optimist, philosophical view rustles underneath: *"How wonderful it is to be digging. / How wonderful to be able to dig."* The poet sings to the facts of life and living. He exults the physical act of digging in the garden – connecting with nature – and rejoices in the spirituality that emerges from it.

We will enjoy the great poet too, magical in his images, ones we can almost touch or feel to be direct witnesses to: *"Dimming cloudless sky rakes bare branches, / black, resting in sliver moon's silver slide. / Thousands upon thousands, waves / of Red-breasted Mergansers dip and glide east, / into darkness / undulating, riding primitive tide of survival / under Jupiter's timeless eye."* Grove is on fire, regaling us with these magnificently combined metaphors.

One of Grove's poems in particular had an impact on me because I was born on September 11, 1965, "High Bluff Island September 11, 2010." Grove delineates natural scenery echoing spine-tingling sequels of the 2000 attack to the US towers: *"the seething cacophony / of writhing life has turned / to a battlefield of skeletal remains… / twisted sun-bleached rags, / progenitors legacy, now hollow / shells, tomorrow's dust / the foundation of life."* Yet, upon such vision, the poet seeks out faith, fortitude and confidence in *"the foundation of life."*

Grove´s section in this book is like a journal. He brings his ideas together in a symphony of love, family, friends, experiences and memories. He cannot write his poems without the outpouring of his everydayness. These elements will strike home with the Hindu soul in such a way that they will revel in his carefree yet committed-at-the-core style. One poem title summarizes, for me, the essence of Grove's signature as a poet: "In the Deep Heart's Core," there lies all the power of his writing.

In the Deep Heart's Core

Owed to Yeats and his poem "The Lake Isle of Innisfree"

I will rise tomorrow and return
to our home on-the-frigid-shores
of Lake Ontario
snow-laden deck. Pines
in the back, looming,
will greet me and I will have
some peace there
where calm   whispers
through the silent red
of dogwood, branches
perched upon by darting chickadees
foraging in winter solitude.
Midnight there will glow in quiet
silver moon's still beam,
a calm that will hush
into   my   long silence.

I will rise tomorrow and go
into the squeaking footfalls
of a walk on a chill afternoon
hand in hand with Kim away from these
sand-swept shores
of Havana east. I can already hear
the ice calling me home,
a shore-washed welcome
of broken frazil. I hear it
in the deep heart's core
this shore-chattered welcome.

Grove says he was honored to be published in this book with John B. Lee, an icon of Canadian poetry. Lee opens his section with a splendid, soul-caressing piece that starts: *"I wake in the morning / to the crimson hallelujah / of divine sunrise."* From there, a rainbow of depictions, narrations, colours, experiences carrying the reader elsewhere and everywhere: *"brilliant-winged tropical hallucination / something from the forests of Sri Lanka / something from the treetops / of Costa Rica / the lost green song of a canopy / ringing the bells / and climbing up the Lilliputian ladders / of their farmhouse kitchen…"*

Lee also pays tribute to family, especially his mother: *"Marilyn Monroe / and my mother / were born the same year / and my mother / born in the little house / on the hardscrabble farm near Mull Crossing / was also a great beauty / my mother / in the apple orchard / wearing a ragged straw hat / her hair / still long to her shoulders / captured in a late-summer photograph"*

Lee reminisces and philosophizes as well in his poetry, trying to find answers to his questions and doubts: *"and I wondered for a moment / am I alive enough / to listen like / an infant-unborn swimming / through water sounds / towards a second darkness lost as I am in the first."*

We will feel the romantic poet in Lee in his poem "Oh Silo My Columbarium," roaming physically and mentally, giving the readers an idyllic vision harmonized with a mature view of his own.

Oh Silo My Columbarium

for me
the ghost on the hill of the family farm
comes shaded
in the white-shadow-shape
of the silo by the barns
for it has lost its all
from the fragrant seasons
of my youth

when the air seemed sorghum sweet
in the early fall
and the silage line
came greening up the inner walls
like the harvest as a water line
in a handsome well
how high the ladder went then
with the rung's force
in the instep of the man
assigned to climb
out of the earth
and into the blue circumference
of a circle of sky
as though he were rising
to the limits of heaven

in that litmus of light
encompassed by an azure describe
of something portioned by desire
for divine ascension
like mist in the mind of morning
and I remember
how winter formed on the ten tined fork
in the redolent curve of wet feed
as it fell to strike its odour
rung by rung descending to the floor
how like a columbarium
that choir of pigeons worshiping dawn
in flights of the silo's dovecote
preening the iridescent beauty of their blue-green feathers
shitting as they flew
up and out of a shattering white like milk splash
and the after-stain of faded lime gone spirit grey
why then
is it with lamentation alone
that I mourn
the vacant ground
where walked my father
like a patch of fog
adrift in the solid reasons that we live
all melted away

like fruit from seed and leaf from shade
and thus our branches break at the graft
in sun-cast weather
when the weight of darkness feels
like the burden of light

These poems are Grove and Lee, blending faith, tradition, time, death, and much more with outstanding expressive means and stylistic devices that never repeat themselves. The fountain of imagery expressed by both writers and the freshness in their style do not cease to amaze me – and I have had my share of poetry reading in my life! I wish the reader as much joy and enlightenment as I had with this book.

A Review on Richard Marvin Grove's *Living in the Shadow* Hidden Brook Press. (2017)

MSc Miguel Ángel Olivé Iglesias. Associate Professor, Author, Poet, Editor, Reviewer

I just finished reading *Living in the Shadow*. I found it hard to read, very hard given the topic and the fact that I have a fifteen-year-old daughter who is the light of my life. I have had to detach (more yank) myself from that fact, so that I can make comments on the book and the writing.

I believe Mark Beatleman, your main character, is a troubled man, with socio-psychological, spiritual, moral and loving "deficiencies" in his life stemming from when he grew up; we can see that in the reading and in the excellent development of the character. These moral deficiencies should be the explanation; not the justification. The way he argues and pins the blame on everything, mainly society, leads the reader to contemplate the concept of a deranged mind.

We know that the brain can be likened to a box with electricity, wires crisscrossing in every direction (the synapses). If by an astronomical misfortune of astronomically varied causes one of these wires burns or the person is born with a limited cycle of life because of his/her biological mapping, or it was tampered with by outside factors, also of astronomically varied causes, then that person is doomed, his/her acts then might be the result of his conscious and willing self. Is that Mark Beatleman´s case? We can only surmise.

What he did and how he described his depravity, what he said about finding comfort or mental ease in his daughter´s agreeing to the rape, is in itself depraved and disgusting. As a father and as a human being, I was horrified by Mark Beatleman´s actions and thoughts. But, let us also consider his right, his ability, to change, or at least suffer a transition. Isn't everyone entitled to that in the legal system? It is a pity there are no moral courts.

The Kafkanesk passage is very powerful and, on a dark level, interesting: a reflection of Beatleman´s turmoiled brain? Is he seeing himself as a monster? – But the monster scampered away…There may be room for an alternative interpretation to this sequence. Well done, Grove.

Moral corruption is apparently around the corner. It is hard to restrain from biological demands that come with the formative years of an individual. It takes a high level of morality and values, and a sense of social and human responsibility to then suppress your urges and put shackles on those ones that break the most basic logics of all: you must not harm others. Grove has written an impacting story that needs to be told. It will be difficult to forget.

A Review on Richard Marvin Grove's *Some Sort of Normal* Hidden Brook Press. (2018)

MSc Miguel Ángel Olivé Iglesias. Associate Professor, Author, Poet, Editor, Reviewer

Richard Marvin Grove takes us from his fictional memoir, *Living in the Shadow*, to his novel *Some Sort of Normal*. Both books are poking a finger at the open wound of pedophilia that festers in just about every corner of our society. Both books by Grove are open to as many acts of judgment, interpretations and degrees of now-pat-Bea/etleman´s-shoulder-because-he-explained-himself, as there are people out there lurking in the shadows.

My previous analyses on the main character, Mark Beatleman, from *Living in the Shadow*, aimed at making it clear that reading the book was hard, so very hard, because I have a thirteen-year-old daughter who is the light of my life. I had to detach myself, much against my will, from that fact, so I could read the book with a cool head and comment objectively, if possible, on its achievements as an excellent literary contribution.

In my review prior to this, I do remember likening the brain to a box with electrical wires – an elementary but helpful comparison – wires crisscrossing in every direction (the synapses) and prone to maybe short circuiting at some unfortunate point in time and space due to a multiplicity of causes. Thus, in *Living in the Shadow and in Some Sort of Normal*, Beetleman´s acts then might or might not be the result of his conscious and willing self, they might or might not be the outcome of a short-circuited brain. Is that Mark Beetleman´s case? We can only shoot in the dark with speculation – or perhaps shoot Mark Beetleman himself.

This new book by Grove, *Some Sort of Normal*, makes me feel as uneasy as his fictional memoir, *Living in the Shadow*. In being human, Beetleman has trespassed principles of decency. This is not normal in a moral society, but he jumps through verbal acrobatics to justify his acts of breaking the sacred realm: a father-child bond. Psychological "deficiencies" may be the explanation yet never the justification to do evil, much less to try to validate such acts on a social level. Beetleman claimed it was an act of love in doing what he did to his daughter. The fact is it was an act of manipulation, humiliation and depravation.

I found the opening chapter to be first-rate. The characters, compared to *Living in the Shadow*, are now more involved in dialogues, more in an exchange, helps me, the reader, flow along the confessions he is about to make. It sets the atmosphere of what is to come. More dialogue and added chapters are the variations from the original book, *Living in the Shadow*. The story flows very well as a novel.

The way the main character, Mark Beetleman, presents arguments in his favor and blames everything, mainly society and the way he was raised, leads the reader, time and time again, to realize we are in the presence of a vicious mind filled with glitches. In the explanations to his dreams, he has done nothing but seek to hide behind a dirty, lame, self-excusing mask. However, it does not give him impunity at all to harm others, who are human and deserve dignity. What remains to be seen is how deeply disturbed this man really is from a psychological standpoint. No one is above the holy laws – written or not – of ethics and affection and ironclad respect for one's children. Here the boundary is black and white, no shades of grey.

The image on the front cover is significant in many ways. It invites Freudian and non-Freudian followers into the enigma of why the table and its reflection. My first thought is to wonder how isolated it is, how out of place in a peaceful and quiet setting. Its brown, mossy appearance underwater speaks to me of moral corruption. I can talk about the dirty boards, faded colors, and rusty bars, all of them images of dissolution and corruption. What did the author want to convey with such an image? What does the table stand for? Is it drowning or surfacing – or both, like the character´s intermittent strife to survive beyond his acts and uncover some rationale, some defense to what he did?

Why the title *Some Sort of Normal*? Is it an invitation to peel layer after layer off Beetleman´s warped mind to see if we can find an iota of "normal" in an abnormal man? Is it an invitation for the reader to look carefully at what is normal and just how normal are we all?

The final lines of the novel reveal Beetleman's effort to try to fit in and feel comfortable around people. "I was never so glad to be myself ever in my life. I can't believe it. I'm not a cockroach and I am glad to be me." Read between the lines, dear reader! The man is clearly stating how he feels! He is not an insect; he is human – glad to be him! Once more, there is manipulation and a futile endeavor to be at peace with himself, and sell that notion to the reader.

Remember Grove's words at the beginning of the book: These are all "feeble justifications and rationalizations by the offender." Nothing more. Therefore, reader, parents, people of decorum and principles, beware! Richard, I welcome your new book on such a delicate topic. You laid it down in a new style, with a different voice that speaks to reach as many sensible and sensitive readers – minds and hearts – as possible. You have created a voice that skillfully states, reveals, prods, exposes and succeeds in warning and teaching in a skillfully balanced language for expert and layman, being in logical turns colloquial and technical according to the chapter and the contextual situation depicted by the author.

We can feel the painfully thorough research done by Richard Grove for the book and his genuine urge and concern to reach people, to send a meaningful alert into the future. I restate what I said in my comments on the original book: Richard, you have written a painfully dissecting, shocking story that needs – claims – to be told repeatedly, as frequently as these acts, sadly, repeat themselves; some made public, some struggling beneath the awful veil of silence and duress and impotence.

This story stands as a red flag for parents, next of kin and our dear children. It will be difficult to forget. Ask the families and victims of such deviations.

Comments on poetry published by Richard Marvin Grove (Tai), John B. Lee and James Deahl in The Envoy, the CCLA newsletter

MSc Miguel Ángel Olivé Iglesias. Associate Professor, Author, Poet, Editor, Reviewer

The year 2016 was a landmark in my life: I was introduced to Canada Cuba Literary Alliance (CCLA) Founding President Richard Grove by CCLA Ambassador in Gibara, Jorge Pérez. From then on I was immersed in an extensive, intense and refreshing exchange with Canadian poets and their craft.

My college studies, Teacher Education English Major, had provided insight of Canada from a bird's-eye-view cultural-literary approach as part of my curricular pursuits but it fell short of really fanning out for me the wealth, depth, width and prominence of Canadian literature.

Richard Grove filled that void with a wonderful host of digital and conventional books coming in from 2016 until today, and also invited authors to send their works to me. It turned me into an avid recipient of poetry chiefly, but also prose, essays and research carried out by scholars (Terry Barker, for example) on outstanding Canadian authors and Canadian poetry in general.

His support, along with many other poet friends – like John B. Lee, who *actually read* my humble poems and took time to suggest, respectfully, changes for improvement! – was motivation enough to work on and soon publish my book *In a Fragile Moment: A Landscape of Canadian Poetry* (Hidden Brook Press, 2020), a tribute compilation of thirty-five reviews and essays I wrote about the thirty-one Canadian writers. Such a project was immediately supported by Grove (who put love, faith, personal budget, publishing house, and unlimited efforts into seeing it come to fruition), Grove's wife (Kim, who gently gifted me with a line from her poetry to title my book), Lee and James Deahl.

Many other Canadian poets celebrated the idea too. During the past months, the inflow has gathered spectacular momentum. I have been receiving books from Canadian poets who, encouraged by dear poet friend James, have generously contributed to my bookshelf, my knowledge of their literary prowess and my further appreciation of Canadian poetdom.

Among the many generalizations I can make out of reading them and all Canadian poets who have entered my life (deep connection to the land; identification with nature and wild life; a rooted sense of belonging to Canadian geography plus social-thought ramifications therefrom; a feeling of proud nationality/nationhood; freshness and versatility in the use of expressive means and images; etc.), some are particularly salient and heart-warming to me: their commitment to family and values – values to champion, besides, what is true and what is moral beyond and above family contexts, and transcend in terms of aesthetics, cognition and axiology to what is loftier and spiritual. In addition are the poets´ reminiscences of childhood and their recollection of friends and friendship.

Both from the very opening dedication pages in their books, poems and in-memoriam poems, we are moved by this convergence of leitmotifs which stand the test of time, finely penned and felt by the poets. May this "warm light upon this land and us" *(Taken from the title of a poetry book by James Deahl, A Shower of Warm Light Upon this Land and Us, 1993, Moonstone Press. Canada)* continue to shine and bless Canadians, Cubans and lit-loving people of good will everywhere.

Richard Marvin Grove (Tai)

Grove is every inch a poet. He captures the world's everydayness, eternalizing it for us and for those to come. He exudes poetry, delicacy/passion and experience in everything he writes and does. His poem "Spring" *(Published in The Envoy 88, June 2019)* is an ode to nature, a deep-rooted love affair Canadian poets have. Irony is handled as an expressive means of the language: "April is the cruelest month / with temperatures rising / finally into life, even at night."

The utility of the means works in the following terms: "A word used ironically may sometimes express very subtle, almost imperceptible nuances of meaning." *(Taken from Stylistics, 1981, Moscow Vyssaja Skola, by I. R. Galperin)* Richard Altick stated that "The effect of irony lies in the striking disparity between what is said and what is meant." *(Idem previous quotation)*

As readers, we sense this "disparity" immediately, as we are aware of the season's majesty, but the next lines in the poem also contribute to help us see the masterful use of irony: "Lilac buds are kissing / the warm air with swelling buds…" Grove meant exactly the opposite in the opening lines! Spring is presented too as opposed to winter, "… frost threatened landscape / that swirls memory with desire / only to be slammed / by her sister, winter's / punishing joke." The poet contrasts the two seasons: "The last of shadowed snow / the melancholy reminders / of hunkering down / are all but gone." And goes on in obvious joy: "Black budding branches bulge / with the promise of life / now full of winged music… / … it will not snow – again."

His poem "My Heart Grows Wings," *(Published in The Envoy 92, October 2019; previously in A Small Payback, Ode to Victoria Lake. Hidden Brook Press, 2016)* is rich in beauty and plasticity of image and metaphor: "Ebony branches part / to brilliant sundrenched view…" Repetition as a stylistic device is appreciated in "… down, down over the tree tip spires / to vast wilderness panorama…" emphasizing the notion of movement and expansion. Epithets enhance his interpretation of the natural scenario: "… vast wilderness panorama… unsullied, pristine. From the general view, the poet now zooms in on a spectacular sight he describes in unique tropes: "Wing tips deep, / loon lances / silver mirrored sky."

The universe leans softly onto his sheet of paper, gently star-guiding his pen in poems that echo "… a gentle whisper of harmony…," for example, in his piece "A silent echo heard" *(Published in The Envoy 93, November 2019)*: "a gentle whisper of harmony / ripples across / the mist covered lake / into the universe."

Tai's sensitive, artistic eye knows how to give a poetic touch to reality, granting it the colors of nature, in its role of gracing human presence: "From our hotel window / we can see a small group / gathered / in a willow-draped park…" There are key **word-images** in the poem to really construe how imbued the poet is in what he watches (we cannot forget he is also an artist) and how he is able to draw out cosmic connotations from a common sight and serve it to us, nature once more a blazoning element: "in slow motion / doing Tai Chi. / Fifteen or more / filling the early morning, / **swaying in unison**, / a gentle **whisper of harmony** / **ripples across** / the mist covered lake / **into the universe**."

We enjoy wonder-poetry reaching the readership through The Envoy. Grove and my next poets honor the newsletter with their submissions and publish edifying creations. Thank you, Tai, for your poetry flowing so freely, so intimately.

John B. Lee

John B. Lee's writing gift has made him a recipient of as many awards as is humanly possible. He has tirelessly crafted piece after piece in his long, prolific career. He has written nearly about everything with unique perspective and style. He has memorialized his travelling experiences in books about his own and other countries. As well, Lee's contribution and adherence to the long-standing tradition of celebrating nature – awesome, edifying, unavoidably present, whether we see it or not, whether we want to see it or not – is transcendental.

Canada's formidable scenery owes to poets as much as they owe to its being so glorious: an all-embracing foundry of beauty and spiritual growth. Lee also celebrates life and turns his language and his style into forging tools leaving us with such poems. No better insight into Lee than my closing quotation: "… a true idiosyncrasy of style is the result of an author's success in compelling language to conform to his… experience." *(Taken from In a Fragile Moment: A Landscape of Canadian Poetry. Hidden Brook Press, 2020)*

Lee's elegance has notably achieved that. For example, his poem "My Love is Like an All-Day Rain," *(Published in The Envoy 93, November 2019)* one of the many he has sent to me during our e-mail exchanges along with his permission to publish them, invites the reader to the unique experience of love from an in-depth look at nature in a sustained orchestration of similes and metaphors.

Lee eases us into the natural world, the coupling of rain and soil and the chain of unfolding events, revealing the magic of what otherwise might seem like ordinary. The perspective he reveals for us is sweetly magnificent. Amidst this explosion of images capitalizing on the wonders of nature, Lee allows us to anticipate sensuousness that blossoms – to honor the poet's chord – in the end-lines: "but keep this rain in mind, my love / these ethers gauzed in grey / were / once the amorous continuum of weather / caught within the petals of your crimson rose." I have read the poem several times, each taking me nearer to a heaven-on-earth state, each uncovering a fresh path. Thank you, John, for this extraordinary gift you share with us.

James Deahl

James Deahl, another prolific poet friend, who regales us with artistry at its best. James writes with a style that envelops and snuggles warmly, even when winter is the subject. The poem "Sarnia By Starlight" *(Published in The Envoy 93, November 2019. Poem taken from Travelling the Lost Highway, Guernica Editions, 2019)* is a harmony of cityscape and natural scenery, superbly, sensually blended by James to sing to his beloved Sarnia: "Sarnia's adorned / by a skein of lights / strung between sky / and night's river."

The city is suspended in a symphony of blue pulses, evening falling, a girl's open blouse, a skein of lights, sky, night's river and starlight giving us a cozy feeling of home, sweet home: "Must every object / that summons desire / be beautiful? / An ashplant / That girl's open blouse?" Nature is a diva in his poetry: "A slow, blue pulse / from cold water. / Call and response of smoke and wind / as evening falls" and he magically bestows it with human traits in a first-class combination of simile, metaphor and personification: "Starlight enters / with ancient airs / like a bride, / the music dancing / on her shy lips."

The second poem, "Quince-bush In Winter," is the poet's sharp eye capturing beauty in winter and trees. Still connected to the human reference in the poem, James grants the leading role to the quinces´ warmth that "spreads through January's cold." He portrays the bright side of things with metaphorical expressions: "My neighbour's quinces have all put on white caps. / She never harvests her quinces / so they hang all winter, orange globes / lighting my mornings as the sun begins to rise."

James Deahl appeared in 2020 as our Guest Poet, together with Norma West Linder, on the 16th The Ambassador volume, the CCLA official magazine. Thank you, James, for your touching poetry.

I have tried to condense in a few words my modest insight of three exceptional poets´ writing. My first review book, *In a Fragile Moment: A Landscape of Canadian Poetry (Hidden Brook Press, 2020)* included longer analyses on specific books they published. Hence, their reluctance to appear here again.

I am lucky to have been able to read their poetry, understand and enjoy it. In the process they contributed to my personal growth, both though their poems and their advice, support and encouragement. I cannot think of a more fitting title for this essay than calling them poetry architects and poet epitomes.

A Journey of Pleasures in Richard Marvin Grove's Cuba Poems. *In Celebration of a Trip to the Caribbean* Hidden Brook Press. (2002)

MSc Miguel Ángel Olivé Iglesias. Associate Professor, Author, Poet, Editor, Reviewer

I have been blessed during my personal and professional life by demonstrations of acknowledgement that I have welcomed with obvious self-pride at having accomplished something, or brought joy and satisfaction to someone, an acquaintance, a total stranger, or as is the case now, to a friend I care about: Richard Marvin Grove (Tai), Founding President of the Canada Cuba Literary Alliance (CCLA). Yet I have also taken it with a mature awareness and objectivity that if I am acknowledged by an experienced, qualified friend, it is because I have earned his praise and what I do has some worth.

Recognition comes in many forms, one of them is being asked in my present status as CCLA member – promoted later by "conspiring" friends and members to CCLA Cuban President and Editor-in-chief of The Ambassador magazine – to edit books and anthologies, cooperate with other writers and editors, translate, revise and finally write reviews about poetry and prose.

Poets like John B. Lee, Bruce Meyer, Ronnie R. Brown, Elana Wolff, Laurence Hutchman, Eva Kolacz, Ed Woods, Michael Mirolla, Laurie Kruk, Henry Beissel, etc., have kindly asked me to write a few words about some of their works and include them in my review books. Actually, my second volume came to life thanks to Grove and CCLA key player, James Deahl, who put brain, brawn and heart into promoting my work and encouraging those fine authors to send me their books, which they did in a most generous gesture, filling my bookshelf with treasures.

It is my privilege today to talk about a book by a prolific writer and artist, Richard Grove. I cherish a personal collection of over twelve of his books, photography, poetry, prose or an integration of these, he has sent or brought to me these last four years, ranging from his early works to more recent publications. I chose a particularly interesting book to write about thus honoring in return his having honored me with his friendship, trust and help in many circumstances and ways.

Nevertheless, my review does not stem from a mechanical, biased reason based on his being my friend; it fully responds to his contribution to Cuba – through *his* CCLA, founded in 2004 and still floating above objective and subjective setbacks; vigorously, invaluably supported by many judicious patriots and friends – of Canadian and Cuban culture, and logically of poetry.

Cuba Poems. In Celebration of a Trip to the Caribbean is a book of fond memories, eagerness to visit, know, meet, mix; conceived in the very same "wide-eyed with anticipation" favorable atmosphere Grove refers to in his opening piece, "Cuba, Here We Come." The title reflects his joyful experience with a key phrase, "in celebration of."

We are invited to a trip across the book's proposal of poems and anecdotes, forged from a tourist's vision of a Cuba he faces. His first-world individuality enters a third-world reality with expectations and curiosity – and an open heart. I remember the first time I wrote about him, some four years ago: I reviewed the collaborative John B. Lee-Richard Grove *In This We Hear The Light* (Hidden Brook Press, 2013, photography-poems) and said the authors "… do not wish to veil their way of expressing themselves from a very personal and outsider-who-has-been-inside perspective, which is raw sometimes, but never irreverent, in my view." *(Taken from my review book In a Fragile Moment: A Landscape of Canadian Poetry, Hidden Brook Press, 2020, my essay Touched by the Light. A review of John B. Lee and Richard M. Grove's In This We Hear The Light (Poetry and Photography) (2013) Hidden Brook Press. Canada)* In the book I am commenting today, we will encounter this mood, and will understand it inasmuch as there is empathy and appreciation in his heart for the Cuba he knows now and loves.

Grove's initial "tourist excitement" is sensed in the end-lines: "Passports clutched in one hand / tickets and reservations / clenched in other with / dreams and hopes / of sun, sand and snoozes." The richness of the poet's style begins to shine right at this point: "Passports clutched in one hand / tickets and reservations / clenched in other…" is a direct primary dictionary meaning sentence; however, two elements jump at me as a reader.

The first one is the employment of two effective transitive verbs (they are in fact non-finite verb forms, *ed*-participles, acting as noun-modifiers, adjectives) to describe the state of elation or nervousness or impatience the poet is in, "clutched" and "clenched." He could have simply used *held* or *carried* but he chose, intentionally, to color the poem with more semantically-charged words, stylistically enhancing the intended message. The second detail is that passports, tickets and reservations are clutched and clenched respectively, yet these verbs are added a metaphorical meaning-role when the poet pairs them with the next sentence unit, a prepositional phrase: "clenched in other with / dreams and hopes / of sun, sand and snoozes." Now the brand-new linguistic-stylistic hue is evident.

An extra element I *dare* refer to regarding the verbs *clutched* and *clenched* is that together with their metaphorical value, there is also a latent zeugma in their use. Zeugma is "…

the use of a word in the same grammatical but different semantic relations to two adjacent words in the context, the semantic relations being, on the one hand, literal, and, on the other, transferred." *(Taken from Stylistics, 1981, Moscow Vyssaja Skola, by I. R. Galperin)* Both verbs function literally in "Passports clutched in one hand / tickets and reservations / clenched in other…" and transfer their meanings to figurative enclosed in the prepositional phrase "clenched in other with / dreams and hopes / of sun, sand and snoozes."

The setbacks I mentioned before are hinted in the second poem, "Never Leave Home Without it." The tour guide, "with wide eyed smile," reminds them and readers that American Express cards cannot be used in Cuba due to blockade issues imposed by the US government. Fortunately, "Visa and MasterCard are welcome."

A tempting blend of nature-loving body and heart, willingness to escape the hectic mazes of Toronto life and gratefulness for being at a Cuban beach resort, are the aspects finely recreated by Grove in his "Hard to Believe We are in Cuba." Thus we are pleased to read "… I woke from my sun-worshipping / dream state to the sudden salty / reminder that I was on a soft, / tan, sandy beach of Cuba," understand the radical – agreeable – change he has undergone as "I was no longer in my Toronto condo bed / being lured by computer, email, / time restraints and the bottom line" and swim in his "… cool, green ocean, / paces away, beckoning me."

The poet's fascination reaches a cusp in the next poem, "More." He broadly contrasts being in Toronto against being in Cuba: "In the middle of November, / everything is sweeter, / better in Cuba than in Toronto." To illustrate his sensations he engages in a sequence of allusions to nature, sun, breeze, evening; even the galaxy: "The blossom kissing afternoon sun / shines more brightly. // The palm shimmering breeze / of early evening is more alluring. // Orion's midnight belt / sparkles more clearly." Between the lines, an environmentalist vision is noticed. Orion is more discernible from a pollution-free geographical location.

The poem ends as it began, the first stanza is repeated. In a way, I see rhythm in the words chosen and in this structural arrangement, much in line with the musical context the poet is a part of.

In my words about Richard Grove's poem "My Heart Grows Wings," I said it is "… rich in beauty and plasticity of image and metaphor." *(Read the whole review in this book: Architects and Epitomes. A Word about Three Canadian Poets: Richard Marvin Grove (Tai), John B. Lee and James Deahl. Comments on poetry they have published in The Envoy, the CCLA newsletter (Poetry) (2019)* My opinion applies entirely to Grove's next poem, "A Cuban Sun Shower." On the course of my explanation, I will present the poem whole, as it is brief and worth-quoting.

The poet rejoices in the exuberance of the place, "Lush, outstretched palm branches, / sweep the Cuban sky, / gently fanning in salt air," deploying a sustained metaphor that lasts through the whole piece: "… the single cloud / that grins overhead / christening our morning…" Personification as an expressive means – "… the attributing to abstract or inanimate objects qualities characteristic of persons." *(Taken from New Horizons, McClelland and Stewart Limited, Revised edition, Canada, 1965)* – is attained through the verbs "grins" and "christening." This language means occurs as a result of interplay of realities fused by the poet, who reveals metaphorical nexuses-implications textually overlapping: "… the single cloud… christening our morning…"

The finish lines heighten this figurative conjuration conceived and achieved by Grove: "christening our morning / with a sun shower / of expectation."

Allow me to revisit prior views I have written about Grove's style. As my conclusion to John B. Lee and Richard Grove's book, *Two Thousand Seventeen* (2018) Sanbun Publishers. New Delhi. India, I said "The fountain of imagery expressed by both writers and the freshness in their style do not cease to amaze me." *(Taken from Timeless Poetry in a Timeless Land. A brief review of Richard Marvin Grove and John B. Lee's Two Thousand Seventeen (Poetry) (2018) Sanbun Publishers. New Delhi, India, in my review book In a Fragile Moment: A Landscape of Canadian Poetry, Hidden Brook Press, 2020).* My assertion holds up to characterize "A Cuban Sun Shower."

I know Richard Grove personally, I call him my friend. I can say for a fact that Tai (that is how friends call him) is a man of many qualities. Apart from his artistry in photography and writing, his generosity (proven in many occasions), his profound faith, his way with words and his gift as a public speaker, we also enjoy his humor. Logically, it is present in his poetry. "I Only Have Eyes For You My Love" is a fine example of humor and use of expressive means, like suspense and repetition.

Suspense operates on the anticipatory mechanisms a poet triggers in the reader or listener (we cannot forget the original orality of poetry) therefore its "main purpose is to prepare the reader for the… logical conclusion of the utterance," *(Taken from I. R. Galperin. Stylistics. Moscow Vyssaja Skola. 1981)* That is what Grove does in the poem aided by repeating (another expedient expressive tool) the opening refrain "I only have eyes for you, my love, / though I must confess."

Grove does not leave out **metaphors**, "I only have eyes for you, my love, / though I must confess / the copper tone buxom senorita, / **licked by the Caribbean sun, / caressed by the Cuban breeze**, / beamed for me." In order to really display more realistically the nature of a poem, which recreates a true event, the poet incorporates a seemingly conversational twist. I say *seemingly* because we are not fully certain of how much his words materialize from his "confessional" attitude into the tangible act of confessing.

To build up a conversational style, the poet resorts to colloquial phrases and idiomatic turns: "… a pretty Cuban **head turner**." "the… senorita, / … **beamed** for me," "bronze **toy boy**, / blond, with tattooed **pecs**…" (this latter, a final clipping in lexicological terms) to which he incorporates one example of foreignism, "senorita," to put the situation in the Cuban context (Spanish language).

How the poem finishes, unexpected ending, is the expression of humor, assisted by the ways in which he depicts both the "senorita" and the boy. The last two lines, "I only have eyes for you, my love / though I must confess," are reminiscent of sincere love and the religiousness that is part of Grove's profound faith I mentioned earlier: notice that in all the previous stanzas the verb, "confess," is transitive (it has a direct object); on the other hand, in the last line it changes to its intransitive function (no direct object), so it transfigures into an allusion to a possible act of religious confession.

The last poem under analysis is "A View of Contrasts." Grove shows his expertise in depicting nature, be it Canadian or Cuban, with superb images. As he does, we distinguish as well the contrasts he made explicit in his poem, "Hard to Believe We are in Cuba." Highly descriptive to the minutest detail, "… the dirge of dry red clay earth / with palm rimmed horizons / capping jungle homogeny. / Lush banana plantations fill gently rolling valleys past / concrete, tin capped, peasant huts…," the poet talks about an everyday Cuban scene: "… modest, laboured gardens from / roving speckled pigs and / white bearded billygoats…"

The contrast is shown in his lines: "… adventures end, takes us back / to North American style opulence called / creature comforts of pressed linen…," strengthened in the closing ones, "Home, past roadside open wells where / post siesta / farmers water their / rib-clad burros, / sending us on our way with gentle / smiling waves…" Grove has portrayed an idyllic setting, his nostalgia seeping beneath the lines, metaphors alive and moving: "… gentle / smiling waves."

I have traveled with Richard Grove. I have embarked on a journey of pleasures in resemblances and contrasts, content and form, text and context, literality and tropes. And I have returned for a celebration, too, of Cuba.

A Review of *Flying on the Wings of Poetry*, SandCrab Books (2020)

MSc Miguel Ángel Olivé Iglesias. Associate Professor, Author, Poet, Editor, Reviewer

I have heard old people comment that home is where your dreams are. While this is quite true in my experience, I must say *Flying on the Wings of Poetry*, a Hidden Brook Press English-Spanish book, tells us dreams are also possible in other places that feel like home. At least this is what the four fine Canadian poets visiting these pages prove to us. John B. Lee, Antony Di Nardo, Laurence Hutchman and Richard Marvin Grove capture life, turn it into a poetic experience and hand it out to us.

Their way to write about themes showing their involvement at an affective-creative level with geographies far from their homes reveals a connection that we appreciate as readers. They cannot elude – nor do I think they have tried – the charm, the magnetic force pulling them in, prompting them to craft fact-depicting, mostly experiential, strings-attached poetry.

Thus their poems travel with their exploring lines: "out there just beyond the edge of ice where the blue beauty of moving water begins to shoulder over the white line" (Lee); "Not clouds that look like clouds but beach umbrellas aloft among the palms that stick out like tongues and plumes and rattle their leaves in spoken words I easily distinguish." (Di Nardo); "The tree still stands austere and gaunt, guarding the harbour by the wall of the military station. Its roots unusually above ground so alive in their slender serpentine shapes anchor the tree in the earth." (Hutchman); "Jupiter perched on timeless horizon west over *Los Caneyes*. Twilight silver grey scanning the stars…" (Grove).

They also glide, rise, plummet with facts and feelings in a phantasmagoria of metaphors: "a lone vulture soars, kiting the thermals the black flag of his dropshadow drifting echo-darkness over the mango groves caressing the orchards by the lake as though with the sorrowful breath of a widow's veil" (Lee); "Above a cavalcade of clouds, blue skies stretched in a patch of metaphors for the journey up and north, a sudden sort of blue, sublime, like pages and pages of the very same colour in books on our shelves." (Di Nardo); "On this giant hotel wall the figure of a woman has a mystical appearance: from her one ear a large fish extends with a flower on its blue fin, from the other a stingray with molecular flowers." (Hutchman); "Only the imagination will know what will happen to those coins hurled into the Atlantic waves of tomorrow's fury. I am not sure that Poseidon will care much about a fistful of coins tossed into his salty treasure trove" (Grove).

And they rejoice or suffer: "here within this sand-white arc of bent bones long-lost in the disinterment of a deep grave at the sad moment when the heart drops through as on some archeological grey-water gloaming when heaven refuses the light loss" (Lee); "*Café sin leche* (milk is impossible to find) and a little *tortilla* starts every day and the place never changes, not in our lifetime, not since Apollo went to the moon, not since we decided to follow the rise and fall of the orb of the sun" (Di Nardo); "When the lights go off, I drift into the night sky, millions of years away, reminding me when I was eight lying in bed, thinking back in time farther and farther, stepping into infinity" (Hutchman); "If there is one axiom of life it is that man will survive with less. In Cuba there is enough love and camaraderie to go around." (Grove).

SandCrab Books published in 2018 the fourth volume of the Bridges Series Books, *Where the Heart Lies*, with two Canadian and two Cuban poets. The poems´ core significance had to do with writing from the heart about places it has been touched by, leitmotifs emerging from a sentient identification with them. Our present book follows on that chord leading beyond the poets´ frontiers.

Poetry nurtures, poetry uplifts; poets are everywhere, and it is their duty and pleasure to discern the many realities offered to us with different eyes and present them to people. This is what these four poets have achieved, outstandingly, with their hearts upon their sleeves, as reads the title of the fifth Bridges Series Books volume, soon to be published too. I cannot call this "heart-related" aspect of poetry publishing by Hidden Brook Press or its imprint, SandCrab Books, a mere coincidence.

The bond between poets and context, between their gift and their product at the service of life, is significantly appreciated in this new book and flaps like a proud banner for the publisher too, who always aims at the best, at the most representative, heartfelt literature.

The Warmest Beat, the Brightest Light on Both Sides of Life's Tunnel. A Review of *Hearthbeat*, Edited by Don Gutteridge. Hidden Brook Press. (2020)

MSc Miguel Ángel Olivé Iglesias. Associate Professor, Author, Poet, Editor, Reviewer

Fifty-nine poets, including the book´s editor, capture in heart-warming wording and fine style the sometimes time-diluted – or apparently passé-in-these-modern-hectic-days – idea of what family really means, in this anthological gem Don Gutteridge and the Hidden Brook Press publisher bring to us in 2020, *Hearthbeat.*

I have written about the subject in my reviews and essays (*In a Fragile Moment: A Landscape of Canadian Poetry*, HBP, 2020, and *This Shower of Warm Light Upon this Land and Us. Essays and Reviews on Canadian Poetry,* work-in-progress) about many (twenty) of the authors invited to this family jubilee.

I have been motivated by the fortunate realization that Canadian poets do have an "umbilical" connection with their roots, understood as a national and family historic construction of an individual identity. It tells them where they come from and defines them, lighting up their paths: the hearth, aptly registered by Webster´s dictionary, digital version, as "*home and family life: the joys of hearth and home.*"

Take John B. Lee´s nostalgic poem, "After the Bath," where the poet´s reminiscences get to us and send us back in time. It is the great poet singing to the great small things marking his early life, outlining his formidable legacy of poems-to-come:

> "… as my mother
> came gripping a towel
> a flag of love
> she meant for the nation of me
> and I newly cloaked like a terrycloth king
> a hero of saltwater stripes

ran quickly away from my youth
in primordial mornings kept close to the heel
by the shade"

The following lines, taken from James Deahl´s "Hiorra Summer," speak not only of a poet recalling his boyhood and family attachments but also that poet laying foundation as well as original leitmotifs (landscapes) and motivations to write, which would become a lifetime career:

"Every boyhood summer
we'd visit the old home Ulysses built
on the high slopes of Chestnut Ridge.
When thunder invaded the night
I would listen to the mountains,
try to catch their words
when they thought no one could hear"

I have quoted Deahl explaining his devotion to poetry: "*I decided that I needed poetry in my life… If I could find a way to speak to people…*" Definitely, from boyhood mementoes to a tall poet is what we receive today.

In "Horses Against the Horizon" we read a transfigured Keith Inman: a poet turned into a painter who leaves pictorial, nearly expressionistic, impressions on me,

"and the children thin
and weak with summer soup spooned
into mouths leaned
over wide white bowls //
It came sharp
like light cracking the sky
as thunder bent her
into wind-whipped wheat"

As we move down the book, we glide with poetic proposals constantly inviting us back to the "family womb." Already pictorially provoked by Inman, now we read John Di Leonardo´s poems.

Di Leonardo offers his spirituality and aesthetics by exploring and evoking, unveiling and *connecting* in that sentient human drive to build, either with words or with images – or with the overlapping produce resulting from blending both. He writes inspired by images, he turns into poetics *what was already poetry*, as he lets us know opening his book, *Conditions of Desire*, with a quotation from Simonides of Ceos: "*Painting is silent poetry; poetry is painting that speaks.*"

Thus Di Leonardo repaints, in word form, the works of art he so admires. He engages in ingenious labor and materializes a second "reading" – that is, a re-construal of a reality that had been interpreted before by a visual artist – this time with words.

Enjoy these graphic lines from "Sweetheart" *(Inspired by E. Manet's, "A Bar at the Folies–Bergère" 1882.)*

"Between storms
your tears like rain,
all colours washed away. //
In our bones we all know
sweetheart, real genius
unfurls rainbows in others.

We are deeply moved by Ronnie R. Brown´s "Home Again." A delicately penned piece – the poet´s eye-heart-hand nexus crafting a highly responsive poem of remembrance and homesickness – that endears our recollections and evokes sweet reflection:

"You pull into that familiar drive
expecting everything to be
the same: crocheted afghan
on the couch, aroma of fresh-baked
cookies in the air, the flowers //
A perfect picture and then
they come into view.
Shrunken somehow, their skin
like ancient cellophane,
so slow you hold your breath
as they wrench themselves
from the cradle of easy chairs
to welcome you home again…"

Joyful anticipation from the title and expressiveness of memories are kindled in "Family Album," by Anna Yin. A poet and critic, Anna has all the ingredients to make us tremble with her poetics. Heiresses of a millenary culture of Chinese origin, her veins carry blood of family stock that she holds and moulds in her poetry:

"They state —
my father, a golden lion,
with a kingdom in mind; rolling and roaring –
the darkness descends, with sight lost,
my father, a silent lamb.
They swear —
my mother, a wooden house,
with windows peering through the foggy road.
When too tempted outside,
closing the door and learning to listen —
my mother, a hut for night."

Our road through so many impressive poetic memoirs I cannot, unfortunately, cover in full in this review, takes us to Richard Grove´s eloquent title, "Fragments of Memories." Because that is what they are, the memories: *fragments* flickering in our minds, which either fade or endure, oftentimes depending on our affective willpower.

The poet puts it vividly, transporting us back in time, telling exactly what it feels like. In between, a mixture of sadness and happiness in recollections melting in the web of time past:

"Mother is living with what is left
of memories, fragments of time
surfing on a milky pool of reality.
It was very cold when skating
with her father, her at twelve
walking when no one else dared
join them at the rink, scattered glimpses
of scarfed faces blurred into focus //
Now all these years later, knuckles white
gripping wheelchair, running to get warm.
Soft silver hair shadows the recollections
of tobogganing. Was it with her brother
or her children fifty or sixty years ago"

The sad-glad alternation of memory – linked to the notion of old events revisiting, or to irreparable loss – is masterly presented in Grove´s "The Sleep," a eulogy to his father. Here the poet blends first-class imagery and innermost feelings epitomized in lines like "*the timeless slumber,*" "*the threshold of the great sleep,*" "*the ocean of no horizons*" *and* "*where consciousness fades then vanishes into the eternal*":

"Sleep dear prince,
now at the leaf-fallen years
of swaying amber grass
you are in preparation
for the timeless slumber,
at the threshold of the great sleep,
the languid undulating endless seashore,
the ocean of no horizons
where sky and water blend
with the mist
where consciousness fades then
vanishes
into the eternal."

The editor, Don Gutteridge, whom I have written about before (he is one of the few authors who appear in my two books on Canadian poetry), understandably left his own poetry for the end. I have then left my comments about his poetry to close this review.

Don opened his book with a statement, "To the core called family." There is no better introduction to a collection of poetry that celebrates the institution of family in its varied manifestations and ramifications. When we read Don´s "Going," our hearts leap out to the grieving soul that writes these beautifully sad lines. However, we seek to find necessary, unavoidable comfort in the closing line…

"When I first saw you
in that incubator
taking baby breaths,
your wee fingers still
wizened from the womb, glancing
off any horizon,
I didn't think we'd see you
growing golden into your bones,
but we did, and you grew anew
each loving day
you gave us, and when Death
drew you into its darkness,
we mourned your lonely going,
knowing you would never be old."

As a compilation, one of the book´s virtues is in the group of poets summoned to make this book come true. Such choice granted from the beginning the literary-sentimental value of what we have in our hands today.

In my *This Shower of Warm Light Upon this Land and Us. Essays and Reviews on Canadian Poetry* (work-in-progress) I quote from a poem by Don, "The Way Home" (from his book *Point Taken*, Hidden Brook Press, 2018): "The way home is thru / the heart, every blood-beat / hums with remembrance."

I stated in my review book that "Gutteridge´s *Point Taken* has brought happiness and homesickness to my mind." So has this new Hidden Brook Press release. *Hearthbeat* honors these quotations from cover to cover: family ties and memories beat in the mists of time never to fade because there are poets, editors and publishers who safeguard and remind us, readers, of the worth of family roots.

Where it comes to remembering about life and living, love and loving; we will always have the warmest beat and the brightest light shining on both sides of life´s tunnel, the one that leads us into, through and out of existence: family. Poetry certainly eases the passage.

Everywhere You Go Beauty Shows. A Review of *The Beauty of Being Elsewhere.* Edited by John B. Lee. Hidden Brook Press. (2021)

MSc Miguel Ángel Olivé Iglesias. Associate Professor, Author, Poet, Editor, Reviewer

The Beauty of Being Elsewhere, edited by Canadian poetic gem, John B. Lee, is a wonderful book everyone should buy. Reading it will inevitably spark two effects. First, the desire effect: to travel and see, "live," places that the authors describe, miss and memorialize so warmly. Second, the learning effect: we are enlightened cognitively and touched affectively during our many journeys beside the poets.

Lee's summoning power groups more than a hundred poets, mostly Canadian, between the covers of this "*Elsewhere*" anthology. *The Beauty* unfolds with Lee's selection of an attractive, I´d say "exotic," leitmotif, traveling. Emily Dickinson speaks to us in the book´s opening quotations, "*Go travelling with us!... By routes of ecstasy.*" The quotation's page finishes with an excerpt from one of Lee´s poems, "… *a Cuban evening feeling the lovely melancholia of being elsewhere* …" Both are poignant and well-chosen epigrams to the book.

Reverence and flashback reflections are felt in the pieces included in the book, outlined in the editor´s preface, lines wherefrom the title was born: "… *inspired by the journey or the sojourn these poems were written and have been gathered here to honour the beauty of being elsewhere.*"

Every poet offers his/her experience, the wide-open hues of each pair of eyes enticed by what they perceive and breathe in. It is an entire anthology singing the marvels of learning, seeing, touching and safeguarding in the mind´s niche "*things of beauty*" dazzling like a rainbow, heart-touching as if an angel´s invisible soaring had sprinkled afterglow dust.

The spirit of the book echoes epigraphically in the lyrics from Ian Bell's song "I'll Fly Away" from his CD "Free Range." These poetic lyrics sing the book into the theme of travel: "*Geese in the stubble and a deer in the corn / Listen to the water as the stream rolls by / Smoke in the air on a frosty morning / I'm going to fly away / Light through the valley as the sun climbs higher / Listen to the water as the stream rolls by / Sumac setting all the hills on fire / I'm going to fly away...*" Poets flew away – and returned with a bagful of responsive poetry we are enjoying from here to the end of the book.

Marsha Barber is context-thrilled in "Las Vegas," where sights, music, dancing, glamour dazzle and baffle flash about, "*I am part of the glittering Eiffel Tower / find the Paris of Moulin Rouge / Cancan dancers perform high kicks and wild splits / as Bellagio's fountains dance / I linger at street cafes / feeding sparrows fresh baguettes / tour art galleries / filled with Impressionist paintings / ride gondolas in shallow canals by Piazza San Marco...*"

Particularly spiritual is Nancy Bell´s poem "Never Linger," Her haunting lines instantly drew me in; "*Never linger by the orphaned house near the slough / Lest the spirits of the past catch your hand / And draw you with them into a sunny summer past / When the apple trees were young and heavy with fruit...*" and markedly idyllic is the last stanza, "*Never linger under the old twisted trees of the orchard / You may find a sunny meadow and August sun / In the deep cold of a January day / The soft moo of the milk cow and the drone of honey bees*".

Consider these lines by Bronwen McRae, "*Sit on the dock, a breezy morning. / Watch momentary mountains climb from the lake. / Later the water is a living carpet rolled between shores. / So real you could walk across, your toes sluicing through silky fibres. / Know you have witnessed loon love, / listened to squirrel gossip...*" The poet has been able to involve me with nature, enthrall me as a reader and give me peace. In a string of film-like images rolling softly; kindling touch, sight, hearing, threaded into appealing metaphors, MacRae treats us as almost-guests sitting on that dock contemplating the beauty of a place in her poem aptly entitled "The Writing Retreat".

The magic of traveling descends upon us taking us close and far across sea and landscapes that defy the four points of the compass. It was Ireland in Lisa McGuire´s "Song 3" and "*The tiny, dark pub... alive at just 11:11 a.m.*" Suddenly, it is Rhonda Melanson´s journey in "Strong Women," "*...play penny whistles and drums / in Alaskan string bands / lilt their chords in clear Juneau air...*" or Bruce Meyer grasping the book´s concept in lines I quote only a few from. They epitomize the beauty of being elsewhere and back: "A Grace for Welcome": *You have been many places, / and the world that followed you... / Come in. Rest here as you wish... / Feel at home. If you have left / the comforts of the familiar, / look around... / You bring the gift of experience / from the places you have seen...*

Later, you are in Michael Mirolla´s "Juhu, Mumbai": "*Fingerling on Arabia's sea, Mumbai / vapours in the distance, sky / scraping*" and miraculously back in Ireland in Mary Ann Mulhern´s "Fishing Village in Ireland": "*In Porturlin, County Mayo, Ireland / I stand on a cliff / Overlooking the sea / My mother says when she was a child / Sheep sometimes perished / On rocks below...*" or waking up with Richard Grove´s "Without a Word."

The fragment I quote shows his unending allegiance to Cuba, his love for the simple things he finds in my country and leave him speechless: "*I had intended / to sit in the Cuban sun / and read the wisdom of José Martí... / but the longing call / of my rooster friend / drew me to the top / of the stuccoed wall… / I was instantly, / without a word / with you and Martí*." Despite the wordlessness he writes about, expressive words flow in the poem!

John B. Lee himself becomes an agile stair-climbing tour guide roller-coastering us from sweet little Cuba in his "So, this is a place of places," "*we climb the four hundred steps / to the Cross of Holguin / and Manuel says / "So, this is a place of places ..." / and we stand / above the city*…" to cyclopean China in "Climbing the Great Wall of China": "*I climb the stairs / to where the great wall / breaks its spine / along the grey-green ridge / of smoke and fog above the Yanshan mountains*…"

It is impossible to comment on every fine and eloquent poet that Lee has carefully, skillfully, chosen. I have tried to capture the essence of this book by simply sharing ideas that came to me as I ponderously pored through the pages and lingered long enough to celebrate. Readers will appreciate and rejoice in this journey that Lee has laid before us. I found familiar names – some I have written reviews about or recognized from the many books I have reviewed – and I also ran into new voices that I will keep an eye open for in the future. Mostly, I have partaken in the stirred nostalgia of my own traveling, which has been limited but experiential; short but indelible.

As to *The Beauty*, it is unlimited in scope, widely experience-based, warmly long, and absolutely indelible for poets, editor and readers. Let´s end this review with Lee´s own elucidation of what traveling may mean, an excerpt from his poem "I Too Can Show the Way": *Where would you lead me friend? / into what future / and from what past / and by what light guide / and for what purpose go / and to what end / and with what faith …*

In traveling we meet with the past and savor it; we envision our many tomorrows, lean hopefully on them pedestaled on our present. In traveling we grow and become informed humans, we are invested with the gift of constructive comparison and contrast, we forge purpose, seek end and stand trustfully on faith. In traveling our individuality waxes as universality that we lacked as "locals," and we learn to appreciate "thereness" and otherness in geographies we had at our fingertips and encounters we embraced.

And after our Ulysses ventures, we value more our *home sweet home*, where we sit before a desk and thank *Calliope*, *Erato* and *Terpsichore* for the blessing of poetics. Let´s thank John B. Lee too for this new chapter of fine poetry, sceneries, people and engaging aesthetics.

A Word About a Special Issue of the Magazine *Devour. Art & Lit Canada*

MSc Miguel Ángel Olivé Iglesias. Associate Professor, Author, Poet, Editor, Reviewer

Poet James Deahl and I were invited as editors by the Editor-in-chief of the Canadian magazine *Devour. Art and Lit Canada* to prepare a special issue. In reading the fine poems my friend James Deahl put together for this new *Devour* issue I could not avoid realizing how cohesive they are, how they were born from each poet and found room in the articulate vessel he skillfully molded. It may have been Deahl´s editorial expertise. It may have been the pieces coming to life and falling into place – because *they knew* they would inevitably enter a phase of thorough selection, of tender treatment only a caring Uncle poet would give to the offspring of his brothers/sisters-in-poetry.

The poems included here are a melting pot of urges, motifs, passions, styles the editor simmered then poured as fresh pieces, which contribute from their individuality to poetic universalness. It is indeed easy to see why I felt so at ease reading them.

I cannot speak about each poet but I can illustrate with poems that express the quality, harmony, rhythm and emotional unity we will enjoy. Let´s take a fragment (all examples provided in this review are excerpts) from Briesmaster´s "esse est percipi":

> I have no real life without you. Am nothing, now,
> unless you notice me. No value, unless you
> confer it. Otherwise: doubt, toward despair.

A poem expressing love, thanking the lover´s sensitivity and acknowledging what is essential, it also stands as what poets seek and find in writing, "*No value, unless you / confer it.*" The concretion of values lies in human connection; without that perception of each other they cannot be reified. Significances are central, they make all things, animate and inanimate, acquire worth; and that is what prompts poets to word their emotions:

> How else can existence acquire substance,
> except as bright horizons of our meaning meet?

We notice the value-conferring act in every poem in this issue. We tremble with Deahl´s "Beyond Mere Death," where he mourns and embraces the magic of nature to "*borrow… surcease of sorrow*" *(from Poe´s "The Raven")*:

Midnight's storm cries out your name and in that
breathless moment when I turn you're in my arms
swift as lightning, bold as August's heat.

Or with Lee´s solid aesthetic concepts in "My Love with her Pocket Full of Glass":

in the multi-coloured
squint, in the
milk-of-magnesium blur
of eclectic bricolage
there is a beauty
that is also only her

As we move down this accord of poetry, beloved ones, nature, family, philosophical inquiries, etc. meet us. Let´s read this stanza of Sorestad´s "My Father´s Voice":

I have spent much of my life a writer,
seeking and finding my own voice
and now, here, in my own latter years,
I sing less, write less, and pass my time
pondering matters like my father singing,
the inherent shortcomings of memory,
and somewhere, a voice that lies
just beyond the rim of consciousness.

Fortitude and hope sparkle in these poems, to make a poet´s day – or his/her whole life. In "What Does One Hold in Poetry?" Yin addresses the underpinnings of poetry and voices her innermost claims:

Looking into the mirror
…torn by
sorrow and sadness //
yet, turning around
a smile in your dream
a hope in your heart

The healing powers of nature surround and fondle Grove in his refreshing piece "Aching to be On the Water, March 22." Surf in these lines:

> I swing east around Boulder Island,
> I swing west, surfing,
> by wind and waves, south back
> into the leeside calm of the cove.
> As I drag my kayak from lapping shore
> placed back into its bed of crunching leaves
> my spirit sings.

We are moved by the vigorous declaration and earnest request for love and life in Jaffe´s "My Letter to the World":

> I am the world, writing in response,
> hoping against hope
> for more light, fresher air, water
> clean and clear as starlight.
> I have whispered to you in flowers and fruits,
> thundered and wept in tornadoes and hurricanes,
> scorched in drought and fire,
> opened my heart to rebirth.
> I want to save my children, not swallow them up.
> Will you listen?

We nod in approval and full support of Wolff in her "Tear near the Knot," where she intimately relates to and posits from her sentient perspective nature´s role, nature´s treasures:

> The world is disarranged, the garden oddly
> still for spring. Where are the sparrows and robins, the crows? The
>
> cardinal pair that used to nest in the hedge? What are they up to now?
> And where will we all be brought?
> What we prize in poems, the absent birds already own: canny rhythm,
> cadence, vision, ambit,   open space

Finally, we revel in a dance of life and reverence with Wood´s “Spring Dance”:

> spring roulette and winter’s empty chambers
> of course, it’s unreasonable
> you spin before you think
> without care of consequence
> blood’s unrest pounds to explosion
>   your body swings and swivels
>   on bone and faith
>   all wet and wobbly
> you gasp and clap time to your heartbeat

My brief journey across this new issue of *Devour* invests my pen with argument, emotion and conviction enough to state Canadian poets continue to flourish *in and like* maple trees. Their *quintessential* sap flows in these pages.

Giving Sorrow Words. A Review of *The Blue Dragonfly – healing through poetry*, by Veronica Eley, Hidden Brook Press (2021)

MSc Miguel Ángel Olivé Iglesias. Associate Professor, Author, Poet, Editor, Reviewer

I have often wondered – privately, sometimes in my poetry – how the question of the meaning of life unfolds in the brain. Secret byways connect inner circuits in our "minds." They may run smoothly through an entire lifetime or – because of a concealed "background weight" – suddenly break. What is this baneful weight? What is the unfathomable aspect of its challenge? Why are some people able to wade through, and others weighed down? Zen, as described in Leo Buscaglia's *The Way of the Bull* (1973), teaches us that "the way" is many, but that an individual must seek his or her own path. The struggle for insight, to find oneself, and to discover one's own nature, gives meaning to life.

The Blue Dragonfly – healing through poetry by the Nova Scotia, Canadian poet, Veronica Eley, offers a challenging answer. It is a monumental example of how to cope with trauma, one woman's crusade to unlock, through poetry, the frozen circuitry of the mind. The longest journey is always personal (as I have written elsewhere). Eley's trek is a thorough, temporal exploration of self, as she strives – "divinely" aided – toward the (spiritual) light of personal health.

There is an overlapping area where the poetry therapy she underwent is what the Editor, Roger Langen, refers to in the Afterword as a moment when "Poetry is first herald then divine to her illness," and I term as a "Vygotskyan corridor to learning" about her past, dealing with it and emerging as if from a cleansing bath. In specialized literature, learning is understood as "Process of knowledge acquisition and formation of meanings; constructive, cumulative, self-regulated, goal-oriented, centered, cooperative and individually marked." *(De Corte, 1995, taken from Valle and González, 1998).* It is also viewed as "Process through which an attitude originates or changes." *(Hilgard, 1967, taken from Fermoso, 1976) (Translations by the reviewer)*

(Both quotations taken from the scientific paper Valores ¿formación, aprendizaje, educación? — Values. Formation, learning, education?— by Miguel Ángel Olivé Iglesias. IN Revista Atlante: Cuadernos de Educación y Desarrollo, 2014. II Etapa. ISSN 1989-4155. Indexed in IDEAS-RePEc, DOAJ, LATINDEX)

Reading the Author´s Note in Eley´s book, I noticed the validity of the above definitions and of Vygotsky´s theory. Concisely, the Russian icon postulated that development is propped by these tenets: "(i) culture is significant in learning, (ii) language is the root of culture, and (iii) individuals learn and develop within their role in the community. Culture can be defined as the morals, values, and beliefs of its community members, which are held in place with systems and establishments. Acceptable attitudes and conduct are communicated by the use of language. Culture is shaped over time as the result of specific events, whose messages are then conveyed to its members. Vygotsky explained that culture consistently affects cognitive development by affecting human behavior. He wanted others to realize that there is a complex relationship between culture and human development. It is a cycle; at the same time that the culture is influencing an individual, that individual is in turn creating culture." *(https://educationaltechnology.net/lev-vygotsky-sociocultural-theory-of-cognitive-development)*

Therefore, human development is closely bonded with culture. Here is where the overlapping magnificently crystallizes in the poems Eley wrote as creative offspring of her therapeutic sessions. I had read about animal-assisted therapy and art and music therapy, which "allow… to express and process… grief and other feelings." *(https://www.webmd.com/mental-health/mental-health-psychotherapy#2-7)*. That Eley retraces and refocuses on her ailment in the wondrous relief/cure of poetry is a blessing. It led her to "understand behaviors, emotions and ideas that contribute to… illness and learn how to modify them; understand and identify the life problems or events… and help them understand which aspects of those problems they may be able to solve or improve; regain a sense of control and pleasure in life; learn healthy coping techniques and problem-solving skills…" *(ibidem, previous quotation)*

Eley has bared her innermost feelings and *given sorrow words*, as she lets us know in citing Shakespeare. Eley´s message – as is the wish of the book´s Editor – is "of value to strangers" and purges old, deep wounds scarring the mental web and – most of all, best of all – rinsing her clean for an opportunity at a higher, transparent life.

The Editor´s closing words are sufficiently explanatory and complete in his "dissection" of the poet´s pieces, their origin and storyline. Following a precise chronological arrangement, we move in time through Part 1: Secret Monsters (Prelude, Childhood, Presentation, Altered States); Part 2: The Bodhisattva (Asylum, Transference, Stories); Part 3: Mother (Memory, Healing, Home). The arrangement gives the reader a sense of direction and facilitates the act of entering a woman´s intimate life and thoughts and fight, which she exposes poetically.

Langen talks about the turns in Eley´s style, compositionally, syntactically and rhetorically. We will notice the poet´s mind whirlpools in her wording, often reminiscent of

Emily Dickinson (whom she quotes at the beginning) in the immortal lines, "She dealt her pretty words like Blades— / How glittering they shone— / And every One unbared a Nerve / Or wantoned with a Bone" *(https://www.poemhunter.com/poem/she-died-at-play/#content)*. And Eley´s words have shone, unclosing nerve and bone.

I will only mention aspects of poetics that prompted me to write my review, leaving to specialists the psychological component. My strong suit not being psychology (although I did take undergrad and master´s subjects on the matter during my college majors), I am more comfortable commenting on the literary side of the book and the poems´ worth.

Cuban poetess Lalita Curbelo claimed, ""It is impossible to separate poetry from life..." *(The Ambassador 014, CCLA official magazine)*. Eley´s heartrending poetry is a testimony of her life. Therapy may have been the catalyst in her exploration of the appealing realms of imagery and structure, but I discern a woman/poet who had the clay of writing coming together inside her, exploding in the form of "116 poems (of about 600 in total)… culled from diaries and notebooks and loose-leaf scraps" she kept and became what we read today. *(Editor´s Afterword)*

"Poetry is my destiny," told me Canadian poet James Deahl. Poetry charted a revelatory, restorative course to a destiny of healing powers for Eley too. Inspiration is noticeable in these lines of "rain on the tin roof": "when it rained / it hammered on the tin roof / horses' hooves pounding on the track / the surf crashing / in and out / the recurring beat of a drum / this was the soundtrack / for the birth of my first child…" While we claim her "naïve poetic provenance," elegance and poise in her writing stand fresh, gentle, almost proverbial.

Eley´s production, explained in the Foreword and in the Afterword, is a moving mirror, which she dares gaze into profusely. Then it flows piecemeal, crossing and "conquering" the stages life itself imposed on her. In the process – both diachronically and synchronically – there is pain and fear in a graphic, quasi-ekphrastic, approach that makes us cringe and doubt, falter and question. Eley's moving poem entitled "tortured words" is a vivid illustration: "we lived in a hormonal boxing ring / her radical hysterectomy and bipolar disease / my teenage hormones and bipolar disease / words were lost down sieves and drains / sewage / rats / her emotions were like a box of steel / mine, darted off walls / storming / explosive / unpredictable…"

"tantrums" is a strong piece. As a reader, I feel a bottled-up atmosphere that makes me hold my breath. Its surrealistic character is sensed as well as we collapse into the last stanza: "she curls up / on her cushion / with her cats / purring / in her ear"; and "down down" is an impressively indicative piece of the poet´s mental maelstrom and needs: "dark thoughts / waters deep / a child / on the edge / falling into / a deep, dark / hole / mommy / hold me / touch me"

As I proceeded, I was drawn by "the censor," the internal struggle of the poet yearning, suffering and sensitively exposed to the dilemma of "my divided self / the past." Herein we are confronted alongside Eley with the dark forces pulling inwards/outwards she had to contend with and overcome. This notion is revisited in "quicksand," an aptly-titled piece, "a life and death / struggle / suffocating… // darkness, panic / tight in the throat / spastic, narrow / air cut off…" whose coda is a cry, "throw me / a branch / quick".

A glint of clearance on her thorny road comes to me firstly in Eley´s choice to open The Bodhisattva section: hope flickers in the piece she quotes from Shikibu, "Although the wind / blows terribly here, / the moonlight also leaks / between the roof planks / of this ruined house." She sees herself reflected in it, metaphors depicting and bringing into context the Shakespearean "slings and arrows of outrageous fortune" she has gone through. However, hope dances amidst the lines. Eley´s "ambulance" tells us about it: "communication / farewell family / loving me / as I am… // love is all there is" when a new phase in her life is about to begin.

Thus we continue to read and know Eley. A poem I enjoyed was "my mind is a mattress," where the poet creates interesting metaphorical variations combined with biblical allusions ("my mind is a mattress / lay down and relax / I will wash your feet / with my tongue / I will touch your / tired temples") and shows a sensuousness that is engaging and welcome, "… and be lovers / in the mind // hold me tight / massage my thighs / let our feelings / fall like a carpet / of petals / from a flowering / tree"

The poem "the past" refers me back to Buscaglia´s book, *The Way of the Bull.* His thought "… the possible step one man might take to gain insight, find oneself and discover one's true nature…" reverberates in Eley´s piece: "… the past / be careful / of the / undertow… // the little / boat / sails / the red rivers / of blood… // I am / my little boat / my little boat / is me". And, we see the writer, the woman/poet, become aware of the danger of the past and how she and "her boat" are one and "they," whole, can paddle on.

The poet´s coming to terms with her past is reexamined, from a new perspective, in "mother, other". A delicate theme, addressed now by Eley with a perhaps more "mature" vision, while-and-after therapy, and a heightened poetic acuity, is sincere, touching and final. It complements, or brings closure to, her previous "tortured words": "I was sick / and you / were / sick / a mad fury / of / claws and fur / my resistance / served / your dogmatism / I spent / 25 years / saying no // it hurt me / when / you said / you didn't / want to / die in / pain / but / you did"

I choose to close with comments on these equally stirring poems: "spring," "full moon" and "the blue dragonfly". The idea of spring is sign enough of hope, one Eley was able to find, supported by her own fortitude and will to survive and by the generous help offered by professionals, family, friends: "I was / delighted / to see / the peonies // the birth / of a baby / red and wet / not yet / beautiful". In "full moon" we partake with a poet writing to hope again, to the crest of human height and growth. The moon, silently alluring, seems to be a leitmotif in her poems.

Finally, the eponymous title, "the blue dragonfly," which entitles the book. Besides embracing through the poem the millenary wisdom of Buddhism, the poet is wreathed by an aura of calm, of transfiguration into a being who, by power of the therapeutic word, has faced her "demons" and her life, coming out freshened and willing. Slings and arrows avoided – or inflicted wounds *rehabilitated* – Eley does what she entreats in the poem: "fly / soar / spread your wings / take flight".

Come to the forceful, bleeding, honest and enlightening word of *The Blue Dragonfly – healing through poetry* by Veronica Eley. Be reminded of the undertows lurking to drag us down or back, and push, push optimistically onwards guided by the coincidental meaning of the name Veronica (a typically upright plant with *blue* and purple flowers), and its auspicious spiritual significance (picture of Jesus' face on a cloth). Veronica has healed through poetry, so can we. This book is of value to strangers – and to us all.

About the Reviewers and Essayists

James Deahl

Poet, critic, editor and independent scholar based in Sarnia, Ontario. He has delivered guest lectures at Oxford University, the University of Akron, the University of Toronto, McMaster University, York University, Nipissing University, and others. His articles on literary history appear regularly in *Canadian Stories*, and his most recent book is *Travelling The Lost Highway* (2019). He is considered as one of the most knowledgeable experts on Canadian poetry.

jedeahl@gmail.com

Alison González Cuba

Two Bachelor´s degrees in Education, Geography and English majors. Master´s degree in Pedagogical Sciences. Currently works as an Associate Professor for the Teacher Education English Department of the Holguín University. Has published in national and international events on matters related to both elements of geography and the teaching of English as a foreign language, as well as bicultural studies.

alison@uho.edu.cu

Kimberley Sherman Grove

She has taught creative writing at Loyalist College, the University of Ciego de Ávila, in Cuba, the Colborne Community Care Centre, and the Trenton Air Force Base. She has been published in the Boston Globe, the Christian Science Monitor, The Globe and Mail, The Toronto Star, Watershed Magazine and other local publications. She was Editor for the Canada Cuba Literary Alliance Member Anthology Sí Cuba. Her stories and poetry have been published in numerous anthologies including Hola Cuba, A Time of Trial, and Grandmother, Mother and Me. She was featured along other three poets in the fourth book of the Bridges Series, Where the Heart Lies, 2018.

kesgrove@gmail.com

Shireen Huq

PhD. Professor of English, Department of English and Modern Languages at North South University in Dhaka, Bangladesh. Senior experience in the teaching of English and foreign languages in general and author of essays on literature.

dr.shireenhuq123@gmail.com

Shane Joseph

Critic and author of four novels and three collections of short stories, and was the winner of the best fantasy novel award at Write Canada in 2010 for his work *After the Flood.* His immigrant story collection, *Paradise Revisited,* was short listed fort the ReLit Award in 2014. His latest collection of stories, *Crossing Limbo*, was released in 2017. For details visit: www.shanejoseph.com.

shane@shanejoseph.com and shanejoseph1@yahoo.ca

John B. Lee

Author, critic, editor and poet who is Poet Laureate of Brantford, Ontario. He is also the poet Laureate of Norfolk County. He has received more than sixty prestigious international awards for poetry. In 2010 he received the UWO Alumni Award of Merit for Professional Achievement in recognition for his career as a poet/author/editor/performer/mentor. Lee is the author of thirty-seven published books and he is the editor of nearly ten published anthologies. Lee has also been a visiting professor at University of Western Ontario, University of Windsor, Canador College, and a guest speaker at the University of the Witwatersrand in South Africa, and many universities throughout Canada and the United States. He was named Member of the President's Circle of McMaster University.

johnb.leejbl@gmail.com

Ronald Mackay

Master's degrees from both Aberdeen and Edinburgh Universities and a PhD from l'Université de Montréal. He has taught at the Universities of Bucharest, Newcastle upon Tyne, Toronto, and at Concordia where he was Professor of Education. Dr Mackay's research and professional work was in the interdisciplinary practice of international initiatives to promote food security and social wellbeing, especially in Latin America. He taught graduate courses in the design, management, and evaluation of development programmes. He has authored many academic and technical papers, reports, and books. Since retiring in 2002, he has published three memoirs, *Fortunate Isle, a Memoir of Tenerife, A Tenerife con Cariño*, and *The Kilt Behind the Curtain* as well as a score of short stories published in several anthologies.

mackay.ronald@gmail.com

Gail M. Murray

Canadian, Gail M. Murray B.A. B. ED. was an English teacher and teacher-librarian. After retiring Gail has become a free-lance writer. Like Keats, seeks to capture the essence of the moment. Gail's writing is a response to her natural and emotional environment. Her poems have been published in *Written Tenfold, Blank Spaces, Wordscape, Arborealis, The Banister,* and on *CommuterLit.com*. Her creative non-fiction has appeared in *The Globe and Mail, Trellis, Heartbeats, Renaissance, The Ontario Gardener, NOW Magazine, Blank Spaces, Just Words Volume 2, Stony Bridges, Ottawa Review of Books, Historical Fiction Magazine, Our Canada, More of Our Canada and Our Canada, Our Country, Our Stories.* She is a Writer, Poet, Book Reviewer.

gailmurray73@hotmail.com

Miguel Ángel Olivé Iglesias

Bachelor in Education. Master´s degree in Pedagogical Sciences related to values and values education in the English lesson. Thirty-two-year experience in the field of education and the teaching of English. Currently works at the Holguin University Teacher Education Department as an Associate Professor. Publishes nationally and internationally on the issues of foreign language teaching, pedagogy, interdisciplinary approaches, axiology and the preservation of humankind´s values, both material and non-material, from an educational perspective.

migueloi@uho.edu.cu / cclacubanprez@gmail.com

Syed Peeran

Graduation from St. Joseph's College, Bangalore, 1969 in Natural Sciences, completed Law from Govt. Law College, Bangalore and Post-Graduate Diploma in Social Service Administration from National Institute of Social Sciences, Bangalore. He became part-time Professor of Law for eight years in Havanur Law College, Bangalore. Peeran is trustee of International Sufi Centre, Editor of Sufi World a Journal on Sufi Culture, Philosophy and Literature(Islamic Spiritualism Tasawwuf). Poets International Bangalore has also nominated him as "Best Poet for 2003". International Poetry Academy, Chennai has also awarded him with "Best Poet" award for 2009. He has won Literary Prize 2017 of 'Naji Naaman' of Lebanon.

www.slpeeran.com / slpeeran@gmail.com

Jorge Alberto Pérez Hernández

Bachelor in Education, Major in English. Instructor. His research has been devoted to the development of skills in foreign language teaching. He worked as an Instructor for the former Pedagogical University of Holguin teaching English in the Teacher Education English Major. He has also worked at Holguin Medical School branch in Gibara teaching English for Special Purposes. Currently he publishes short stories, poetry and reviews in the Canada Cuba Literary Alliance (CCLA) formats and is Editor-in-chief of The Envoy, CCLA monthly newsletter, and Contributing Editor of The Ambassador, CCLA yearly magazine.

joyph@nauta.cu

Adonay Bárbara Pérez Luengo

Full Professor from the University of Holguín. Master and PhD degrees in Pedagogical Sciences. Also, a poet, writer, editor, proofreader and translator. She publishes her poetry with the Canada Cuba Literary Alliance, and her academic works in numerous national and international issues and events.

adonaypl076@gmail.com

Aylene Rodríguez Sondón

Associate Professor with a BA in English and a Master degree. She currently works in the English Language Department of Holguín University. She teaches translation and interpretation. Her publications and participation in events introduce papers on the issues of linguistics, translation and interpretation, and gender-related themes.

arodriguez@uho.edu.cu

Basudhara Roy

PhD, Assistant Professor in the Department of English, Karim City College, Jamshedpur, Jharkhand, India. The author writes reviews and critique and has been published in his country and abroad.

https://basudhararoy.com/

Kevin Spence

Born in London, Ontario (Canada) and still resides there. He was educated in the public schools of that city and attended Western University, where he studied Philosophy. Upon graduation, he was awarded the Gold Medal in Philosophy (The Mr. and Mrs. Bruno Schacter Award). He subsequently took a post-baccalaureate year in which he studied English literature. He is currently planning to enroll in Western's Faculty of Education.

kevinspence97@gmail.com

Marla Vega Romero

Associate Professor with a BA in English and Master and PhD degrees in Pedagogical Sciences. She currently works in the English Language Department of Holguín University. She teaches translation and interpretation and is Department Chair. Her publications and participation in events introduce papers on the issues of linguistics, translation and interpretation, and gender-related themes..

mvega@uho.edu.cu

Manuel de Jesús Velázquez León

PhD in Pedagogical Sciences, Full Professor who worked at the University of Holguín for more than forty years, currently working in a Chinese university teaching English and cultural studies. Professor of the History and Culture of the English Speaking Countries. Poet, writer, essay writer, translator. Has published his literary and academic works in numerous national and international issues and events.

manueld@stu.edu.cn

Anna Yin

Mississauga's Inaugural Poet Laureate who has authored four collections of poetry, the latest entitled "Seven Nights with the Chinese Zodiac" (Black Moss Press 2015). Her poems have appeared at ARC Poetry, New York Times, China Daily, CBC Radio, World Journal etc. Anna won the 2005 Ted Plantos Memorial Award, two MARTYs, two scholarships from West Chester University Poetry Conference, three grants from OAC and 2013 Professional Achievement Award from CPAC. She performed her poetry on Parliament Hill and has been featured at 2015 Austin International Poetry Festival and 2017 National poetry month project etc. Her website: annapoetry.com

anna.yin@gmail.com

Note: Three anthologies and a magazine that feature a large number of Canadian poets were also reviewed:

– *On the Wings of Poetry.* Hidden Brook Press. Edited by Miguel Ángel Olivé Iglesias.

– *Hearthbeat.* Hidden Brook Press. Edited by Don Gutteridge.

– *The Beauty Of Being Elsewhere.* Hidden Brook Press. Edited by John B. Lee.

– *Devour. Art and Lit Canada.* Hidden Brook Press. Editor-in-chief, Richard Grove. Special issue edited by James Deahl and Miguel Ángel Olivé Iglesias.

List of authors/editors reviewed/mentioned

Margaret Atwood
Sharon Bala
James Deahl
J. Graham Ducker
Veronica Eley
Douglas Glover
Kimberley Sherman Grove
Richard M. Grove
Don Gutteridge
W.L. Hawkin
Keith Inman
Ellen Jaffe
Nicholas Jennings
Shane Joseph
Rupi Kaur
John B. Lee
John Di Leonardo
Norah McClintock
Bruce Meyer
A.F. Moritz
Alice Munro
Gail Murray
Antony Di Nardo
Michael Ondaatje
P.K. Page
Jennifer Robson
Stuart Ross
Glen Sorestad
Raymond Souster
Robert Sward
Morgan Wade
Jan Wood
Elana Wolff
Donna Wootton
Anna Yin

About the Editor

Miguel Ángel Olivé Iglesias is a professor, researcher and poetry, fiction and non-fiction author. He is a Canada Cuba Literary Alliance (CCLA) editor, *The Ambassador* Editor-in-chief, *The Envoy* Assistant Editor, and President in Cuba of the CCLA. He does translation, proofreading, reviewing and revision for the CCLA, along with compilation and anthologizing.

He is a member of the Mexican Association of Language and Literature Professors, VP of the William Shakespeare Studies Center and guest member of the Canadian Studies Department of Holguin University in Cuba.

Born in 1965 in Bayamo, Cuba, he travelled to Holguin City in 1977 for his Junior, Senior High and College studies. Today he is an Associate Professor at the University of Holguín, with a Bachelor's Degree in Education, Major in English, and a Master's degree in Pedagogical Sciences. He has been teaching for thirty-three years and writing academic papers, lit reviews, poems and stories in Spanish and English.

Miguel has written and published numerous academic papers in Cuba, Mexico, Spain and Canada. He publishes nationally and internationally on the issues of foreign language teaching, pedagogy, interdisciplinary approaches, axiology and the preservation of humankind´s values, both material and nonmaterial, from an educational perspective.

He publishes too his poetry, short stories and literary essays with Canadian publishing entities, like Hidden Brook Press, SandCrab Books, QuodSermo Publishing, Canadian Stories Magazine, and Adelaide Group New York-Lisbon, and translates, edits, reviews and proofreads newsletters, magazines, anthologies and books of Canadian and Cuban poetry and prose for the Canada Cuba Literary Alliance, project for which he is the President on the Cuban side. So far he has being the Editor of seven CCLA books, published more than a hundred poems, six short stories and over forty critical reviews of poetry books and novels in different issues:

The Ambassador, official flagship of the CCLA; *The Envoy*, official newsletter of the CCLA; The Bridges Series Books, published by Hidden Brook Press and SandCrab Books; Adelaide Group in New York-Lisbon, and other anthologies by Hidden Brook

Press, SandCrab Books, QuodSermo Publishing and *Canadian Stories* magazine. He has published a review book, *In a Fragile Moment: A Landscape of Canadian Poetry* (Hidden Brook Press, 2020); his first full-length solo poetry book (bilingual), *Forge of Words* (Hidden Brook Press, 2020); *Pedagogical Sciences* (QuodSermo Publishing, 2021) and *Five Canadian Poets. Analytical Essays on James Deahl, John B. Lee, Don Gutteridge, Glen Sorestad, A. F. Moritz* (QuodSermo Publishing, 2021).

His poetic themes touch upon women, people, life, family, love, nature, and human values. He is currently involved in many CCLA projects: his second review book, *A Shower of Warm Light Upon this Land and Us*; his second solo poetry book, *This Pulse of Life, The Words I Found,* etc.

He works in the Teacher Education English Department as a professor of English, English Stylistics and grad courses. He is also Head of the English Language Discipline. He uses his academic papers, essays, stories and poems in class for reading, debating and practicing the language, adding a didactic and formative element to his scientific and literary production. He also does poetry reading in co-curricular on-campus and community activities.

CanLit Revealed

A Series of Review and Essay Books on Canadian Literature.

Title: *In a Fragile Moment: A Landscape of Canadian Literature*

ISBN – 978-1-927725-92-4 – Softcover
ISBN – 978-1-927725-93-1 – epub
ISBN – 978-1-927725-94-8 – mobi

Publisher: QuodSermo Publishing

In a Fragile Moment is an insightful collection of essays and reviews, written from the poetic heart of Professor Olivé. The authors covered in this astute critical study are treated with heart felt respect. Professor Olivé has the uncanny ability to portray his incisive observations in a poetic and perceptive manner.

Title: *A Shower of Warm Light: Reviews and Essays on Canadian Literature*
Author: M.Sc. Miguel Ángel Olivé Iglesias

ISBN – 978-1-989786-55-0 (softcover)
ISBN – 978-1-989786-56-7 (ebook)

Publisher: QuodSermo Publishing

A Shower of Warm Light follows in the footsteps of *In a Fragile Moment* as a profoundly insightful collection of reviews and essays by M.Sc. Miguel Ángel Olivé Iglesias on Canadian Literature. Professor Olivé continues to open the readers eyes to the warm light of contemporary Canadian Literature.

Title: *On the Breeze of Canadian Literature: International Reviews and Essays*
Editor: M.Sc. Miguel Ángel Olivé Iglesias

ISBN – 978-1-989786-20-8 (softcover)
ISBN – 978-1-989786-21-5 (ebook)

Publisher: QuodSermo Publishing

On the Breeze of Canadian Literature follows in the tradition of In a Fragile Moment and A Shower of Warm Light but this time as an international collection of reviews and essays by scholars, professors and academics from around the world. Through these well written and accessible essays Professor Olivé brings us an enlightening perspectives on Canadian Literature.

Title: *Ploughing the Home Ground: Essays on Canadian Literature and Poetics*
Author: Don Gutteridge

ISBN – 978-1-989786-59-8 (softcover)
ISBN – 978-1-989786-60-4 (ebook)

Publisher: QuodSermo Publishing

Ploughing the Home Ground is a collection of republished essays on Canadian Literature and Poetics by Don Gutteridge including two essays about Don and his work.

Title: *Five Canadian Poets: Analytical Essays on, James Deahl, John B. Lee, Don Gutteridge, Glen Sorestad, A. F. Moritz*
Author: M.Sc. Miguel Ángel Olivé Iglesias

ISBN – 9781989786369 (softcover)
ISBN – 9781989786376 (ebook)

Publisher: QuodSermo Publishing

Here you will find outstanding essays on both the biographical history as well as the literary history of five of Canada's top poets. This collection of essays brings literary life to Canadian poetry in the making. Examples of each poet's work are critiqued, examined and observed gently and sympathetically. They have been described as "well-researched love letters to poetry and the poetic spirit." These essays will open your eyes to poetry.

Title: *The Canadian Poet Who Wrote Himself Whole: Revealing the Poetics of Don Gutteridge*
Author: M.Sc. Miguel Ángel Olivé Iglesias

ISBN – 978-1-989786-57-4 (softcover)
ISBN – 978-1-989786-58-1 (ebook)

Publisher: QuodSermo Publishing

The Canadian Poet Who Wrote Himself Whole is a fine collection of essays and reviews by scholar and essayist Miguel Ángel Olivé Iglesias on the poetry and prose of world class Canadian poet Don Gutteridge.

www.ingramcontent.com/pod-product-compliance
Lightning Source LLC
Chambersburg PA
CBHW080340030726
47595CB00012B/4084

* 9 7 8 1 9 8 9 7 8 6 4 5 1 *